# PC to Vax:
## A Communications Guide

# PC to Vax:
## A Communications Guide

**Corey Sandler**
**Tom Badgett**

**Scott, Foresman and Company**
**Glenview, Illinois**       **London**

Cover Photo: Image Bank

1-2-3 is a trademark of Lotus Development Corporation.
AppleShare and Appletalk are trademarks of Apple Computer, Inc.
Bitcom is a trademark of Bit Software, Inc.
CommUnity-DOS is a trademark of Technology Solutions, Inc.
DECmate, DECnet, DECnet/PCSA, and DEPCA are trademarks of Digital Equipment Corporation.
EM220 is a trademark of Diversified Computer Systems.
LAT and LK201 are trademarks of Digital Equipment Corporation.
Macintosh is a trademark of Apple Computer, Inc.
Microsoft Windows is a trademark of Microsoft.
MicroVAX is a trademark of Digital Equipment Corporation.
MNP is a trademark of Microcom.
MS Windows and MS-DOS are trademarks of Microsoft.
Netware/VMS is a trademark of Novel, Inc.
OS/2, PC/XT, PC/AT, and PC-DOS are trademarks of IBM.
PC-Talk is a trademark of Headlands Press.
Polystar/240 is a trademark of Polygon.
PowerStation is a trademark of KEA Systems.
Presentation Manager is a trademark of Microsoft.
Professional 380 is a trademark of Digital Equipment Corporation.
PS/2 is a trademark of IBM.
RAF is a trademark of Datability Software Systems.
Rainbow is a trademark of Digital Equipment Corporation.
Reflection 4 Plus is a trademark of Walker Richer & Quinn, Inc.
ReGIS is a trademark of Digital Equipment Corporation.
SmarTerm 240 is a trademark of Persoft.
Ultrix, VAX, VAXmate, VAXstation, VMS Services for MS-DOS, VMS, VT100, VT220, VT240, VT241, VT300, VT320, VT330, VT340, and VT52 are trademarks of Digital Equipment Corporation.
Wordperfect is a trademark of Wordperfect Corporation.
WPS-Plus is a trademark of Digital Equipment Corporation.
XENIX is a trademark of Microsoft.
ZStemPC is a trademark of KEA Systems.

**Library of Congress Cataloging-in-Publication Data**

Sandler, Corey
    PC to VAX.

    Bibliography: p.
    Includes index.
    1. Local area networks (Computer networks)
2. Microcomputers. 3. VAX computers. I. Badgett, Tom.
II. Title.
TK5105.5.S263    1990    004.6    89-10512
ISBN 0-673-38579-5

1  2  3  4  5  6  MVN  94  93  91  90  89

Copyright © 1990 Corey Sandler and Tom Badgett.
All Rights Reserved.
Printed in the United States of America.

**Notice of Liability**

The information in this book is distributed on an "As Is" basis, without warranty. Neither the author nor Scott, Foresman and Company shall have any liability to customer or any other person or entity with respect to any liability, loss, or damage caused or alleged to be caused directly or indirectly by the programs contained herein. This includes, but is not limited to, interruption of service, loss of data, loss of business or anticipatory profits, or consequential damages from the use of the programs.

Scott, Foresman professional books are available for bulk sales at quantity discounts. For information, please contact Marketing Manager, Professional Books Group, Scott, Foresman and Company, 1900 East Lake Avenue, Glenview, IL 60025.

# Contents

1. **Introduction**  1
   The Concept  1
   What This Book Is About  2
   Who Should Read This Book  2
   Conventions Used in This Book  3
   What Is in This Book  4
2. **Networking in Digital's Environment**  7
   Digital's Philosophy  8
       Third-Party Computing Agreements  8
   The Technology of PC-VAX Communications  9
       Ethernet  10
       FDDI  15
   PC-VAX Communication: The User's Perspective  17
       The User's Need to Communicate  17
       Benefits to Users  18
   PC-VAX Communication: The MIS Perspective  19
       MIS Needs for Communication  19
       Benefits to MIS  19
   The OSI Influence  20
       Digital and OSI  20
       Protocols  21
   Specific Standards  24

Network Distance Limits    25
Chapter Summary    26

3. **Coordinating PCs in the VAX Environment: Networking    27**
   Computing Islands: PCs in the Workplace    27
   PC Networks: Departmental Distributed Processing    28
      Peer-to-Peer LANs    29
      Server LANs    30
      Distributed Processing    31
      Components of LANs    33
   The VAX Network: DECnet    35
      Overview of DECnet    35
      DECnet versus OSI    37
      Features of DECnet Network Management    41
      Enhancements of DECnet    44
      TCP/IP    45
      AppleTalk    46
      Netware    47
   Chapter Summary    49

4. **The Theory of Telecommunications    51**
   The Hardware Side of Communications    52
      Putting Bits on the Move    54
      Taking the Serial Bus    54
   The Telephone Network    55
      Terms and Technology    56
      The Nature of the Phone Network    56
      Stringing Out the Phone Line    58
   Private Solutions    59
      Leased Lines    59
      Independent Common Carriers    60
   Converting Data for Communications    60
      The Modem    61
      Transmission Speeds    62
   Chapter Summary    64

5. **How Do You Connect?** 65
   Direct Links   65
      Serial   65
      Ethernet   72
   Modem Links   74
      Dedicated and Leased Line Connections   74
   Network Server Links   75
      Software Components   75
      The VAX as a Peripheral   76
      The VAX as a Peer   78
      PC Network-to-VAX   79
   Chapter Summary   80

6. **Looking Down: The View from the VAX**   81
   The VAX Perspective   81
   All about Personal Computers   83
      Overview   84
      Operating Systems   87
   Personal Computer Products   89
      The Original IBM PC   90
      IBM PC XT   90
      IBM PC AT   91
      IBM PS/2   92
   Chapter Summary   93

7. **Looking Up: The View from the Personal Computer**   95
   The Personal Computer Perspective   95
   All about VAXs   96
      Overview of VAX   96
      VAX Operating Systems   97
   VAX Product Line   99
      PCs by Digital   99
      MicroVAXs   102
      Midrange Systems   107
      High-End Systems   109
      Older VAXs   110

Terminals and Digital   111
   VT-Family Terminals   112
Chapter Summary   113

## 8. Personal Computer Operating Systems   115
Overview   116
MS-DOS   116
   DOS versus VMS   116
   Features and Commands of DOS   117
   MS-DOS Files   118
   MS-DOS Devices   119
   MS-DOS Directories   120
   Other Features   122
OS/2   123
   Features of OS/2   123
   Positioning of OS/2   125
XENIX   126
   XENIX Commands   127
Chapter Summary   128

## 9. The VMS Operating System   129
Getting to Know VMS   129
   Logging In   130
The Digital Command Language   134
   Logging Out   136
   VMS Help   137
VMS Files and Directories   139
   File Names   141
   Defaults in File Specifications   142
   Global Characters   142
   File Manipulation   145
VMS Utilities   146
   VMS MAIL   146
   The Utility PHONE   148
Chapter Summary   149

10. **Terminal Emulation**   151
    **What Is a Terminal?**   152
    **What Is a Workstation?**   153
    **Terminal-to-Host Communications**   153
    **Workstation Terminals**   155
    **Terminal-Emulating Workstations**   157
        Configuring the Workstation   157
        Terminal Emulation Software   160
        Terminal Emulation Hardware   165
    **Chapter Summary**   166

11. **Transferring Files**   167
    **Software Protocols**   167
        The Human Model   168
        Synchronicity   169
        Starting and Stopping Computer Words   170
        Traffic Control   171
        Shaking Hands Properly   172
        Filling the Bucket   173
    **Protocols**   174
        High-Tech Microcomputer Protocols   174
        Data Compression   175
        Error Checking   175
        Parity Checking   176
    **Chapter Summary**   180

12. **Other Communications Environments**   181
    **Overview**   182
    **Digital's VAX/VMS Services for MS-DOS and DECnet/PCSA**   182
        General Features   182
        Client Software   183
        Data Sharing   183
        Remote Boot Support   184
    **Datability's Remote Access Facility (RAF)**   184
        General Features   185
        Utilities and Other Functions   185

Applications 186
Performance 186
LAT Support 187
Technology Concepts' CommUnity-DOS 188
General Features 189
Network Access 189
Novell's NetWare/VMS 190
General Features 190
System Requirements 191
Product Positioning 191
Terminal Emulator Software 192
EM220 192
Power Station 240 192
SmarTerm 240 193
PolyStar/240 193
Reflection 4 Plus 194
Chapter Summary 195

**Appendix A  DCL Command Notebook  197**
Abbreviated Forms 197
Self-Prompting Commands 198
A Few Housekeeping Essentials 199
APPEND 199
COPY 200
DELETE 201
DIRECTORY 202
PRINT 203
PURGE 203
RENAME 205
TYPE 205
Directories and Subdirectories 206

**Appendix B  VMS MAIL Notebook  209**
Reading Your Mail 210
Consulting the Directory 210
Using Folders to Organize Your Mail 212
The Hierarchy of Mail Folders 213
Moving Messages 213

Copying a File     214
Sending a Letter     215
Sending a File by Mail     216
Sending an Electronic Chain Letter     217
    Extending the Powers of SEND     219
Using the Keypad for Commands in MAIL     220
Reading a Map of MAIL     223
A Short Note about Long MAIL Messages     224
A Special MAIL Dictionary     224
    ANSWER and REPLY     224
    COPY     225
    CURRENT     226
    DELETE     226
    EDIT     227
    ERASE     228
    EXIT     228
    EXTRACT     228
    FILE and MOVE     229
    FORWARD     229
    PRINT     230
    PURGE     230
    QUIT     231
    READ     231
    REPLY     233
    SEARCH     233
    SELECT     233
    SEND     234
Navigational Commands within MAIL Files     234
    BACK     234
    FIRST     235
    LAST     235
    NEXT     235
System Commands within MAIL     236
    SPAWN and ATTACH     236
    ATTACH     238

COMPRESS 238
 SET and SHOW 239
Everything You Need to Know about
 Your MAIL Account 242
The Help Is in the MAIL 242

**Appendix C   VMS PHONE Notebook   245**
PHONE Commands 246
Dialing a Call 247
Conference Calls 248
Directory Assistance 248
Answering the Call 249
Hanging Up 249
Sending a File from within VMS PHONE 250
How to Phone for Help 250
Placing a Call on Hold 251
The Computer As an Answering Machine 252
Rejecting an Incoming Phone Call 252

**Appendix D   The VT-Series Terminals   255**
Character Attributes 258
Operating Modes 261
The Standard Digital Keyboard 261
 Main Keyboard 262
 Editing Keypad 264
 Auxiliary Keypad 264
 Function Keys 265
 Visual Indicators 266
 Audible Indicators 266
 Control Commands 267
 Composing Characters 270
 Type-Ahead Buffer 271

**Appendix E   Serial Communications Notebook   275**
A Matter of Standards 275
The RS-232C Nonstandard Standard 278
An Expedition across an RS-232C Cable 279
Nonstandard Standard Cables 280
Leftovers 281

Shopping for Cables 282
Good-bye, RS-232C? 282
Standards for Modems 283
The International Arena 283
    The 2,400 Baud Battle 284
Centronics Standard 285

**Appendix F    Modem Notebook   289**
Buying a Modem 289
    Specifications for Modems 290
    A Measure of Speed 291
Types of Modems 292
    Direct-Connect Modems 292
    Acoustically Coupled Modems 293
Going for a Short Haul 293
    Intelligent Modems 294
The Hayes Standard 295
    The Hayes Indicator Lights 296
    AT Commands 297
    Hayes Modem Registers 298
Alternatives to Modems 299
    The Null Modem 299
    Line Drivers 300
    Multiplexers 301
    Concentrators 302

**Endnotes   303**
**Glossary   305**
**Index   339**

# 1
# Introduction

Distributed processing. Heterogeneous networking. Connectivity. Multivendor environments. Interoperability. These are new terms to the computing industry, born of the rising need to provide more power to each user and the necessity for sharing information among users, computer sites, and even across company boundaries.

Various interested groups within the industry have worked hard to move their individual computing platforms into this new shared environment. Today these concepts touch just about everybody who uses a computer. Especially prominent, because of the development of more powerful hardware and the spreading interest in computers, is the personal computer (PC).

## THE CONCEPT

When the PC began its rise to popularity and finally to acceptance within corporate computer operations, these desktop machines were purchased to fill specific, well-identified needs. There was little need for such *personal* machines to use existing data stored on VAXs and other large computers. System planners and those responsible for the day-to-day operation of corporate computer resources first rejected, then tolerated desktop systems purchased with individual or departmental budgets and designed for personal needs.

In the beginning PC users also were VAX users, and the PC shared desk space with the ubiquitous VT-series terminal. Within a few years, however, there arose a new class of computer user, who learned about computing in the PC environment and who had no experience with or need for larger computers.

For a while these two user classes coexisted, separated by the boundaries of their computer experience and needs. Then two things happened. PCs became powerful enough and capable enough to gain the attention of traditional Management of Information System personnel who had shunned them as annoying toys. At about the same time, PC users became aware of the difficulties associated with *solitary* computing and they began to push for access to shared resources.

There still are two classes of computer user, each now more aware of the other but neither fully integrated into the other's world. Moving from one environment to the other can be painful and difficult. The material in this book is designed to ease the transition.

## WHAT THIS BOOK IS ABOUT

Incorporating PCs into a shared computing environment involves communication at several levels. This book will introduce you to personal computer communications hardware and software and show you how to use these tools in a PC-to-VAX environment. The fundamentals of serial communications, Ethernet, DECnet (Digital's networking protocol), and terminal emulation are discussed. In addition there are sections on VAX and PC hardware and software that can serve as reference or tutorial guides.

This book is not intended to provide step-by-step instructions to all of the major PC-to-VAX connectivity solutions. Rather we hope to make the reader aware of some of the options and capabilities available.

## WHO SHOULD READ THIS BOOK

This book is for the PC user who must learn to use the corporate VAX host; it is for the VAX user who must coordinate with PC users just joining the VAX environment. The topic is communications, but the book also is an introduction to personal computer hardware and software for the VAX user; it can serve as a good beginning for those who are just learning about VAXs.

## CONVENTIONS USED IN THIS BOOK

Describing concepts pertaining to and interaction with computers can be difficult unless it is agreed in advance how certain things will be handled. This section outlines some of the general conventions used in this book. Others should be obvious as you read through the material.

**Commands.** Information presented by the computer will be shown in **boldface** type. Anything you type will be shown in normal type. Most computer commands end with a return. That means you type the command and press the return key, which lies to the right of the main alphanumeric keypad on your workstation or terminal. You should assume that all examples of commands in this book end with a return unless we tell you otherwise.

**"Digital" refers to Digital Equipment Corporation.** Although in years past it has been common to refer to this company as DEC, and while some Digital products still carry this moniker (DECwindows, DECnet, DEConnect), the company is making a concerted public effort to replace DEC with Digital.

**Control characters.** Throughout this book control characters will be indicated with the following convention:

Ctrl-A (for example) for the character yielded by holding down the key marked Ctrl while typing the letter "a."

Shift-Ctrl-A for a character yielded by holding down the control key and shift keys while typing the letter "a."

The Alt key is used in the same way as the control key to provide an alternate character set or command code. Alt characters will be indicated in the same way as control characters:

Alt-A represents the character yielded by holding down the Alt key and typing the letter "a."

**Shift Characters.** Shift characters will be indicated throughout with the following convention:

Shift-A for the character yielded by holding down either of the shift keys and typing the letter "a."

**PC and workstation.** These terms are merging in general use. There may be subtle differences in some applications, and purists will argue that a workstation is more powerful than a PC. However, with the increasing power of personal computers, this argument is less and less valid. In this book we tend to use the terms PC and workstation interchangeably except where there are obvious differences in application or performance requirements.

**PC-DOS, MS-DOS.** PC-DOS is IBM's compatible implementation of Microsoft's MS-DOS operating system for microcomputers. In this book we will use the term MS-DOS to represent both IBM and IBM-compatible systems.

## WHAT IS IN THIS BOOK

**Chapter 1.** Introduction

**Chapter 2.** Networking in the Digital Environment
The Digital computing philosophy; introduction to Ethernet, DECnet, and PC-to-VAX communication. The PC user and MIS perspectives on PC-to-VAX connectivity.

**Chapter 3.** Coordinating PCs in the VAX Environment: Networking PC and VAX networking, including additional details on Digital's DECnet protocol and the Open Systems Interconnect influence. A brief introduction to other network protocols.

**Chapter 4.** The Theory of Telecommunications
The hardware side of telecommunications; the telephone network, used increasingly for remote PC attachments. Modems and data conversion for host sharing.

**Chapter 5.** How Do You Connect?
The various physical connection options, including direct serial links, modem links, and network server concepts.

**Chapter 6.** Looking Down: The View from the VAX
The PC computing platform from the VAX user's perspective. Introduction to PCs for users and MIS personnel who have not used PCs.

**Chapter 7.** Looking Up: The View from the PC
The VAX computing platform from the PC user's perspective. Introduction to the VAX for people who have not used the VAX. System architecture and available VAX models.

**Chapter 8.** PC Operating Systems
Common PC-based operating systems from the new PC user or VAX user perspective. Some of the capabilities of PC system software.

**Chapter 9.** The VMS Operating System
VMS, Digital's most popular VAX operating system. Some of the capabilities of this operating system; reference section to VMS commands and procedures.

**Chapter 10.** Other Communications Environments
Specific PC-to-VAX software: Digital's VMS Services and Apple-Talk/VMS.

**Chapter 11.** Terminal Emulation
PC terminal emulation; Digital's VT-family terminals. Hardware and software concepts.

**Chapter 12.** Transferring Files
Hardware and software aspects of file transfer between PCs and VAXs. Such protocols as Kermit and XMODEM.

**Appendix A.** DCL Command Notebook
Reference section for DCL (VMS) commands.

**Appendix B.** VMS MAIL Notebook
Reference section, including commands and help available, on VMS MAIL.

**Appendix C.** VMS PHONE Notebook
Reference section, including commands and help available, on VMS PHONE.

**Appendix D.** THE VT-Series Terminals
Reference section on Digital's VT family of terminals. Operating modes, models, and keyboards.

**Appendix E.** Serial Communications Notebook
Reference section on serial communications. Serial connector pin-out diagram and information on Centronics Parallel interface, common in the PC environment.

**Appendix F.** Modem Notebook
Reference section on modem operation, types, and selection.

**Glossary**

# 2
# Networking in Digital's Environment

We have come full circle in the computer world. In the late 1970s and early 1980s, computer users began to chafe at central control of computer resources and at the slow response of MIS to their processing needs. Today, users at every level are beginning to recognize the need for communication among all members of the computer enterprise.

Just as the development and acceptance of the personal computer more than ten years ago helped fuel user flight away from the central computer room, recent developments in networking and other communications hardware and software are enabling us to come together on a more congenial common ground. This reunion is still in its early stages, however.

This chapter discusses some of the general technology and terminology of computer interaction. Later chapters will expand some of these topics and relate them more closely to PC-level computing. If you have a good background in Digital networking, including Ethernet concepts, distributed processing, and the open system interconnection (OSI) standards, you may want to skip this chapter for now.

## DIGITAL'S PHILOSOPHY

During the 1970s Digital's design, programming, sales, and management personnel tumbled headlong into a major architectural problem of their own making. Within the company were so many different computing platforms that various company segments were having difficulty sharing information and processing power. Out of this intracompany need grew DECnet and Digital's networking architecture (DNA); and a strengthening philosophy of interconnection and distributed processing began to evolve. (See chapter 3 for additional information on DECnet.)

Over the years Digital has developed many additional products that support resource sharing in a multicomputer environment. These products include clustering hardware and software; gateways to Cray, IBM, and other specific foreign architectures; and direct and local area network (LAN) links to personal computers. Digital's stated aim is to provide users the tools and techniques required for multivendor communication, and it has moved closer to this goal than some other companies by starting early to support international communications guidelines while maintaining compatibility with its own standards.

### Third-Party Computing Agreements

Digital as a company has formally recognized the importance of personal computers in the overall Digital computing environment.

In a joint announcement in January of 1988, Digital and Apple Computer, Inc., announced that they would work closely to ensure connectivity among the two company's products via DECnet/OSI. The initial pact made no provisions for actual product development; rather it was an agreement for the two companies to share technical resources as needed to make sure Apple Macintosh computers and Digital computers can communicate seamlessly through DECnet and Apple's AppleTalk networks.

In May of 1988, Digital and Compaq Computer Corporation reached a similar agreement for "technology exchange" to "ensure the worldwide connectivity of their products." Like the Apple agreement, the initial Digital-Compaq pact holds little substance. It is merely a public announcement of the intent of both companies to exchange the technical information required to keep the two classes of computers communicating. There is no joint marketing agreement involved, but Compaq computers will be certified compatible with Digital's network applications support (see chapter 3) to "communicate across all levels of an organization and utilize enterprise-wide resources."

Such agreements doubtless are good for both companies. For Digital they are an opportunity formally to embrace the desktop computing environment without sanctioning the equipment of such arch-rivals as IBM. Its agreement with Digital gives Apple visibility and credibility in the business computing environment, and Compaq, already an established business computer company, achieves enhanced visibility in the minicomputer world.

Digital is expert in bringing together the resources of third parties with their own expertise and enhancing the offerings of both. We can expect to see Digital reach deeper into the desktop computing world in the future. Its own attempt at PC-level computing early in the '80s was overshadowed by the wide acceptance of the IBM and Apple platforms, but the company is recovering by linking physically and conceptually with the offerings of other vendors.

## THE TECHNOLOGY OF PC-VAX COMMUNICATIONS

If you are using a VAX with a standard Digital terminal, you are already using one of the most common communications links in the computer world, a direct serial link. (See chapter 5.) This interconnection scheme involves simply attaching the terminal to the computer with three or more wires. Without additional equipment this link usually is limited to about fifty feet, but the wires can run through the floor, inside walls, or overhead in a ceiling.

Distance is one limitation with direct serial links; speed is another. Most direct-connect terminals, and the serial ports to which they attach, can exchange data at a rate of about 960 to 1,920 characters per second (cps). Some newer terminals can operate at speeds up to about 3,840 cps, but relatively few VAX serial systems are actually configured for this speed because of the mix of older equipment—including cabling systems—that can't operate at that speed.

Sometimes 960 cps or even less is satisfactory, of course. Interactive computing that involves simple exchanges of a few keystrokes, such as database data entry and report design and preparation, require relatively small amounts of traffic across the communication link. Repetitive, fast-paced query operations or graphics-oriented applications, on the other hand, put a much heavier load on the system. Where long-distance high-speed links are required, many users turn to networks such as Ethernet.

## Ethernet

Ethernet is basic to the Digital computing environment. The Ethernet standard has been sanctioned for local area network (LAN) applications by virtually every computer vendor and through the standards-setting work of the Institute of Electrical and Electronics Engineers (IEEE). The IEEE standard 802.3 specifies how information will be exchanged over Ethernet and ensures reliable and accurate data transfer, even between computers from different vendors. The standard does not specify how this information will be interpreted, however. That is up to individual host hardware and software.

Ethernet can transfer data among attached devices at rates up to 10 megabits per second (Mb/s), or about one million characters per second. The actual effective rate of exchange is less than this because of network overhead required to sort out the various messages from different users, route them to the proper location, and avoid conflicts from multiple pieces of equipment trying to communicate at the same time. Direct Ethernet links operate to over 4,000 feet, depending on the medium used to carry the traffic and other hardware that may be present on the network. Multiple networks can be connected through appropriate hardware to make the effective distance of Ethernet virtually unlimited. Digital calls this configuration Extended Ethernet.

Ethernet runs at the basic standard speed of ten Mb/s for Digital local area networks in the form of DECnet. (See chapter 3.) Additional international standards (see discussion of OSI standards later in this chapter) are broadening the appeal of Ethernet by establishing firm rules for communicating at all levels, including how each host interprets the data sent over the network and how the information is presented to the user within applications.

The physical connection to Ethernet is made with one of five types of cable: thick coaxial (coax), thin coax, CATV, fiber-optic, or twisted pair (telephone wire). Which physical connection is used depends on the type of Ethernet. There are two broad divisions of Ethernet, baseband and broadband.

Broadband Ethernet uses radio frequency (RF) signals to transmit information between nodes and travels over CATV (cable television) cable, which is actually a form of coax. If you have cable television in your home or if you are using a video recorder, you probably have this type of cable connecting to your television.

It is called broadband because of the wide frequency spectrum that can be used to carry information. Like commercial radio and television, which share the atmosphere to transmit signals of various frequencies to your receiver, broadband Ethernet installations share the frequency spectrum available on the cable, enabling users to add voice, video, telemetry, and other types of information to the same cable that carries the Ethernet signals. Figure 2-1 shows an Ethernet connector frequently used with broadband links.

A receiver tunes in a particular radio or television signal from the myriad that fills the air. Broadband cabling systems work in a similar way, with various types of equipment that attach to the network capable of selecting out the signals they need to process.

The main difference between broadband and baseband Ethernet is the number of data types that each carries. Whereas RF-based

*Figure 2-1* **Ethernet twist-on connector of the type that is sometimes seen in UHF (ultrahigh frequency) communications applications. (Source: Black Box Corporation)**

broadband networks can share the medium among an almost unlimited number of information types, baseband cable carries only the Ethernet signals.

ThickWire Ethernet is so named because of the size of the cable. Where ThinWire and baseband cables are about a quarter of an inch thick, ThickWire cables may be several times thicker. As an end user, you may not actually see the thick cable, however, because normally it is used as a network backbone, with smaller cables attaching between your workstation and the backbone.

An increasingly popular Ethernet cable is the unshielded twisted-pair wire (Figure 2-2) used with standard telephone systems. In a building with a flexible telephone wiring system already installed, this is the easiest and least expensive way to attach network devices. You

*Figure 2-2* **A simple telephone-type wall connector can be your computer's link to a twisted-pair network. (Source: Black Box Corporation)**

can tell if you are using unshielded twisted-pair because the wire that attaches to your workstation will look like standard telephone cable of the type that connects your home telephone to the wall. Although some systems require a customized telephone-type cable that is different inside, in all probability the computer connection is using standard telephone cable. There may also be a small box attached between your workstation and the wall jack. The cable from the workstation to the box is probably coax; the cable from the box to the wall is probably flat telephone wire.

Unshielded twisted-pair (see Figure 2-3) offers the advantage of quick and easy connections that can be changed readily. In most offices the telephone wires that go to individual desks or workstations congregate in a wiring closet or patch panel at a central location on each floor. This is usually a star configuration in which the wiring closet or patch panel forms a hub and individual connections radiate from this hub like the spokes of a wheel. You connect to this patch panel by plugging a wire with a modular connector into a wall jack. When you make the connection, you are attaching to four wires (two twisted-pair) or six wires (three twisted-pair) that run through the wall, into the ceiling or floor, and to the central wiring location.

This wiring configuration allows you to move your computer hardware by unplugging this wall connection, physically moving the equipment to the new location, and plugging into the wall jack there. Changes to the physical connection to the network are made at the central wiring location by moving wires on a punch-down block (Figure 2-4) or by attaching modular jumpers to the proper blocks (Figure 2-5).

Although telephone wiring is not used as often as coax cable today, this wiring scheme is destined to become the standard for office- and floor-level connections. For connecting users between floors, coaxial cable is the most common—either ThinWire or Thick-Wire—but fiber-optic cable is gaining popularity.

Fiber-optic cable uses laser diodes at either end of the link to transmit information over a light-conducting cable. The advantages of fiber are its small size, large data capacity, and resistance to outside interference. A standard fiber cable is only a fraction of the size of standard coax, yet it can carry the equivalent of hundreds of standard coax cables. In addition, whereas standard wire is subject to signal problems if it passes close to power lines, electric motors, fluorescent lights, and other electrical noise sources, fiber cable is not affected by outside electrical fields. Moreover, wires radiate signals of their own

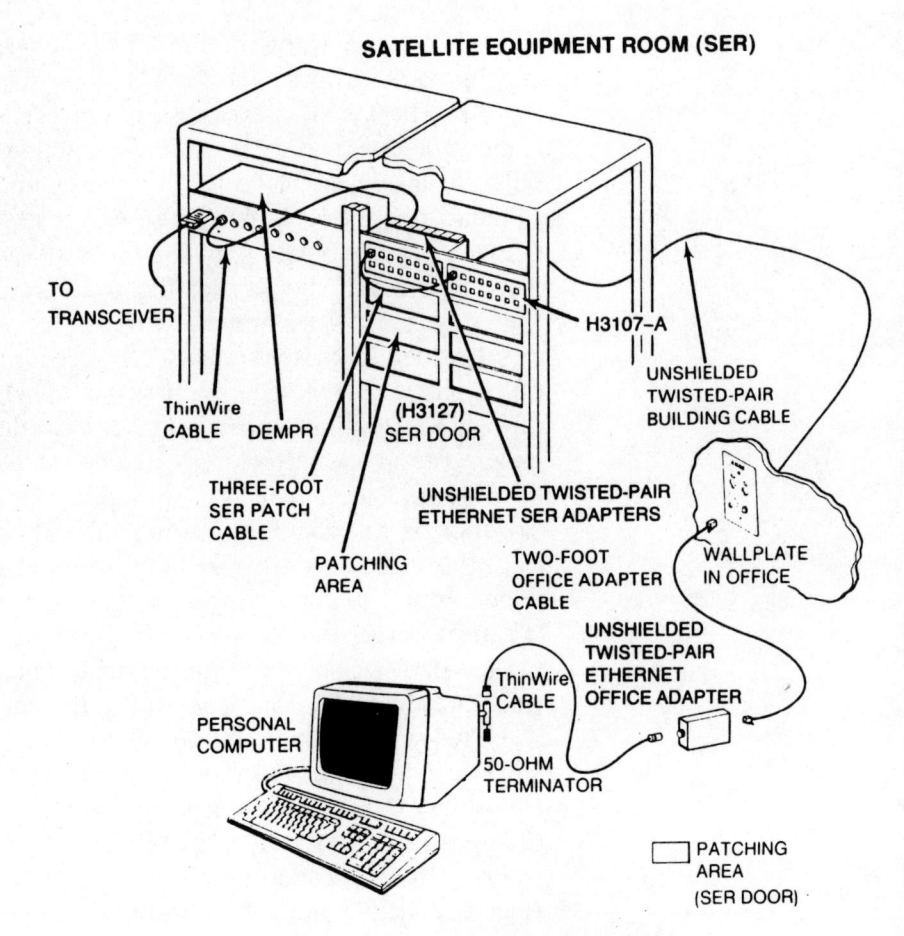

*Figure 2-3* **Unshielded twisted-pair configuration. (Source: Digital Equipment Corporation)**

as data is transmitted, and this radiation, under certain conditions, can be detected by sensitive receiving devices, compromising the security of the network. With fiber cable, only a physical connection to the network can intercept the signals, making unauthorized access to data much more difficult.

The only real disadvantage of fiber cabling systems at this point is the cost of the equipment required to convert the computer's electrical signals to optical signals and vice versa. Prices are falling rapidly, however, and an increasing number of companies are providing optical networking equipment. Most experts are predicting that

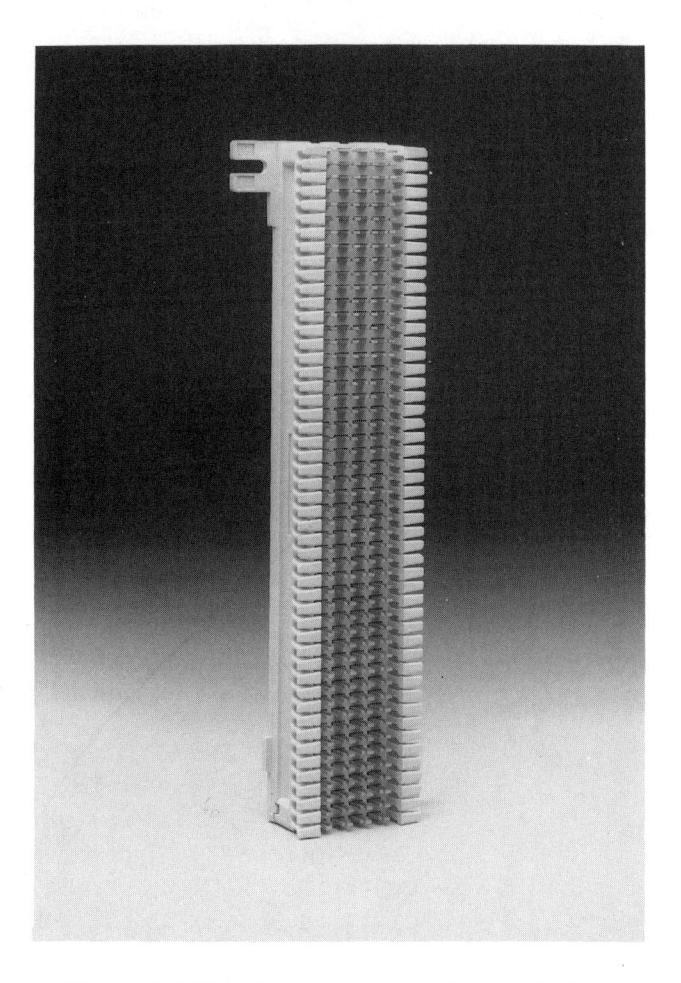

*Figure 2-4* **Telephone-company-type punch-down block. (Source: Black Box Corporation)**

optical cable soon will become the standard for relatively long-distance connections—between floors and from building to building—while unshielded twisted-pair will carry the majority of network traffic for shorter distances.

**FDDI**

A new high-speed fiber-optic networking standard is rapidly taking shape. Fiber-distributed data interface (FDDI), boosts network speeds to 100 Mb/s over optical cable. Already vendors are installing FDDI

*Figure 2-5* **Modular patch panel. (Source: Black Box Corporation)**

cable backbones to connect floors in large office buildings or to link multiple buildings on campuses. FDDI will quickly become the standard for such links, and 200 Mb/s FDDI is not far behind.

FDDI uses a dual fiber-optic transmission medium and token-ring architecture over distances up to one hundred kilometers. Such high-speed links between departmental LANs will enable even closer ties among the central processing units (CPUs) within a given installation. This in turn will increase the feasibility of true distributed processing, in which processors of modest capability combine through the network to form a computing environment that is effectively much more powerful. Desktop and deskside machines are destined to figure heavily in this scenario along with more powerful departmental-level and mainframe-class machines.

Standard Ethernet LANs, especially those based on twisted-pair wiring, likely will remain the standard for departmental or floor-level computing, while FDDI or other high-speed optical links will be used to interconnect these smaller LANs. At present the equipment required to interconnect between wire and fiber is relatively expensive, but the speed justifies the expense in many installations, and with increased popularity of FDDI, these costs will decline.

This trend is part of a natural progression to bring ever-faster links to the desktop. Many current Ethernet installations, for example, use the 10-Mb/s link for interdepartmental communications but slower serial links to the desktop. As prices for Ethernet equipment decline and users demand increasingly higher-speed connectivity, look for 10 Mb/s to become the standard to the desktop, with channels 100 Mb/s or faster providing the links among other larger groups of users.

# PC-VAX COMMUNICATION: THE USER'S PERSPECTIVE

Many PC users broke away from the mainframe fold when their needs, coupled with a broader awareness of central computer capabilities, pushed MIS beyond its ability to respond with timely services. Computing in isolation worked well for a while as users and vendors developed software and refined hardware to turn the early desktop curiosities into serious processing machines.

## The User's Need to Communicate

When relatively few people within a company used a computer of any type, the issue of communication was a small one. Today workers from receptionists to presidents are using PCs or terminals to do part or all of their work. Under these conditions, users rapidly are becoming aware of the need for these disparate machines to communicate.

The receptionist's telephone messages, for example, can be forwarded automatically over a network anywhere in the company; secretaries can coordinate meeting schedules for department heads by viewing central meeting calendars; designers and engineers can exchange design drawings and specifications in real time; a central database can provide inventory, sales, and other information to all users simultaneously; all users benefit from electronic mail.

## Benefits to Users

Such benefits are taken for granted by minicomputer and mainframe users. They have operated in this shared environment for years. If you have used a PC LAN, you have seen some of the benefits of linking individual processors to a central server, but if you have used only a stand-alone computer, the concept of sharing programs, data, and mail may seem foreign.

With networking you gain direct communication with other users on the network as well as local and possibly national electronic mail.

There are also subtle benefits. As a PC user attached to a VAX or VAX network, you will gain access to very large disk space. Although 20- and/or 40-megabyte (MB) disk drives are fairly common on PCs, not every user has one. It can be expensive to supply every PC user in a business with a large, local disk drive. Having these users share central storage on a VAX not only provides ample storage, it also ensures that their data will be backed up automatically.

Most MIS operations have evolved a reliable method for making regular backups of central drives. PC users, on the other hand, are notorious for failing to back up local drives adequately. When PC users had only diskette drives or relatively small hard disks, this was not a particularly serious problem. With PC disks of 40 MB and larger becoming fairly common, the problem of data backup becomes rather more serious. If the majority of PC data is stored on a central VAX disk, backup can be taken care of when the rest of the system is serviced. Moving PC-based data to the VAX allows the PC workstations to handle the user interface and applications processing duties of, say, a database, while the VAX is used for storage of very large data files. In addition, the files can be shared among PC and terminal users.

As PC-to-VAX links become more common, applications developers are incorporating routines that can make use of the host's CPU to solve complicated or time-consuming problems. Uploading data from a 25MHz PC based on an 80386 chip to a MicroVAX for processing is not a wise use of resources. An XT- or AT-class machine, however, can't possibly handle large problems as quickly or efficiently as a VAX 6200 parallel processor. As applications catch up with hardware and communications software, we will see even better use of this type of distributed computing.

In a large enterprise, linking PCs to a local VAX offers another benefit: bringing PC users together with other terminal users everywhere in the network. This opens up companywide data and expertise to all computer users.

# PC-VAX COMMUNICATION: THE MIS PERSPECTIVE

There were a couple of common responses from MIS personnel as computer users within the enterprise turned to PCs. One was to exert very strong control over users who wanted to apply PCs in their work, in many cases denying permission for the addition of decentralized machines. This response, quite possible in companies where the MIS personnel sit at a high enough level—or where the company is relatively small—effectively stymied the growth of PC applications in these companies for several years. When users finally brought in their own processors, frequently by manipulating budgets and purchase approvals to hide the fact that they were buying computer equipment, there was no central coordination. Applications were chosen piecemeal; hardware was not compatible among departments or even individual users; and there was no way to link these users to the central processor.

Another common MIS response as desktop computers gained popularity among users was to look the other way as individuals bought their own computers and applications. Rather than fight the the decentralization of computer resources, this group of MIS people simply chose to ignore the new technology. The result with this approach was the same: a variety of hardware and software grew up around the company, ultimately frustrating end users because they could not share programs and data among incompatible systems. In addition, the variety of machines and software made satisfactory central support for the end user impossible.

## MIS Needs for Communication

The need for enterprise-wide communication is the same from the MIS perspective as from the user perspective. MIS personnel benefit from electronic mail, central data storage, and the other benefits to end users. In addition, when PC-based and other workstations are involved in the enterprise, MIS can reap other benefits of linking these machines through local area networks and to a central VAX.

## Benefits to MIS

In addition to central control of companywide data files and backup, linked PCs permit easier upgrades of user applications. In a large company with hundreds or even thousands of personal computers, the task of upgrading these users with the latest versions of software can be almost impossible. When an application is stored on a central host, that application has to be upgraded only once to provide the latest version to all users. Even when an application is stored at individual PCs, a single copy frequently can be made available on the VAX for each user to download, making the upgrade via the network rather than by carrying individual copies of the software to each work site. Some software can automate this process.

When MIS personnel make positive use of the connectivity of PC users, it can influence these users to coordinate purchases of their hardware and software, reducing MIS support problems.

Probably not very many companies saw the benefit of distributed processing with PCs in the very beginning; therefore all companies are suffering from the problems of multiple hardware and operating systems, incompatible applications, inadequate backup, and frustration for both the MIS and the end user. The popularity and new ease of linking disparate systems through standard networking protocols is helping to eliminate many of these problems.

## THE OSI INFLUENCE

Open system interconnection (OSI) is the international model for communication linking heterogeneous computer systems. OSI is the product of a standards committee of the International Standards Organization. (ISO is based in Geneva. The American representative to the ISO is the American National Standards Institute, or ANSI.)

OSI in its earliest form dates to the 1970s. Competitive networking models from Digital and IBM—the DEC network architecture and IBM system network architecture (SNA) respectively—were already under way. Both companies have declared their intention of making their products comply ever more closely to the OSI model; Digital has made more progress in this area.

### Digital and OSI

Digital's strategy for OSI is to maintain the current proprietary DECnet protocols so as to provide continuing support for existing users, meanwhile laying an OSI-compliant architecture on top of it. When DECnet/OSI (DECnet phase V) is fully functional, Digital says, users will be able to choose which communications protocol to use depending on the requirements of the information exchange. For Digital-to-Digital communications, the best choice is to stay with DECnet protocols, the company says, because that system has more features and is faster. If information is destined for a network that includes foreign equipment, OSI protocols are preferable. Digital believes this simultaneous compliance with the two standards is the best way to support existing and future applications.

## Protocols

The OSI model has layered architecture. Its functions and facilities are divided logically into seven layers, each of which conducts separate but related functions. Each higher layer makes use of the functions of the layer below it, but the details of how this lower layer functions are transparent. This design provides modular architecture that permits changes—or even significant redesign—to each module without affecting associated modules. As long as the basic functionality is maintained, it is not always necessary to change all modules when one is changed.

Key elements of a protocol are syntax, semantics and timing.

Syntax specifies the signal levels to be used and the format in which data is to be sent.

Semantics is data handling and coordination among machines.

Timing matches the communication speeds of machines and arranges for proper sequencing of packets of information if they arrive out of order.

The OSI protocol is based on a seven-layer model that specifies precisely how information will be exchanged across a network. OSI standards groups have spent more than ten years hammering out the details of the protocol. The basic seven layers are now firmly established, agreed to by various international standards organizations. Additional areas must be defined, and some industry observers say the work could continue ten more years, but with the seven layers stable, hardware and software can safely be based on the standard.

There are subgroups within the seven layers. The first three layers deal with the physical aspects of connectivity: wiring and cables, data encoding, addressing, and data management. Layers four, five, and six provide interoperability among different systems: session control, dialogue management, and format conversion. The highest layer, number seven, handles such distributed applications as file transfer, remote file access, and database management.

The seven layers are physical, data link, network, transport, session, presentation, and application. Each of the layers is summarized below.

1. Physical layer. The wiring, cables, or fiber optics that physically make up the connection among members of the network. Physical-layer standards provide specifications for electrical interconnection, including plugs, connectors, and sockets. All of the signals of an OSI network are carried by the physical layer, with all of the definitions made by higher levels. In addition to mechanical specifications, the physical layer covers encoding techniques and modulation standards.

    Within the physical layer are various electrical standards. Most common in PC networks is the RS-232C standard, which is essentially a definition of the assignment of specific signals to specific pins and a setting of voltage levels to indicate "on" or "off," or "1" or "0" in computer terms. A European near-equivalent to RS-232C is the X.21 standard.

2. Data-link layer. The controlling level for the data stream from one system to another. This level supervises the assembly of characters of data into packets, or blocks, of information. The packet is checked before it is put onto the network to ensure error-free transmission. The standard also calls for this layer to be ready to send a "message received" note to the supervisor at the other end to indicate that a packet has arrived safely. Alternatively, it may work with the supervisor at the other end to arrange for retransmission of a message if a packet does not arrive safely.

    Protocols applied within this layer include advanced data communications control procedures (ADCCP), bisynchronous and high-level data link control (HDLC), International Telephone and Telegraph Consultative Committee (CCITT) X.25 for packet-switched network communications, and the IEEE 802.3 LAN standard.

    IEEE 802.3 (also known as ISO 8802.3) is closely related to various Ethernet schemes, including those of Digital Equipment Corp., Xerox, 3Com, and others. The 802.3 data-link standard controls how data is transferred over a network. It is based on Ethernet carrier sense multiple access/collision detection (CSMA/CD) technology.

In PC networks much of the work of the data-link layer may be performed by special-purpose chips on interface cards, by error detection protocols such as Xmodem, or by elements of some of the more sophisticated communications packages that include their own error detection facilities.

3. Network layer. The mechanism of OSI for the selection of the physical pathway from one geographic location to another. Network-layer protocols interpret data packet addresses as they are put onto the network and route the information to the appropriate node. This can be a fixed route, or it can be altered on the basis of network conditions, priorities of service, or other situations. The location of the network layer varies greatly with the design of the network; in a common-carrier network or other major trunk network, this oversight is typically provided by an external controller.

4. Transport layer. The traffic cop of the system. It takes over after the network-layer specifications are satisfied. The transport layer performs functions similar to those of the network layer, working at the local level. Transport-layer protocols control the flow of information between nodes once the path is established.

If the network fails, the transport-layer software searches out alternate routes or finds a way to save transmitted data until the network connection is reestablished. It also supervises the quality of the packets of information, examining the format and ordering of information.

One of the protocols of the transport layer is transmission control protocol, part of the TCP/IP package.

5. Session layer. The layer that enables work to be done across the network. The session layer allows two applications or two pieces of the same application to communicate and supervises security and housekeeping functions, including password exchange and logging.

Two PC software products that deliver session-layer functions are NetBIOS and APPC.

6. Presentation layer. The controller for the look and feel of the application on the network. The control codes, character

sets, and graphics characters and commands yield the distinctive look of some programs. Interestingly, the presentation layer is employed by most terminal emulators that make a PC appear to be something that it is not.

Presentation-layer protocols smooth out differences among multivendor systems by converting information as necessary at each end of the link to maintain a consistent presentation.

7. Application layer. The one with which the user interacts. It contains the network operating system and the applications programs, including electronic mail, file sharing, databases, and other facilities.

With general acceptance of OSI standards, purchase and system design decisions can be made on the basis of preferred vendor, applications capabilities, or hardware features instead of on the basis of interconnect capabilities. Integration of new systems with existing ones will be easier, and the application of widely diverse systems within an enterprise will provide more flexible system design. Individual users or departments can select the hardware and software systems they want for a particular application without having to pay too much attention to what other groups or individuals within a company are doing.

## SPECIFIC STANDARDS

Within these general guidelines, specific standards influence how systems communicate. Some of these standards evolved with OSI development; some were influential in defining the OSI standards.

The Institute of Electrical and Electronics Engineers (IEEE), for example, has published a set of standards for the two lowest levels of the OSI model. These definitions include cabling as well as electrical and physical design.

IEEE 802.5 (ISO 8802.5) defines token-ring architecture of the sort proposed by IBM in many situations. A logical token is circulated around a physical ring topology, giving the node that possesses the token exclusive access to the network.

IEEE 802.4 (ISO 8802.4) also has token-passing architecture, but the physical arrangement is bus topology. Logically, however, an 802.4 network functions as a ring.

The International Telephone and Telegraph Consultative Committtee (CCITT) also has originated standards that have been adopted by many hardware and software vendors around the world.

The CCITT X.25 protocol, for example, establishes methodologies for communicating across packet-switched data networks (PSDN). Like the IEEE 802 specifications, X.25 is a low-level protocol. Interpretation of the information exchanged over an X.25 network must be handled by individual applications.

X.400 is important because it establishes standards for electronic mail interchange and because it is the first higher-layer application to become available under the OSI international standards. The standard specifies how private mail systems and public carriers will transfer mail messages internally and between private and public systems. X.400 also provides for store-and-forward mail service. X.400 was established as a mail system standard in 1984, prompting a number of companies to introduce products based on it. Digital's MailBus and related applications are examples of X.400-compliant products.

File transfer access and management (FTAM) standards handle the actual control of file transfers between systems at the application layer. FTAM standards, finalized in 1988, provide methodologies for file exchange among multivendor systems.

Other application-layer standards include virtual terminal protocol (VTP), common application service elements (CASE), and job transfer and manipulation. At this writing these standards are in various stages of acceptance by international committees and are virtually assured of broad acceptance. They will futher enhance the ability of vendors to operate successfully together in a network environment.

# NETWORK DISTANCE LIMITS

The distance a signal can travel on a network is generally limited by the design of the network and the type of cabling employed. A typical Ethernet network can carry an unamplified signal about a thousand feet, a typical token-ring system about six hundred feet. Various devices can extend the distance:

- *Repeater*. Amplifier with electrical continuity to the cable. Signals enter one side of the amplifier and come out the other side stronger but with no switching or alteration.
- *Buffered repeater*. Amplifier not electrically continuous to the cable. It can control the flow of signals by issuing "start" and "stop" commands to avoid collisions.
- *Bridge*. Connection between networks, allowing nodes on either network to work with nodes on the other. A standard bridge does not amplify signals or control their flow.
- *Gateway*. Intelligent devices that bridge the gap between networks running incompatible protocols, working at the OSI session layer.

## CHAPTER SUMMARY

This chapter provides an overview of Digital's networking environment and introduces technologies and protocols such as Ethernet and DECnet. This chapter also discusses the need for PC-to-VAX connectivity from the perspective of the PC user and the VAX user. The work of OSI committees to standardize network communication is presented. Chapter 3 provides more details on networking procedures and technologies.

# 3

# Coordinating PCs in the VAX Environment: Networking

A personal computer means different things to different users. It is all the computer many users ever have, and it serves their needs very well. To others the PC is just one small component in a much larger computing environment that may include minicomputers, mainframes, and other PCs. For these users the PC is an intelligent workstation and a terminal; it is a personal processor that provides local CPU power and storage; it serves as a platform to run personal applications such as word processing, spreadsheets, data management, and graphics programs; it provides a window into larger computer systems.

This chapter shows you how PCs are becoming part of VAX computing environments through networking. Later chapters talk about telecommunication and direct links.

## COMPUTING ISLANDS: PCS IN THE WORKPLACE

The need for interconnecting PCs is stronger now than it has ever been. It took a number of years for traditional computer users and corporate MIS departments to embrace personal computers as viable members of a computing enterprise, but once that happened, growth was rapid.

The most common complaint PC users offer about multiuser computing is that response times are slow. This is a valid complaint when you are accustomed to having the full power of a one-MIPS or faster CPU dedicated to your use. Many traditional VAX machines are rated at little more than today's new high-speed desktop computers, yet they may service twenty or more users.

PC users also complain that they have spent months or years learning how to use familiar PC-based software such as Lotus 1-2-3, which are often more versatile than their host counterparts. Many PC users are accustomed to a color screen and graphics-oriented applications, while most VAX users have VT-100-class monochrome terminals with only limited graphics support.

Most of these complaints are valid, so it is no wonder that users experienced only in the PC environment shy away from shared computing. However, fairly recent advances in hardware and software are providing users with the best of both PC and VAX. Individual computers linked over a network to a central VAX-class server form the ultimate computing environment. Many mundane computing tasks such as screen updates and other user presentation duties, communication with the network, and the core of applications processing can be conducted at the desktop, relieving the central processor and providing faster response time.

## PC NETWORKS: DEPARTMENTAL DISTRIBUTED PROCESSING

The first step in bringing PCs into the MIS fold was the development of PC-based local area networks. Companies such as 3Com, Apple, IBM, and Novell provided central file servers, electronic mail, shared print services, and secure applications for the PC.

Most local area networks use bus-level (internal) interface cards for each desktop computer. To install a LAN, you plug in an interface card, run a cable around the network to connect all the PCs (nodes), and load up networking software at each workstation. The cable can be coax or twisted-pair (see chapter 2) and the communications protocol can be Ethernet (see chapter 2) or one of a number of proprietary protocols.

When there are more than a few PCs working within an enterprise or campus, a network can provide definite advantages over stand-alone operation. In fact, some users say that two PCs are enough to benefit from networked operations, and with the new low-cost LAN hardware available today, the cost can be fairly easy to justify.

PC networking provides immediate advantages:

- Electronic mail can be exchanged among the stations.
- Users can share common applications such as databases, calendar and time management programs, and word processors.
- Commonly needed data is available to all users simultaneously.
- Data security is easier to maintain.
- Data backup for all users can be handled at a central location.

There are two basic networking schemes common with PC LANs:

- Peer-to-peer networks, in which every user has full access (subject to security limitations) to all of the facilities of every computer on the network.
- Server networks, in which workstations atttach to a central server computer, sharing only the facilities of the central host.

## Peer-to-Peer LANs

A true peer-to-peer PC network (see Figure 3-1) is rare, and for good reason. A network where all users are equal can be extremely difficult to manage, for one thing. In addition, PCs are not all created equal. A PC AT- or 80386-class machine with a laser printer, a high-speed impact printer, a 12Mhz CPU, 4 MB of memory, and 80 MB of disk space provides a facility to the network that is very different from that of a PC XT with a 4.77 MHz CPU, no printer, dual diskette drives, and 256 kilobytes (KB) of RAM. Peer-to-peer networks are somewhat more common in a large-machine environment, but usually equal access is provided only among approximately equal machines. PCs and other workstations on the network are not accessed in the same way as a large minicomputer host.

There are advantages to peer-to-peer arrangements, however, and this type of network can be successfully applied in some circumstances, such as with a small PC LAN whose members are configured similarly. In this situation network members benefit from distributed storage, access to multiple disk drives, printers and other peripherals, and shared applications.

If a minicomputer host is a part of the network, and if careful management techniques are employed, even greater benefits can be

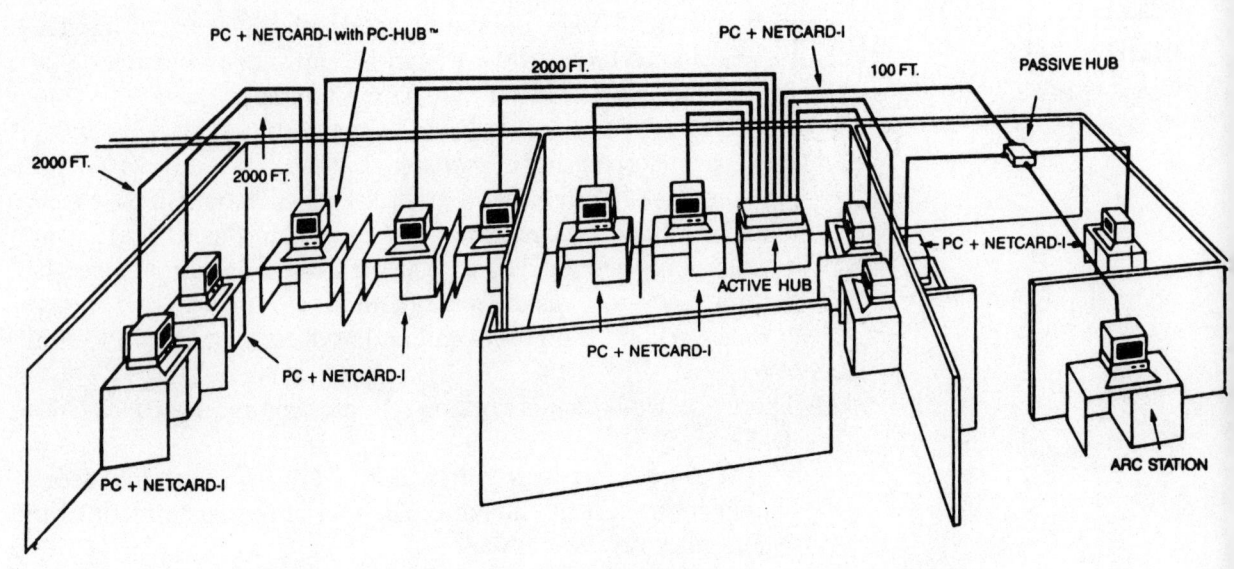

*Figure 3-1* **Peer-to-peer PC LAN configuration. (Source: Black Box Corporation)**

realized. PC users have access to the larger facilities of the host, so the host, can be used as a repository for PC-based applications, making PC software upgrading easier and establishing a backup route for PC-based data.

**Server LANs**

The more common PC network (see Figure 3-2) establishes one or several host machines that can be accessed by the network users. A PC LAN host can be a conventional PC AT- or 80386-class machine running host software, or it can be a machine designed for server duty by the networking company or a third party. If the server is a custom machine, it may or may not possess the same architecture as the PC nodes it services; it may not even use the same microprocessor as its CPU.

In addition to the benefits of file and program sharing, some server-oriented networks also provide specialized processors that may function as part of the main host or may be separate, dedicated CPUs. These include communications servers; gateway servers, which provide access to other networks; and database servers.

## Distributed Processing

Initially, easy transfer of whole files from one computer to another seemed enough, but as users increasingly turned to multiple vendors to provide the computing power they needed, it became obvious that a lower level of sharing was needed.

The problem with most PC networks is the amount of data traffic that crosses the cable. Consider a PC network in which several workstations are running a database program, for example. The database application software is usually stored on the central server for simultaneous access by all users, and the common data files reside on the server disks. To access the shared data, each user calls the database program from the server, which operates like a large remote

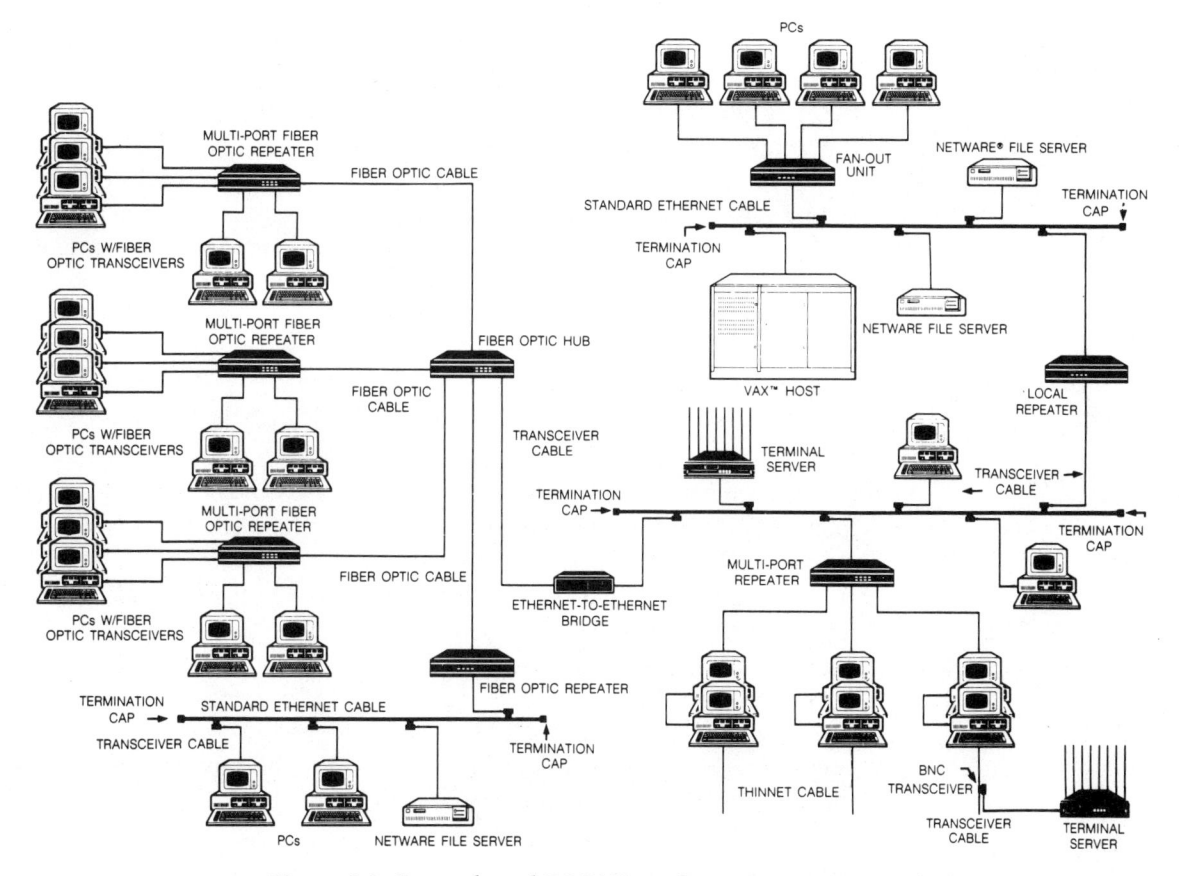

*Figure 3-2* **Server-based PC LAN configuration. (Source: Black Box Corporation)**

disk drive. When the program is loaded into local memory, it runs on the local CPU. Now each desktop computer is functioning as an individual entity, each running a copy of the database application and calling for data from the central disk as needed.

When a report is generated, the local copy of the program sends a request to the server for a portion of data from the central file. A piece of the data file is transmitted across the network to the local PC, where the database software sifts through it looking for the information requested. When the data residing in the local computer's memory has been searched, another request is sent to the server and another piece of the data file is sent across the cable. These steps are repeated until all of the requested data has been found. Next the local program instructions build a report from the found data and send the information back up the network to be printed on a shared printer at the server or at another print station.

Although this arrangement gives users access to the same data simultaneously, as you can see, it also generates a tremendous number of transfer operations, filling the network data path and slowing down operations.

A better design would be to distribute the processing further on the network so that only the data requested by a local workstation is transmitted from the server. In this arrangement an individual user requests certain data from a central file by sending the request to the central server, where the file is searched and the requested records are transmitted to the local workstation for further processing. It may even be possible to send only pointers or other codes to the local workstation, never transmitting a full record until the local workstation asks to display it on a screen. Then, if the search results in printed output, a network print server can process the report, reducing even further the amount of information that must be exchanged with the workstation.

The ultimate multiprocessor solution provides this kind of true integration of hardware and software in a distributed environment. Distributed processing systems use the power of multiple CPUs simultaneously, effectively increasing the CPU power available for any processing task. Four one-MIPS (million instruction per second) machines working in concert on a database problem, for example, can provide the throughput of a much larger machine.

With the acceptance of personal computers within minicomputer and mainframe environments, desktop and deskside processors are becoming part of Digital's distributed processing architecture. As Digital and third party software vendors add distributed processing power to their programs, personal computers will offload more processing duties from the host CPU. Programs like DECwindows, which moves screen updates and user interface processing to desktop machines, for example, can increase dramatically the overall power of a computer installation.

## Components of LANs

There are two major components in any network, the hardware and the software. Although neither component can function alone, with the push for international networking standards, the hardware is fast becoming a commodity, while vendors are vying for differentiation in the software they offer.

### Network Hardware

PC LAN hardware traditionally has been a mixed bag, generating a lot of disagreement among vendors over the best method for connecting workstations to the server and to each other. The hardware and its associated cabling system and firmware determine which protocols the network will use to exchange data. Ethernet (see chapter 2) is among the most popular networking schemes, even in the PC environment, because it affords the potential, at least, for compatibility with networks of larger machines.

Whatever network protocol is used, the hardware arrangement is basically the same. A bus-level circuit board called a network interface card (NIC) is plugged into one of the expansion slots inside each PC on the network. Another card is installed inside the network server machine. Depending on the design of the network, this card may be identical to the ones in the other workstations, or it may be a special server version of the network interface. If the server is not a standard PC bus machine, then the network interface may be part of the main circuit board or it may use a proprietary bus.

A cabling system connects network members. A connector is attached to each circuit board mounted inside each PC network member and to each server on the network. If ring or bus topology is used, each network member, including the servers, attaches to only a single cable. If some workstations are members of more than one network, there must be a separate interface card and cable attachment for each network. In a star configuration, the workstations have a single cable attachment and the server has one cable for each PC on the network.

**Network Software**

Two basic software components make up the other part of any network installation. Network access software—sometimes called a network driver—is installed on each workstation in the network, and server software permits the server PC or dedicated server to process information for the remote nodes.

Usually the PC-based network driver is loaded as the operating system is booted and becomes part of the operating system. Such drivers use 60 KB or more of available memory as long as you are running the network application. Node software conducts a number of functions:

- Sends and receives characters through the bus-level network interface card
- Catalogues network resources such as disk drives and printers and makes them available to the local workstation
- Processes network messages, including error conditions, and displays them to the user
- Handles the interface between applications software and the network
- Interfaces with the PC's operating system, passing data from the network for local processing and accepting local information for processing at the network level

Whether the network server is a dedicated PC or custom hardware, it must run control software to allow it to perform its duties. Server software performs many of the same functions as node software, but in the opposite direction. The server software works more like a complete operating system than the node software. The server software:

- Sends and receives characters through the network interface card. This can involve exchanges through a single port, much like an individual node, if the network is a bus or ring configuration; or it can require management of individual workstation connections if the network is a star.

- Catalogues network resources and manages access among the attached workstations. Two users cannot use the same disk drive at precisely the same time, for example. Therefore the network server must accept requests for access, put them in the proper order, and process them quickly and efficiently. The server also must manage the print queue, buffering data for one or several printers.
- Monitors the network and processes network messages, including error and status conditions, and sends them to the users as required.
- Manages logon and logoff, including passwords and other security codes and procedures.

## THE VAX NETWORK: DECNET

DECnet is one of the most important parts of the Digital product line. DECnet and its associated components form the foundation for connectivity among computers, printers, terminals, and PCs throughout the enterprise. The features of DECnet evolved as Digital's connectivity philosophy solidified. (See chapter 2.) In addition, DECnet is growing to address the needs of multivendor, heterogeneous computer systems through the addition of OSI-compatible stacks. (See chapter 2.) Digital's goal is to make DECnet compatible with the communications architecture of other vendors who adhere to this international standard while maintaining the benefits of their own proprietary networking features.

This section discusses DECnet and the Digital networking architecture in detail. The information here should provide good background for later discussions of networking communications, and it can serve as a reference to features and functions for other applications of DECnet.

### Overview of DECnet

DECnet has a long history. It grew out of a need to communicate among a variety of internal hardware and software systems. DECnet has been evolving since 1974, and the company has done a pretty good job of keeping it abreast of technology and user requirements. It is interesting to note that DECnet predated OSI by about five years, and many of the original DECnet concepts are embodied in OSI.

What was first designed as a program to help Digital connect its own people and hardware grew into a major sales tool that was offered to customers and was supported heavily by third-party vendors. During the mid and late 1980s, as a worldwide push for computer communications standards gained strength (see chapter 2), Digital expanded its philosophy of interconnection to include multivendor environments. Although still committed to some proprietary features, such as the VMS operating system (see chapter 9), Digital has officially recognized the need for easy integration of hardware and software from multiple vendors and is supporting standards that further this capability.

DECnet is software that runs with Ethernet and is the core of DNA. DNA has undergone a number of revisions over the years. Phase V (DECnet/OSI) is the latest version. It addresses the need for international communications standards by adhering closely to the OSI model while maintaining proprietary features essential for maximum function. With the introduction of phase V in 1987, Digital established a three-year program for providing full OSI compliance in DECnet/OSI. That means full phase V features will be available sometime in 1990, but portions of the new version are to be released periodically until then.

Digital usually refers to DECnet and OSI as similar, parallel, and simultaneous architectures. Ultimately DECnet will be smart enough to understand which protocol stack is being used by any applications software, and the applications that call on the network will be routed automatically via OSI or DECnet.

One interesting fact about DECnet is the level of sophistication and planning built into the network from the beginning. Although the OSI recommendations developed separately, there are many similarities between the OSI model and Digital's version of a heterogeneous network. It is this planned architecture that is permitting DECnet to interface relatively easily with the OSI model and to be flexible enough to address changes in communications technology, which have been rapid over the past few years. The modular design of DECnet further enables the company to respond to customer needs and technology changes.

Among Digital's stated design goals for DNA:

- *Transparent operation*. Network access should appear simple and be virtually invisible to the user. In addition, the network should require a minimum of management intervention.

- *Broad-based and flexible support for technologies and applications.* DNA is designed to handle a wide range of applications, communications facilities, and network topologies as well as to permit growth and to support migration to new architectures. DNA can also be implemented as subsets for installations that do not require all of its features.
- *Support for standards.* Digital stated its intention to support the developing OSI standard from the beginning and has been instrumental in helping to evolve the specifics of OSI recommendations.
- *Decentralized and secure facilities.* Within DNA such functions as routing and network management are not centralized. This is one factor in maintaining high availability (reliability) and security. Specific security features are built into the architecture.

## DECnet versus OSI

DNA, which includes DECnet, has three layers of support: the link layer, the management layer, and the application layer.

- *Link layer.* Supervises the communications hardware and the packaging of messages. For point-to-point connections in an all-Digital system, DECnet creates packets, transmits them, and decodes them using the Digital data communications message protocol (DDCMP). In a heterogeneous environment, DNA's link layer could be replaced by Ethernet or X.25 communications.
- *Management layer.* Supervises the routing of messages between sending and receiving DECnet nodes. Programming calculates the lowest-cost route for a particular message from among the various physical links available. DECnet also finds alternative connection paths in the case of failure of individual lines or network nodes that are used in routing. This feature is called adaptive routing capability.
- *Application layer.* Allows programs running on different nodes of the network easy exchange of logical messages and cooperation with each other. This facility, similar to IBM's LU 6.2 software, permits applications such as shared databases and electronic mail.

DECnet itself is divided into five basic layers and has many similarities with the OSI model. The bottom four layers have the same name and perform almost identical functions as their counterparts in OSI. The fifth layer conducts session control and incorporates session, presentation, and application layers, which are separated under OSI. Frequently the session-control layer is subdivided further to show the close relationship between DECnet and the OSI model. (See Figures 3-3 and 3-4.)

| OSI | DECnet |
|---|---|
| Application | User layer |
| Presentation | Network applications |
| Session | Session control |
| Transport | End of communication |
| Network | Routing |
| Link | Data link |
| Physical | Physical link |

In addition, Digital specifies separately a naming service that is part of the session control layer and maintains a database of network resources that can be made available to all systems on the network.

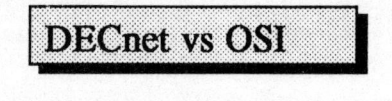

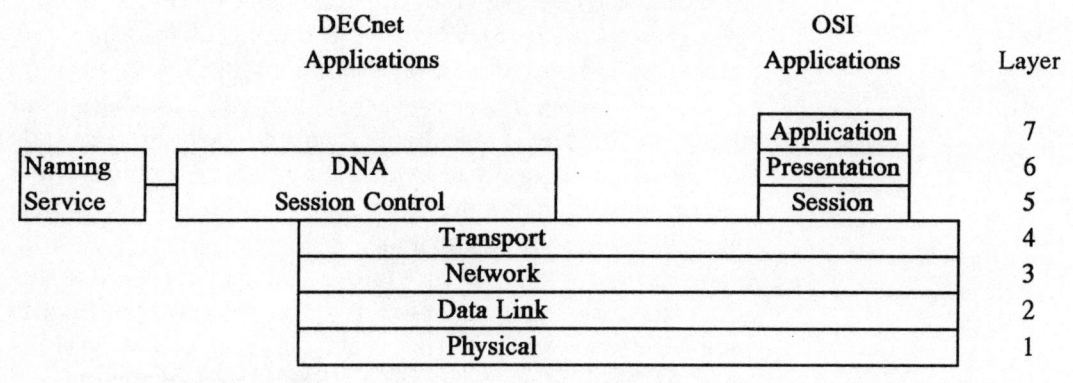

**DECnet vs OSI**

*Figure 3-3* DECnet Layers versus OSI layers

*Figure 3-4* **Open Systems Interconnection model
(Source: Digital Equipment Corporation)**

With DECnet/OSI phase V, all applications use the first four layers just as they would in a straight OSI network. After the fourth layer, applications can decide whether to make calls based on the OSI stack or to use Digital's proprietary protocols. In this way existing applications are not hampered by the switch to OSI standards, many of which were not settled when DECnet was designed, and new applications that adhere to OSI should function satisfactorily. In addition, designers can choose to use the proprietary aspects of DNA if it is a better choice for a given application. Digital and other companies contend that DECnet is a better choice for some applications. The DNA design permits either route.

### Physical Layer

The physical layer is the lowest layer of DECnet, just as it is in the OSI model. This layer sends and receives data across the network medium; it handles such mundane tasks as converting computer-level data into electrical signals that can be sent across the network and back again on the other end. Other functions include monitoring of communications channels and management of such physical-layer connections as dialup lines and X.21.

### Data Link Layer

The second, or data-link layer, ensures that communications across the network will be error free. This is accomplished through communications protocols that can detect and correct data errors from the physical layer.

### Network Layer

The network layer is the traffic handler for network data. It interprets the network addresses of data packets and sends them to the proper location. The database and interpreting logic of the network layer are capable of supporting networks of hundreds of thousands of nodes.

### Transport Layer

The transport layer takes over where the network layer leaves off. It retransmits packets that did not reach their destination because of other network traffic, helps match the network transmission rate to the sending and receiving nodes, and manages the network to avoid congestion while achieving maximum use of network resources.

**DNA Session Control**

This fifth layer of DNA begins the proprietary portion of DECnet. It replaces the OSI session, presentation, and application protocols. (See chapter 2.) These layers of OSI carry data farther up the line toward an application, providing interfaces between the application and the network.

DNA's session-control layer performs similar functions. (See Figure 3-5.) It manages the logical connections between network users and the application services they employ.

It also selects the proper communications protocol between users, manages transport-layer connections, and enforces access control policies, among other duties. Session control also must provide for interfaces between the transport layer and the user of session-layer services.

## Features of DECnet Network Management

With the growth in size and popularity of computer networks, the concept of network management assumes increasing importance. The management of even a small network can involve several important functions, including

- Ensuring that network users have access to the faciliites they need
- Establishing passwords and other security structures and procedures to protect user data
- Monitoring network activity and tuning the operation for maximum efficiency
- Detecting and correcting operational and procedural problems
- Organizing network operational and configuration data into useful statistics to aid in planning for growth

As the size of a network increases, proper management becomes more important and the problems associated with management increase. The more users on a system, the more potential for problems to develop, and with very large networks, it can be very difficult to

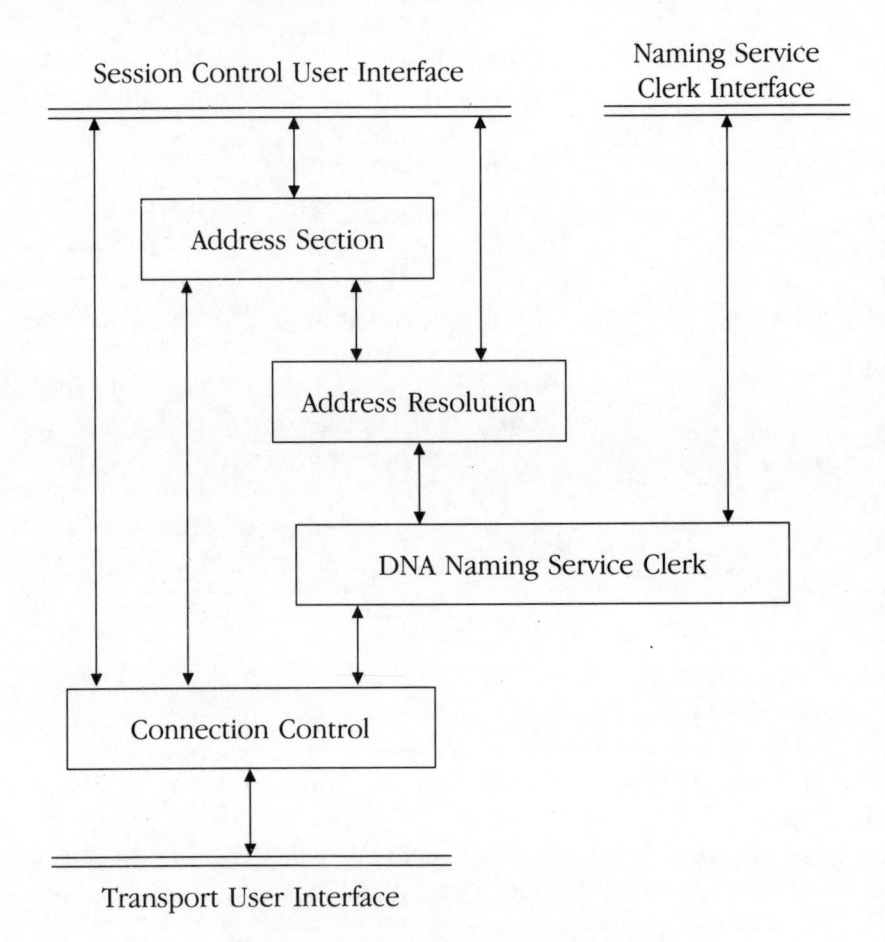

```
                  Session Control User Interface                Naming Service
                                                                Clerk Interface

                         ┌──────────────────┐
                         │  Address Section │
                         └──────────────────┘

                         ┌──────────────────┐
                         │ Address Resolution│
                         └──────────────────┘

                         ┌──────────────────────┐
                         │DNA Naming Service Clerk│
                         └──────────────────────┘

                  ┌──────────────────┐
                  │ Connection Control│
                  └──────────────────┘

                       Transport User Interface
```

*Figure 3-5* **Components of session control
(Source: Digital Equipment Corporation)**

determine where problems exist and what is causing them. Over time, as users and facilites are added, for example, portions of the network may begin to slow down. This may be caused by inefficient software, inappropriate network activities by one or more users, or equipment problems.

With large networks such processes as updating user access rights, adding software components, adding or removing a user, changing network configuration, and data backup can become very complicated and time-consuming. Proper network management tools and procedures can make these tasks more manageable.

It is important to maintain high network efficiency. Monitoring traffic, identifying different types of network activities, detecting differences in speed across different network segments, and storing data for later analysis can all help identify and correct problems.

Digital is now operating what may be the largest network in the world. During 1988 the company installed the forty-thousandth node on its worldwide network, which that year grew at the rate of 150 nodes each week. The company has said publicly on several occasions that one reason it is able to maintain successfully such a large network is use of the built-in network management features that have been a part of DECnet from its inception. Additional tools are available to expand DECnet management capabilities.

Network management can be a full time job for one or more people depending on the number of users. Digital promotes DECnet and its management tools as being very efficient, allowing a minimum number of people to handle the management functions. When Digital's internal network supported only two thousand nodes worldwide, there were six full-time network management people. Today, with a network fifteen times as large, the number of network management personnel is only eighteen.

A network is managed by people who use information collected from a number of resources to detect problems, to tune network operation, and to plan for future operations. They use networked hardware and software to support these tasks. Software such as DECnet has some network management facilities built in, and other software tools for data collection and analysis can be added.

The manager's terminal or workstation has access to management software and other special facilities. The manager can display real-time usage information about the network, design and print reports, conduct statistical analysis on the data, produce graphs and charts, even disable and enable network functions from the manager's workstation or terminal.

The manager does not have to sit in front of a screen all day, watching network events, to find out about the operation of the system. Usually monitoring tools — either dedicated hardware that is a separate network node or software that runs on one of the network's CPUs — capture operational data throughout a day or other period. The manager can display statistics at any time, compare the current statistics with those of previous periods, and project facility requirements into the future.

With DECnet phase V, Digital added a network control language (NCL), which makes it easier to control other network management features. NCL provides authorized personnel with access to the management directives (commands issued to control or monitor network components) that are defined for all network components.

The phase V DNA model also includes an ISO-compliant common management information protocol (CMIP) that runs at the application layer. CMIP is a request-response protocol that enables managers to get and set management attributes, to request execution of management actions, and to report various network events.

## Enhancements of DECnet

Although Digital characterizes DECnet as a full-featured flexible package, a number of enhancement software products are offered. The following section provides a brief summary of some of these products.

### VAX Packet-Switching Interface

Packet-switching interface (PSI) hardware and software to support X.25 and other communications standards. VAX PSI or Ethernet provides low-level OSI network protocols for integration of DECnet in an OSI environment.

### VAX DEC/MAP

Hardware and software to integrate VAX systems into MAP networks. The specifications for MAP networks in factory environments are not yet set.

### VAX OSI

Transport service; VAX OSI applications kernel. A refinement to DECnet's central network management protocol layer to provide an interface from a networked VAX to programs running on other nodes, including non-Digital systems, using OSI's transport and application layers.

### Message Router X.400 Gateway

An electronic mail gateway service between VAX mail products and other mail services. Based on conformity with the National Bureau of

Standards specification for the message format for computer-based message systems.

## SNA

Digital supports IBM's LU 6.2 Advanced Program-to-Program Communications (APPC) protocol, for peer-to-peer communications with IBM SNA systems. Individual workstations on a DECnet network cannot participate in peer-to-peer relation with nodes on an SNA network.

## Other Networks and Protocols

Although DECnet/OSI is important for all VAX users simply because it is the mainstay of Digital's networking strategy and there are so many DECnet users already in place, other networks are common to Digital installations. Some of the protocols discussed in this section, such as TCP/IP, are generic and are supported by a number of vendors. Others, such as Novell's Netware, are proprietary and are used only by a single vendor. In either case these are popular networks and some implementation of them can be found in many Digital shops.

In many cases third-party networks provide some form of connectivity to DECnet, and the number of these networks is growing. Such network-to-network connectivity is making the task of choosing personal computer resources easier because departmental work groups can set up a PC-based network that satisfies their needs, while retaining the link to corporate computing facilities and data through an internetwork connection.

## TCP/IP

The transmission control protocol/internet protocol (TCP/IP) is a common networking scheme in the UNIX environment because it is supported as part of the popular Berkeley version of UNIX. TCP/IP was originally developed for ARPAnet (Advanced Research Products Agency), an early network architecture, and in recent times some industry observers have predicted that TCP/IP is destined to be phased out. Instead, an increasing number of vendors are producing TCP/IP communications products, and it has evolved over the past few years as one more unifying standard in network communications. One reason is that it is nonproprietary; another is the fact that the protocols have been around long enough to be well defined and understood.

Although TCP/IP lacks the detail and sophistication of the OSI model and DECnet, it remains a useful protocol because almost all vendors support it in some form or another. TCP/IP can be useful in linking heterogeneous systems, and it is the primary communications protocol on many networks, particularly UNIX-based systems.

## AppleTalk

AppleTalk, the basic network that is built into every Macintosh computer, is extendable to peripherals and to other computer systems.

Available cabling systems:

- Shielded twisted-pair (AppleTalk Personal Network Cabling)
- Unshielded twisted-pair (from manufacturers including Northern Telecom and Farallon PhoneNET)
- Fiber-optic (DuPont Fiber-Optic LAN)
- Coaxial (Ethernet)

AppleTalk architecture is an open, layered protocol system that includes network services. AppleTalk is consistent with OSI.

AppleShare, the information-sharing component in AppleTalk, handles file sharing and program sharing across the AppleTalk network, permitting several users access to the same data file or the same program simultaneously. Part of Apple's network architecture is the AppleTalk Filing Protocol (AFP), the basic component of AppleShare.

Apple Macintosh users can access the VAX environment in a number of ways. A direct serial link (RS-232C or RS-422) with software to provide VAX-compatible terminal emulation is about the simplest way and one of the most popular. Apple as well as third-party vendors provide Mac-to-VAX communications software.

AppleTalk users can achieve a tighter, more integrated link to the VAX through AppleTalk for VMS. This product brings the VAX into the AppleTalk network and the Macintosh into the DECnet environment. With this arrangement an application running under VAX/VMS (the VAX operating system) appears as a node on the attached AppleTalk network. A Macintosh node can exchange packets of information with the VAX host and its application. In addition, the Macintosh running as part of an AppleTalk network can access such VAX facilities as DECnet network services, applications software, and large disk storage.

Macintosh computers can use a variety of hardware attachment schemes to attach to an Ethernet link running DECnet. Or a Q-bus interface card such as the KFPQ from Kinetics can be installed inside a MicroVAX computer, permitting the VAX to attach directly to the AppleTalk network.

AppleTalk-to-VAX products also are offered by Alisa Systems and Technology Concepts, Inc. Community-Mac from Technology Concepts is software that interfaces with DECnet through an Ethernet controller installed inside the Macintosh. Alisa's TSSnet software operates over asynchronous communications lines or with a Mac-based Ethernet controller.

## Netware

Novell is one of the original PC networking companies. Today it offers one of the most popular network hardware and software solutions for PC users. The company was incorporated in 1983.

Novell's network products include PC-based file servers, network interface cards for coaxial and twisted-pair links, and a variety of network software. Although Novell provides complete network packages, it is the firm's NetWare software that has made its reputation. NetWare PC and host software is supported by most network hardware vendors. The company claims to have more than 1.5 million NetWare workstations in operation.

Novell has a three-tiered approach to providing the PC user with network services. The company supplies an S-Net, a dedicated server that uses a 68000-family CPU in a star configuration. This network operates with NetWare/68 and is linked to PC workstations with shielded twisted-pair cable. Novell also supplies a line of 80286- and 80386-based server PCs with large disk drives for networks that use NetWare/286 as the operating software. And the company supplies NetWare to more than thirty third-party network companies for inclusion in their network packages.

NetWare is recognized as one of the premier network operating systems, providing high speed even on large networks, a good user interface, a number of useful utilities and tools, and compatibility across a wide range of network configurations. In addition, the product is well documented and is relatively easy to install and configure.

The most recent Novell product of interest to VAX users is NetWare/VMS, a version of networking software that runs on VAX computers under the VMS operating system. (See Figure 3-6.) With NetWare/VMS, PC network users can attach directly to a DECnet network and access a Digital host as a member of the Novell network. This arrangement means that PC users on a department-level LAN can access VMS files on a VAX as if they were PC-DOS files and use other host facilities such as high-speed printers. In addition, Novell provides terminal emulation facilities to enable LAN-based PCs to log on to the VAX as if they were VT-series devices and to operate normally in that environment. In this configuration the PC functions as a VT-class terminal directly attached to the VAX, even though it may actually be at a remote location, accessing the VAX over DECnet and NetWare.

NetWare coexists on the Ethernet link with DECnet and LAT (local area transport) protocols and operates as a single process on the VAX. As far as the PC user is concerned, all of the VAX hosts on

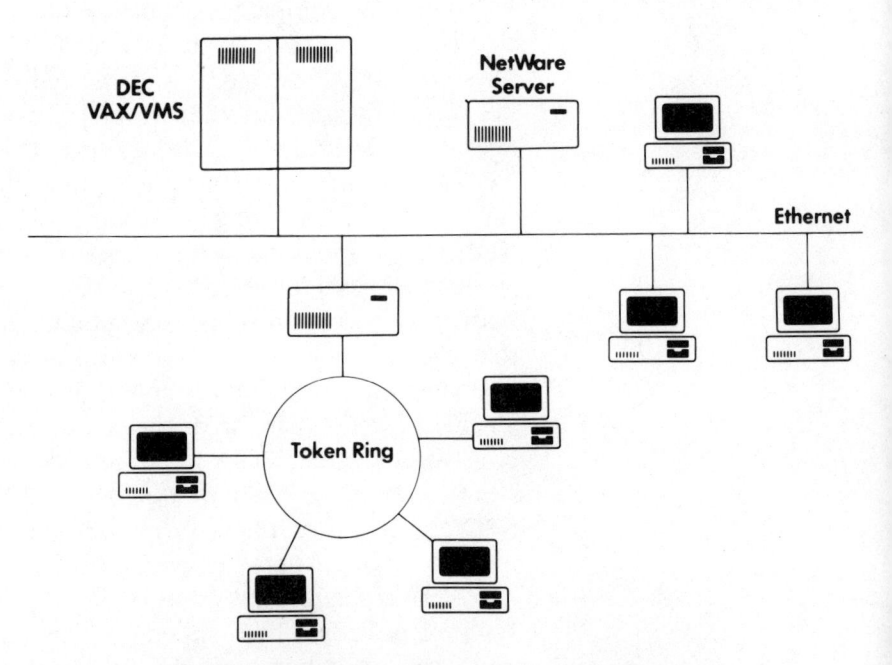

*Figure 3-6* **NetWare/VMS connects PC LAN users to VAX hosts via DECnet. (Source: Novell, Inc.)**

the network are part of the PC LAN. Such a configuration is an easy, transparent method for integrating PC workstations into the VAX environment.

## CHAPTER SUMMARY

This chapter shows you how PCs can be networked in the VAX computing environment. The concept of distributed processing, one of the most important and growing areas of PC networking, was introduced. Such topics as LAN types, LAN hardware and software components, and the technology of Digital's DECnet protocol are discussed, as well as other network protocols, including AppleTalk. The next chapter provides details on telecommunication theory.

# 4

# The Theory of Telecommunications

Ask ten computer users, people who personally handle a wide range of configurations and software, what is the most difficult and time-consuming part of using the machine, and seven of the responses probably will be communications. Although there are standards for connecting one computer to another, the specifications allow room for different hardware and software vendors to design custom devices and procedures.

The basics of computer-to-computer communications are not difficult to comprehend or implement, but the process is unnecessarily complicated by poor documentation, very loose adherence to standards, and a lack of understanding on the part of the user.

This book will not provide step-by-step instructions on how to connect one computer to another; that topic is best left to a technical manual targeted at system designers and integrators. This book will introduce many basic concepts, however, and give you enough information to discuss your communications needs with the MIS department, purchasers, and other company personnel involved in implementation.

This chapter discusses the basics of PC communications, introducing concepts and terms that will make your use of communications hardware and software easier and more productive.

## THE HARDWARE SIDE OF COMMUNICATIONS

Your microcomputer has never heard of the letter A or the number 65. It has no idea what a circle looks like. When it comes right down to it, the machine understands only two very simple concepts: the number 1 and the lack of the number 1. It doesn't even deal in 1s and 0s. Instead the computer is limited to taking a voltage reading to distinguish between on and off. That is all that a computer does—it moves pulses of high voltage or low voltage around the system and in and out of storage places and then takes a voltage reading.

The power of the computer comes from its ability to work with predefined machine logic to allow combinations of on and off to represent almost any bit of data or instructions.

One such pulse is one bit. Bits can be stored in the computer's internal random access memory; they can be put in magnetic form on a floppy or hard disk; they can be permanently etched into silicon inside a read-only memory chip, or they can be in transit from point to point within the computer system. This chapter is principally concerned with bits as they travel into and out of a computer's communications interface—the doorway to the outside world.

This native computer counting system is based on binary arithmetic, dealing solely in 0s and 1s. Decimal arithmetic, which runs from 0 to 9, is the system we most commonly use in our own transactions. There are several other formats, though, that are used by computer programmers for various reasons.

Mathematicians call the multiplying factor for a numbering system the *base*. Almost all systems begin values on the right and work to the left. The rightmost value represents single units up to one short of the base value. For example, in our ordinary decimal counting system, the number 27 can be deciphered as seven units and two times the base number.

Binary has a base of 2, decimal a base of 10, octal a base of 8, and hexadecimal a base of 16.

Let's examine the binary system used in internal representation of numbers by the computer. The only symbols used are 0 and 1, which represent "yes" and "no" in filling out the positions of a binary number. For example, the decimal number 154 in binary is:

1 0 0 1 1 0 1 0.

The way to translate that number into decimal is to read it, from right to left, as

No 1s, one 2, no 4s, one 8, one 16, no 32s, no 64s and one 128, or, in mathematical terms,

$(0 \times 1) + (1 \times 2) + (0 \times 4) + (1 \times 8) + (1 \times 16) + (0 \times 32) + (0 \times 64) + (1 \times 128) = 154$

Now we'll convert that value into a hexadecimal number, which is the system used by many computers for internal storage of numbers. Hexadecimal breaks the same decimal number into two parts, or nibbles. First comes a high order nibble of 1001, and then a low-order nibble of 1010. Each can have a value of 0 to 15, determined by adding the maximum values possible for each of the four columns of the binary number:

$(1 \times 8) + (1 \times 4) + (1 \times 2) + (1 \times 1) = 15$

In this example the 1001 high-order nibble equals 9; the low-order 1010 nibble equals 10. It could be called Hex 9-10. Instead, the letters A through F are used to symbolize values 10 through 15. Hex 9-10, then, becomes Hex 9A. The 9 is multiplied by the base number for the hexadecimal system, 16, and yields 144. A equals 10, which is multiplied by 1, since it is in the units column. The total is 154.

All signals and data on the interface are in binary form. A data bit that carries a value of 1 is called a mark and is the normal condition of the line when there is no data. The mark condition is set by a voltage of -3 to -25. A data bit with a value of 0—the only other kind allowed—is called a *space,* and is indicated by +3 volts to +25.

Therefore, when the computer detects an incoming signal changing from a negative voltage to a positive voltage—from a mark to a space—it determines that a 0 data bit has arrived.

The next step for the computer is the translation of those high- and low-voltage states into the 0s and 1s of binary arithmetic. A signal consisting of mark, space, space, space, space, space, mark would be read as a binary value of 1000001, which is equivalent to 65 in base-10 arithmetic. If the information is merely being stored by the computer, the value continues to its resting place in a binary form; if the information is to be displayed on a video screen, the computer then looks up the base-10 value 65 in its ASCII code table, determines it to represent the letter A, and communicates that information, to the monitor.

Luckily, you don't have to use the computer's language, at least not at that level. It is useful to have some understanding of what goes on inside the machine, but software facilities isolate most users, even programmers, from this low-level computer communication.

## Putting Bits on the Move

The information inside the computer can be translated into characters on a video screen or on paper via a printer. The information can send commands to a plotter, or to a robot arm, or to any one of thousands of devices that can now be mated to a computer. But how can we send that information from one computer to another?

Here are a few ways:

1. *By direct connection of the computers.* The digital output of one machine can be plugged into an input port of the other, and data can be transmitted. Direct connection is a fast, relatively simple means of communication for computers, but it is limited, since it requires point-to-point links between machines relatively close to each other.
2. *By interchange of storage medium.* A floppy disk full of information, for example, can be physically moved from one machine to another. Other forms of physical interchange include magnetic and paper tapes, optical disks, and RAM and ROM cartridges. Interchange of media is a one-way form of communication, since machines are not directly linked. Copying and reading data from a disk drive is comparatively slow, too, and there is time lost through the actual movement of the storage medium from one location to another. In addition, not all types of computers are compatible with each other. A disk prepared on an IBM PC, for example, cannot be read by a VAX without conversion to the VAX format.
3. *By connection through an intermediary wired network such as a telephone system, a public telecommunications network, or a special-purpose LAN.*

## Taking the Serial Bus

The task of moving those 0s and 1s from point to point is the heart of telecommunications, and it does not proceed in a very straightforward manner.

The digital signals moving around within a microcomputer travel along a parallel path—think of it as a multilane highway. In a computer with an eight-bit data bus like the IBM PC, the Apple II, and most computers that use the CP/M operating system, eight wires carry all eight bits of each computer word alongside each other so that all of the elements of a word arrive at the same moment. The IBM PC AT, the Apple Macintosh, and many other state-of-the-art micros have a sixteen-bit data bus, and so sixteen bits of a computer word travel in parallel along sixteen wires inside the computer.

The parallel bus is sometimes extended outside of the computer to form an easy link to a printer or plotter. It is not a big deal to bring eight wires a few feet from the computer to another desktop machine. However, to send the same information over longer distance, particularly when telephone cable is the carrier, the limit usually is only two wires instead of eight.

Therefore, for most longer-distance communication, the parallel output of the computer bus must be converted into a *serial* signal, in which each bit of the computer word follows the one before down a single-data wire; the second wire is the return circuit from the receiver.

The device that makes the conversion is usually called a serial or asynchronous port. The workhorse on that port is a microchip called a UART (universal asynchronous receiver/transmitter). It splits up the parallel data into serial bits and frames each word with start and stop bits to indicate the beginning and end.

The output of the UART is marks and spaces in the form of electrical voltage. The signal goes to a connector; the connector mates to a cable that carries the signal on agreed-upon channels.

## THE TELEPHONE NETWORK

With today's technology any two persons in almost any two places on the face of the earth can communicate directly with each other in a matter of seconds. The necessary device is a telephone, and few residents of the developed world are ever more than a few minutes away from one of the nodes of its system. There are more than 500 million phones installed around the world.

In theory this network of overhead wires, underground and undersea cables, microwave links, and satellite transmitters and receivers could be used for interconnection of at least 500 million

## Terms and Technology

The typical phone line has two to four wires. Only two of the wires are used to carry data and perform all other telephone functions, including ringing the bell. A voice telephone line is technically limited to 9,600 baud (bits per second) using most standard modulation schemes, although 2,400 baud is a more realistic speed. In many places voice phone lines will not support rates even that high, and may be best used at 1,200 or 300 baud.

The connection from the user's office or home to the local phone company is called the local loop. If you call from your house to the neighbor's across the street, the call travels to the central office and back along this line. At the central office, there are two primary outbound links: an interoffice trunk line, which connects with other local central offices, and a toll trunk, which connects to a toll office and intertoll trunk lines for long-distance calls. At each office the phone company must install amplifiers and switching devices.

Here is an outline of a typical local telephone link:

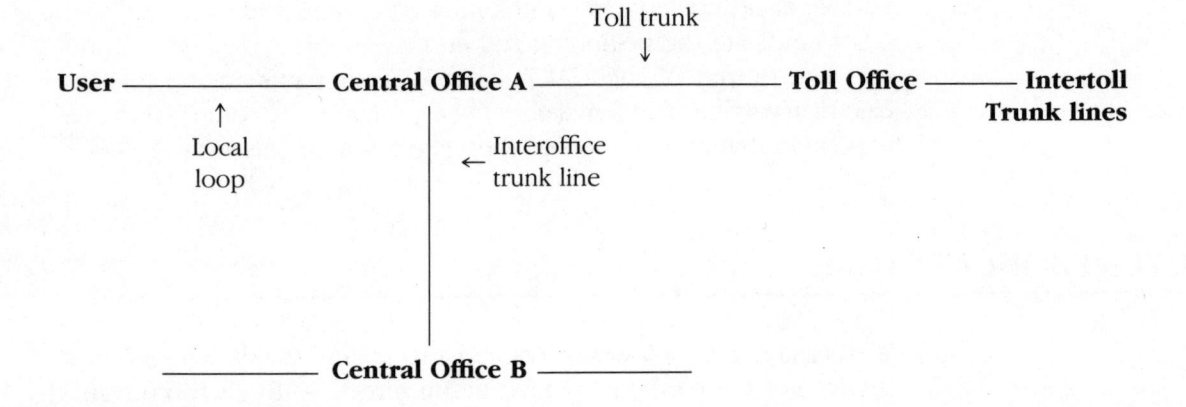

```
                           Toll trunk
                               ↓
User ——————— Central Office A ————————— Toll Office ——— Intertoll
          ↑                   |                            Trunk lines
        Local              ← Interoffice
        loop                 trunk line
                              |
                              |
             ——————— Central Office B ———————
```

## The Nature of the Phone Network

Remember that information stored and manipulated inside a computer is in the form of digital bits, high- or low-voltage levels in memory chips or registers of microprocessors. Two computers directly connected across a short distance with a high-quality cable can easily transfer information using the digital pulses. But once the cable extends more than about fifty to one thousand feet (depending on the type of connection technology used), the quality of the signal degrades; and even if that were not a problem, it is hardly practical to stretch private wires across town or across the country.

The obvious solution is to use the telephone system. However, this presents a different problem. With most voice-grade telephone systems, direct transmission of digital signals is not possible. The precise on/off pulses that leave the transmitter become muddy noise when sent on a voice line.

Why can't voice-grade phone lines carry high-speed data transmissions? Back up for a moment and look at the design of the phone system.

Phone signals are electrical and were designed to carry a representation of the human voice. The human voice consists of recognizable sounds, which are themselves acoustic signals. In human spoken communication, the diaphragm moves air through the voice box and our mouths, where we modulate the air to create sound. Modulation is the use of one signal or medium to change another.

The telephone system uses transducers to convert one form of energy into another. One, the transmitter, is the microphone in the mouthpiece of the telephone that converts sound waves into electrical waves. Another transducer, the receiver, is the speaker in the earpiece, converting electrical waves back into sound waves.

Say "Hello" into the microphone of a telephone, and the sound waves generated by the modulation of air by the human voice box physically move a membrane in the microphone, using modulation to produce an electrical signal. That electrical signal is sent down a wire in a telephone circuit to another telephone, where the signal moves a speaker coil. The physical movements of that coil move air once again, creating sound that can travel to our ear. The full chain of human to human communication via a telephone link: Brain waves, which are electrical; the voice box's output, which is acoustical; the transmitter's output, which is electrical; the receiver's output, which is acoustical; and the human ear's final product, an electrical signal to the brain of the receiver.

The actual telephone signal is called an analog message—a representation of the real sound. Louder is higher, for example. If you were to examine a graph or an oscilloscope pattern of a moment of human speech, you would see that the variations in frequency (what we call pitch) are comparable to the variations in the frequency of an electrical analog conversion of that same moment of human speech.

The typical human voice has a maximum range from deepest bass of 25 Hz to shrillest soprano of 20,000 Hz (Hz is pronounced Hertz after physicist Heinrich Hertz. It is a measurement of cycles per second). Most ordinary speaking sounds fall in the range from 30 Hz to about 3,000 Hz. The original designers of the telephone system felt that a more limited range of conversational communication was all that would ever be needed. Therefore they set a bandwidth of 2,300 Hz, from 700 Hz to 3,000 Hz. A smaller bandwidth let engineers squeeze more than one two-way conversation onto a single wire, with different channels at different frequencies.

By comparison, a stereo system has a range of about 20 Hz to 30,000 Hz, for a bandwidth of 29,980 Hz. (Acoustical theory says that some sounds we cannot ordinarily hear still affect the way we perceive other sounds; hence high-fidelity sound equipment regularly extends beyond the bounds of human hearing.)

## Stringing Out the Phone Line

In addition to stacking several transmissions on the same phone line by limiting bandwidth and placing signals at different frequencies, phone companies can also multiplex a circuit so that each individual signal is chopped up and mixed in with other signals for transmission. Such a scheme, now in widespread use, requires precise timing and quality of signal to allow the incoming signal to be reconstituted at the receiving end.

Any phone signal suffers from attenuation—a loss of power, measured in decibels—when sent over distance. This loss of strength is caused by impedance, a combination of electrical resistance from wires, switches, and connections, and by capacitive and inductive reactance. Reactance is electrical resistance that varies by frequency. As frequency increases, inductive reactance increases; capacitive reactance decreases as frequency increases.

Echo suppressors can also interfere with data. Echo is the feedback that is caused by the delay in reception between two points. To help eliminate echo, phone lines use devices called echo suppressors. Some modems can send a special signal to disable echo suppressors.

All of these factors—the limited bandwidth, the possibility of short pulses being chopped into shorter pieces under multiplexing schemes, the interference and distortion that may be introduced by switches, and the general assortment of noise and interference that distorts most voice grade calls — indicate why digital signals cannot be readily sent over voice lines and why analog signals are limited in speed.

## PRIVATE SOLUTIONS

When communications needs are high among a relatively few locations, it may be economical to bypass the telephone company in favor of private lines. You can provide your own connections if the locations are relatively close together. For longer distances you can contract with the telephone company and other third parties to supply and maintain alternate communications links for you.

### Leased Lines

One choice open to heavy users of telecommunications circuits is a private or leased line.

The basic voice line we all use is a switched line, meaning that there is no one fixed link between your phone and another. The phone company accepts a request for a dial tone and provides a connection to a central office, where the outgoing call is switched to the dialed number in whatever manner best suits the needs of the phone company. In fact, it is quite possible for a call from New York to Miami to be switched through Dallas or Chicago from time to time.

A leased line is a direct link from point A to point B. The user is guaranteed ready access and some protection against the possible degradation of quality that could result from a great deal of switching from one line to another. The phone company, though, since it must dedicate a set of lines for your exclusive purposes (another name for a leased line is a dedicated line) will charge a hefty premium for such service.

The most expensive telephone option is the conditioned line. This is a special dedicated line with additional telephone company equipment and circuitry promising higher-quality circuits, possibly including an increased bandwidth.

Decisions on which type of line is necessary should be made on the basis of economic analysis of your needs. If you will need to connect two points once or twice a day for transmission of a relatively short duration, a standard dial-up (switched) telephone circuit at each end is probably your best bet. A dial-up line also allows the user to connect with other gateways. On the other hand, if two offices in the same city need to be in constant communication for transmission of critical information, a leased line may be necessary and in certain circumstances less expensive than paying time charges on a dial-up line.

## Independent Common Carriers

Another major alternative is to use one of the value-added networks, also called public data networks. Companies such as Tymnet, owned by McDonnell Douglas, and Telenet from GTE, or others may serve your long-distance data communications needs. These networks typically have entrance points in most major metropolitan areas that can be contacted with a local call. These points, called concentrators, take incoming data circuits and add them to the heavy traffic of packets of information on the nationwide circuits.

These competitors to AT&T plug into the system at the toll office level. If you have problems with your local telephone service, you're not going to get much satisfaction from an alternative carrier until you come up with a direct link that does not use the local loop.

If your company is large enough, you might consider hiring a telecommunications consultant to examine your needs, including the possible purchase and installation of PBX (private branch exchange) systems, WATS (wide-area telephone service) lines for incoming and outgoing calls, and other special services.

## CONVERTING DATA FOR COMMUNICATIONS

We have shown how information inside the computer is stored as varying voltage levels (digital information) and how this data can be moved in parallel or serial form. To transceive this data through a communications link such as a telephone system, however, the information must be converted into a form compatible with the link used.

A modem is one device that makes that conversion. A modem modulates an incoming digital signal into an analog waveform for transmission and performs the opposite function as a receiver, demodulating the analog signal into digital pulses. Its name is a contraction of modulator/demodulator.

## The Modem

A modem translates the 0s and 1s of the digital signal into one of four distinct frequencies within the telephone line's narrow bandwidth. A modem identified as an originating device uses one end of the band, with a modem operating in the answer mode using the other end.

The mechanism for movement of the high-low warble of a stream of bits is called a carrier signal. This is a continuous audible tone exchanged between a pair of modems. In technical terms the modem carrier signal is a fixed frequency sine wave—a signal of one strength or amplitude. The waves cycle from positive to negative and back again, and the more cycles per unit of time, the higher the pitch or frequency of the tone. This tone is altered, or modulated, by the modem to represent the 0s and 1s of the signal.

The carrier tone itself can be modulated in a number of ways:

- *Amplitude modulation*, in which the height of the wave, representing the strength or voltage level of the signal, is altered
- *Frequency modulation*, in which the number of cycles per second (measured in Hertz) is varied to represent information
- *Phase angle modulation*, in which information is conveyed by the angle relative to the previous cycle at which the cycle crosses the 0 axis.

Modulation of a signal is sometimes called keying; this is a link back to the old telegraph system, the first commercial use of electrical means for transmission of data. The telegraph system used a telegraph key (switch) to send out the digital pulses of the Morse code.

In modern telecommunications the types of modulation most often used are a form of frequency modulation, frequency shift keying (FSK), and a form of phase angle modulation, phase shift keying (PSK).

FSK uses two different frequencies to represent 0 and 1. The originating device has one pair of frequencies, while the answering device has another. FSK is the basis of the Bell 103 standard and is used in most 300-baud modems.

To understand PSK, picture a continuous horizontal line as representing the 0 point. Rising from the 0 point in a smooth curve is a sine wave. At its peak above the 0 line, the signal represents a +1; dropping back down in a smooth curve, it represents 0 when it crosses the base line. Continuing in a curve below the baseline, it represents −1 at its lowest point; arcing back up to the baseline, it registers a 0 once more. Therefore, an unmodulated sine wave passes from 0 to

+1 to 0 to −1 and back to 0 in one complete phase, or 360 degrees. Phase shift keying changes or modulates that sine wave so that its angle as it crosses the baseline represents information, specifically the 1s or 0s of binary communication.

The PSK standard used in modems goes one step further, having the changes in phase representing two bits at a time, in a character called a dibit. The dibit can be 00, 01, 10, or 11. From any one point of a phase, an alteration can be ± 90 degrees, + 180 degrees, or no change. The corresponding code:

| Change in angle | Dibit represented |
|---|---|
| +90 | 00 |
| 0 | 01 |
| +180 | 10 |
| −90 | 11 |

Here are the frequency assignments for FSK and PSK modems using Bell standards:

| FSK Frequency Shift | Answer | Originate |
|---|---|---|
| Transmit 1 | 2,025 Hz | 1,070 Hz |
| 0 | 1,225 Hz | 1,270 Hz |
| Receive 1 | 1,070 Hz | 2,025 Hz |
| 0 | 1,270 Hz | 2,225 Hz |
| PSK Phase Key |  |  |
| Transmit | 2,400 Hz | 1,200 Hz |
| Receive | 1,200 Hz | 2,400 Hz |

## Transmission Speeds

Data inside a microcomputer typically travels at tens of thousands of bits per second or even faster. Why, then, are we talking about modems with speed limits as low as 300 bits per second?

One reason is the use of serial communication, which is generally slower than parallel transmission, since the bits that make up each computer word must line up one behind the other before they can be sent down the line.

Another major limiting factor on transmission speed is physical capacity of a telecommunications channel, principally its bandwidth. You could think of bandwidth as the diameter of the pipe—the larger the pipe, the more information or the more channels of information it can carry at one instant. In electrical terms bandwidth is the difference between the highest and lowest frequencies that can flow through a channel.

By limiting bandwidth of voice-quality lines, phone companies can cram extra lines onto the same cable. It makes little difference to the quality of voice communication, but it does limit the speed of data transmission.

## The Baud Rate

The speed of transmission of communication data is called the baud rate, which is defined as the number of discrete signal changes per time unit. The term baud is derived from the name of Emile Baudot, early pioneer in telecommunications. It was originally a measure of dots and dashes on telegraph lines.

In the case of 300-baud and slower standard communication, each discrete signal change using FSK modulation represents a single on or off bit, and therefore the baud rate is equivalent to the number of bits per second. At 300 baud, using computer words with eight bits to a character plus one start bit and two stop bits, the modem is transmitting on average about twenty-seven ASCII characters per second, or about five words a second.

Comparison of baud rate and information throughput with high-speed modems becomes a bit more complex, because most such devices transmit dibits, tribits or quadbits—signals that represent more than one bit. The fact is that a so-called 1,200-baud modem is in most cases actually a 600-baud device—it transmits 600 dibits, each representing two characters, per second. This equates to four times the throughput of a 300-baud device, and manufacturers have adopted the shorthand of calling their units 1,200-baud modems. The most precise way to describe these modems would be as 1,200-bit-per-second devices.

A less precise way of looking at baud rate is to equate it with words per minute. Based on a computer word length plus framing bits totaling eleven bits per character, and based on an average English language word length of five and a half characters, a 300-baud modem can transmit about 300 words per minute, a 1,200-baud unit about 1,200 words per minute, and so on. Obviously, this equation does not work for transmission of numbers or programming and also may not work for transmission of technical language or foreign languages, which may have a different average length.

| Baud | Bits/Second | Characters/Second | Words/Second* | Words/Minute* |
|---|---|---|---|---|
| 300 | 300 | 27 | 5 | 300 |
| 1,200 | 1,200 | 109 | 20 | 1,200 |
| 2,400 | 2,400 | 218 | 40 | 2,400 |

*At 5.5 characters per word

## CHAPTER SUMMARY

Although telecommunications is an important and necessary part of getting full use from a computer system, it can be a complicated process. By understanding some of the basics of telephone system operation, binary data stoarge, serial and parallel communications, and how a modem functions, you can make the process more manageable.

This chapter covered some of this basic information and can serve as a quick reference for you as you use communications systems or as you discuss and define your company's computer communications requirements.

There almost unlimited options available in establishing the rules for telecommunications. We can choose the number of bits that make up a word (typically seven, or eight, but occasionally five or six); we can decide to include parity checking or other error-checking or correction schemes (and select from dozens of different algorithms); we can determine the framing of computer words—how the computer is told where one word ends and the next begins—from one of several start/stop schemes; and we can choose the transmission speed.

The communications port is usually responsible for establishing the various protocols, but these selections must also be supported by the modem. Choosing 2,400-baud communication on the adapter will not make a 300-baud modem work any faster, for example.

This information is convered in more detail in Appendix F, where you also will find information about selecting a modem.

# 5
# How Do You Connect?

We have established the *need* to connect PC workstations to VAX host computers. (See chapter 2.) This chapter summarizes some of the methods—hardware and software—for making that connection. Chapter 12 provides details on one aspect of the PC-VAX link.

## DIRECT LINKS

Although the incidence of remote computing is growing where users are attached to a host through dial-up or dedicated lines from across town or around the world, most minicomputer and mainframe users probably are still attached directly to a local host through serial or network links. This is the simplest connection because it requires a minimum of additional hardware and because the problems associated with the connection are reduced.

### Serial

The majority of VAX users still talk to the host through a terminal instead of a workstation, so the majority of user-to-host connections still are made with direct serial links. (See chapters 4 and 12.) It follows, then, that serial communication is a popular method for workstation users because the wiring already is in place, additional hardware and software that may be required on the host is installed, and procedures for supporting serial users are established. (See Figure 5-1.)

In addition, a serial link is relatively simple. Most PC workstations today come equipped with at least one serial port, and the software required to support this type of connection from a PC is readily available and inexpensive, especially if dedicated terminal emulation is not required.

Note that we will call all on-site serial links *direct links* even though there may be additional hardware between your PC and the VAX host. The most common type of interim hardware is a serial terminal server from Digital or a third party. The terminal server acts as a front end to the VAX, concentrating multiple serial lines from a group of local terminals or workstations and sending the various signals across a single line to the host.

If there is a terminal server on the serial line between your PC and the VAX, it may change slightly the specific logon procedure you use to access your VAX account (see Chapter 10), but otherwise you will operate as if the hardware were directly attached to a serial port on the VAX.

Your local installation may use short-haul modems in the serial line. These are designed to increase the distance over which reliable serial communications can be maintained. As a user, you should notice no difference between a direct cable connection to the host and one that uses such a modem. To the end user a modem is a passive device and requires no interaction.

## Hardware

Your PC probably came with a serial port. A few years ago the serial port was a relatively expensive option, and not everyone had one. Today the cost of serial port components is low; more users require this form of system input and output (I/O), and a larger percentage of PCs sold are supplied with a serial port.

You can tell easily if you have a serial port by looking at the rear panel of your PC. Unless your unit has some kind of specialty interface, you probably will find only three types of connectors on the rear

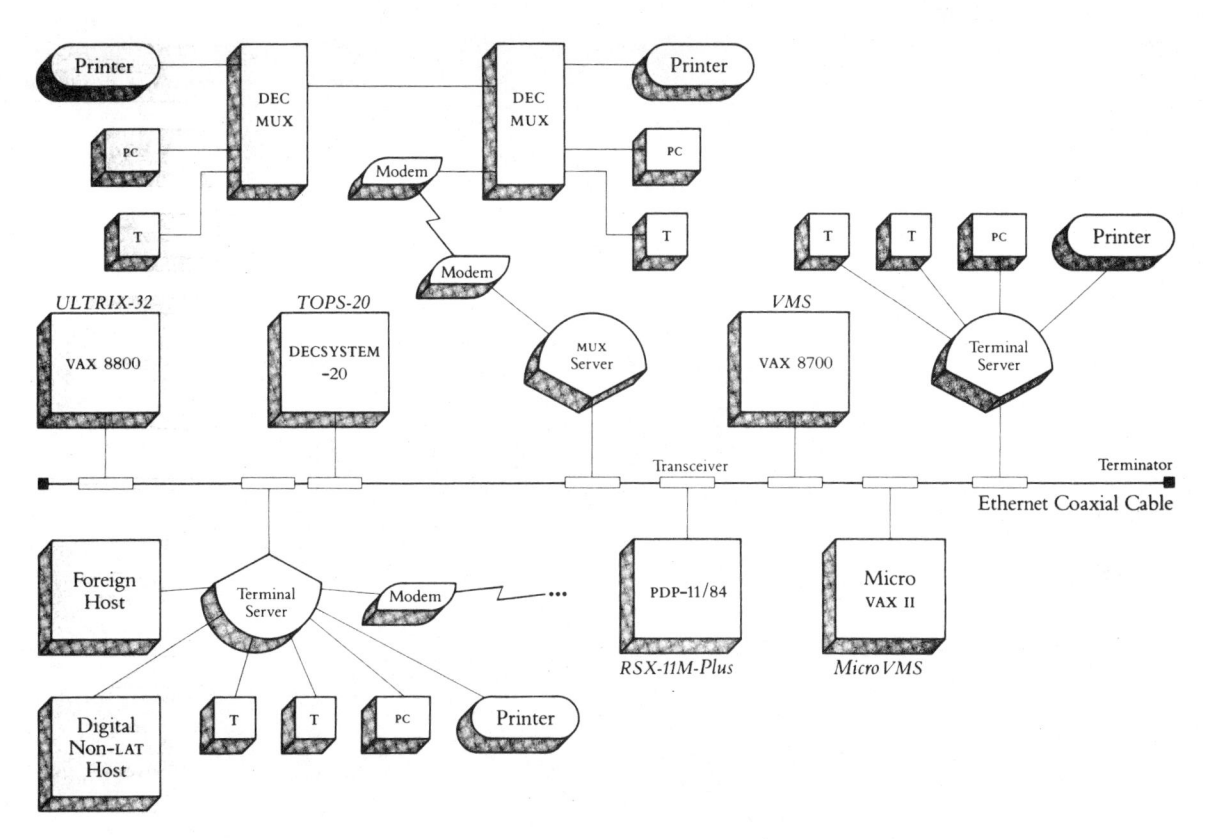

*Figure 5-1* **Serial attachments, showing terminal server, PCs, terminals, and modems. (Source: Digital Equipment Corporation)**

panel. If yours is an XT-class machine, you probably will see connectors that match those shown in figure 5-2. These are DB-25 D-shell connectors. On most PCs, one of these will be a plug (DB-25P) and one will be a socket (DB-25S). Common terminology calls the DB-25P a male connector, while the DB-25S is called a female connector. Before IBM introduced its personal computers, these connectors were reserved for serial communications. Which type of connector was used showed which class of serial device should be attached to the port. By IBM convention, however, this has changed for PC-class machines.

The female connector is used as a parallel printer port and the male is used as a serial port. The parallel port is a Centronics standard port specified for eighteen wire pairs. (See Appendix E for a pin-out

68 □ HOW DO YOU CONNECT?

*Figure 5-2* **DB-25 connectors used for serial connectons. The IBM PC–class computers also use this traditional serial connector for the Centronics-compatible parallel attachment. (Source: Black Box Corporation)**

diagram of the Centronics interface.) With modern printers, however, not all of these wires are required, so IBM used the DB-25 connector as a parallel port to save space on the back panel and to save money during construction.

The male connector on the PC XT back panel is the serial port. There may be more than one of these, and just to make things confusing, the second serial port sometimes uses a DB-25S connector. With a standard, unenhanced configuration, however, there will be two DB-25 connectors. The male connector is the serial port and the female connector is the parallel port.

If you have more than one D-shell connector, how do you tell which connector is which? Ultimately, you should consult your computer manual or the person in charge of configuring your systems. Once you have identified each I/O port on the rear panel, use a label maker or tape you can write on to label these connectors.

If you have to go it alone, you may be in for some trial and error to locate each port. Here are some hints that may help; however, there are so many different PC systems that nothing is assured.

First, the parallel printer port may be associated with your monochrome display card, and this card is probably at one end of the bus, so check the slots on either end of the panel. If you are using a local printer, the cable going from your printer to the rear of the PC probably attaches to the parallel port. There are serial interface printers, however, so this observation is not entirely reliable.

Do you have an external modem? If so, the cable from the modem to the PC is probably attached to the first serial port, called COM 1:. This port is probably the one with the male connector.

If you have to, take the case off of the PC and observe how the boards and cables are arranged inside. The primary serial port and the primary parallel port probably attach directly to their associated printed circuit boards. That means the I/O board plugs into an expansion slot and the appropriate DB-25 connector sticks directly through the rear panel. Secondary connectors attach to the rear panel through ribbon (flat) cables that are connected to a jack on the expansion board.

If you still aren't sure which connector handles which I/O requests, try to find a parallel (Centronics) interface printer. Plug it in to the female DB-25 that is closest to one of the rear panel edges (far left or far right). Boot the system and at the DOS prompt type:

```
DIR >PRN
```

If the printer is plugged in to the proper port, it should print the directory of the selected disk drive. If nothing comes out of the printer, first check to make sure the printer is online and that pause or other nonprinting mode is not selected. If the printer appears ready to receive data but nothing is printed, then connect the printer cable to another female DB-25 connector.

It is highly unlikely that you will have to try more than two ports to find the right one for the printer. First of all, you can't attach the printer cable to a male rear-panel plug because the cable coming from the printer is a DB-25P. Also, because most applications do not support even two parallel devices, a PC with more than two parallel ports is extremely rare.

Remember that you can't really damage anything experimenting with your PC in this way. If you plug a printer cable into the wrong place, the worst that will happen is that the printer won't work. It may be possible to lock up your system by sending output to a vacant port, but you can recover from this condition by turning the system off and back on again or by rebooting (Ctrl/Alt/Del or hardware reset, if your computer has one).

To locate the serial ports, you will need a serial device such as a printer or modem. If you have a serial printer, use the technique described above to find out which serial port does what. If you don't have a serial printer, locate an external modem and attach it to the most likely serial port. This is the port that is attached directly to a circuit board and also uses a male plug. Once the modem is attached, execute a communications program, configure it for COM 1: (see software section below), and type a modem wake-up command. With Hayes-compatible modems, the wake-up command is

**AT**

When this command is entered on the communications screen with a Hayes-compatible modem attached to the same COM port for which the software is configured, you should see the modem's response

**OK**

on the screen. Keep trying different serial connections until you get the appropriate response from your modem.

Now you know which connectors on your PC should be attached to what kinds of devices, and you can follow the host connection procedures below.

If you are using an AT-class machine, this task may be a little simpler. Most ATs use a female connector for the primary serial port. This is a much smaller connector (nine pins instead of twenty-five), and therefore won't be confused with the printer port or secondary serial ports. You will, however, require a short pigtail cable to attach the twenty-five-pin connector from standard serial cables to the nine-pin PC AT serial port. These cables are supplied with many computers and modems. Otherwise you should be able to obtain one from any computer store.

*Figure 5-3* DB-9 connectors used for AT-class serial connections and for video attachments on many PCs. (Source: Black Box Corporation)

Once you have identified the necessary ports, you can attach a serial cable to your PC. If your site is already wired for VT-series terminals, you should be able to plug the cable directly in to the primary serial port. If you are using an AT-class machine, you will need the converter cable between the terminal connection and the PC's rear panel.

## Software

You will need some kind of software to support the PC's serial port before you can establish a direct serial connection with a host. If all you need is to log on is a VT-serial terminal and interact directly with the host, such programs are inexpensive and readily available. Refer to chapter 10 for more information on terminal emulation software types and selection.

Terminal emulation software turns on the serial port to enable direct interaction with an external device and may also provide the ability to emulate, to varying degrees of accuracy, the screen attributes and other functions of the VT-series terminals.

## Ethernet

An Ethernet network can provide another link to a host. Whether you use Ethernet or a direct serial link depends on how your site is wired and what PC resources you have.

### Hardware

Most PCs do not come equipped with Ethernet hardware. To use Ethernet with a PC requires an additional plug-in circuit board to make the physical network connection and some software to allow your PC to recognize and use the additional I/O port.

Remember, three types of Ethernet connection are standard Ethernet, ThinWire, and unshielded twisted-pair. You will need a PC Ethernet adapter that is compatible with your type of Ethernet. Refer to chapter 3 for additional information on Ethernet connections.

In general the Ethernet adapter simply plugs into one of the PC expansion slots in the same way an internal modem or memory expansion card installs inside the PC. The required Ethernet connections are on the rear of this card, permitting you to attach you local Ethernet cable directly to the PC.

With the increased popularity of PC networking, some companies are providing PCs with an Ethernet interface built in. The interface resides on the main PC circuit board, so you don't have to use an expansion slot for the network connection. If you know you will be networking over Ethernet when the PCs are purchased, it is a good idea to investigate integral Ethernet adapters.

The separate plug-in adapters are relatively expensive, about $300 to $600. At the high end, this is as much as a functioning XT-class machine costs. PCs designed as network nodes, such as Novell's diskless network node, have this card as part of the main motherboard, providing Ethernet connectivity at a much lower cost than adding the adapter later.

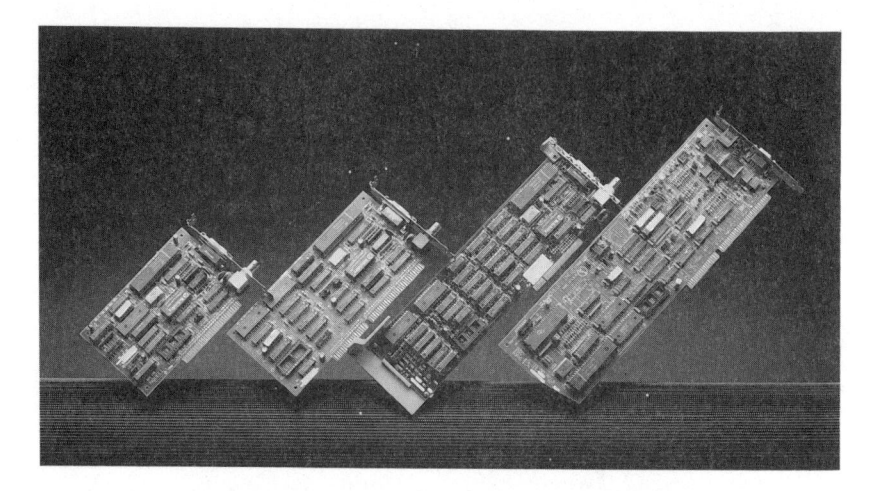

*Figure 5-4* IBM PC and compatible network interface card (NIC) options from Novell: NE1000, NE2000, NE/2, NT2000. The NE1000 is an eight-bit XT or compatible adapter; the NE2000 uses a sixteen-bit interface designed for AT-class machines; the NE/2 is for IBM's PS/2; the NT2000 includes a twisted-pair Ethernet interface. (Source: Novell, Inc.)

If you are using twisted-pair Ethernet, an additional external adapter may be required. In some PC implementations of twisted-pair Ethernet, a coaxial connection from the PC interface card to an external device converts the coax link to twisted pair.

**Software**

Ethernet software for your PC can take a variety of forms, but generally it is system-level code that loads with the operating system. At this level the software makes DOS aware of the foreign adapter and handles the actual movement of characters across the link.

In addition to the interface-level software, your Ethernet connection probably includes some configuration and user-interface software that forms part of the local area network you are using. Novell's NetWare, for example, is a full-featured Ethernet network that permits department-level PCs to interact without a VAX host. The package includes a wide array of menus and utilities to handle LAN activities such as directory assignments, security and other user authorization duties, backup, and other server functions.

If you purchased an Ethernet adapter to support a straight connection to a VAX network without the local PC support, the software you use may be more limited. It will function more at the system level, while you interact with a terminal emulator or other software that supports the VAX link.

## MODEM LINKS

The modem is a common tool for providing PC-to-VAX connections. Modems can be used to provide longer-distance serial communications for a local site or dial-up and direct-connect attachments for remote terminals and PCs. (See Appendix F for more information on modems.)

From the user perspective, a short-haul (local) modem will not change the way you use the PC-to-VAX link. The modem serves as a booster to increase the distance possible between your workstation and the terminal server or host port. In fact, you may not even see such a modem, as it could be located away from your workstation location.

If you are using a dial-up link, however, the modem probably will dial the call in addition to providing the data conversion required. In addition, a dial-up link generally is slower than a direct-connect link. Most modems available today operate at 1,200 baud or 2,400 baud, although 9,600 baud and even 19.2-K baud products are available. Modems that operate at this speed usually, though not always, are attached to dedicated lines and are used between a single host and a single workstation. (Chapter 4 provides additional information on dial-up connections between a workstation and a host.)

### Dedicated and Leased Line Connections

As mentioned in the previous section, you could be at a remote site and still use what amounts to a direct connection to a VAX. By contracting with the telephone company to provide your own dedicated telephone line between the remote site and your host, you have the benefits of a continuous link and avoid the need to use autodial modems.

Depending on the class of line you have, long-distance links at relatively high speed can be maintained over leased or dedicated lines. If your modem or multiplexer supports it, communications speeds of

19.2 K or 38.4 K baud are not uncommon. Another kind of dedicated link, T1, can support even faster data rates and can be used to share data types, such as voice and video, with computer-to-computer communications.

# NETWORK SERVER LINKS

Regardless of the physical medium used to connect your workstation to the VAX host, there are various ways that the logical connection can be made. For many applications you will set up the workstation simply to emulate one of the VT-series terminals and log on to the VAX as if you were using a conventional terminal. In situations where you want to run applications and access data that reside on the host, straight terminal emulation is the best approach. (See chapter 10.)

In addition, you may want to use some of the facilities of the VAX, such as printers and disk storage, while running most of your applications at the PC. This is fairly common and can greatly enhance the use of your local workstation.

A higher level that goes beyond using the VAX as a PC peripheral also is becoming popular. In these applications you use the local processing power of the PC for some applications, store files on the VAX, and use other VAX resources such as printers. In addition, the data generated by the PC application is made available to users with VT-series terminals. This level of function requires some data conversion at both ends of the link, and you have to be using applications that run on the host as well as the workstation.

Chapter 10 shows you how to use your workstation as if it were a terminal. This section discusses some of the other options for connectivity.

## Software Components

PC-to-VAX communication frequently requires two levels of software, a PC component and a host component. If you are doing straight terminal emulation, a host component is not required because once the workstation is set up as a terminal with the proper software, the VAX sees it as a standard VT family member.

If the PC is to access VAX facilities such as disk drives, however, a host software component generally must be installed in addition to the software for the PC. Installing and configuring the host software will be handled by the appropriate MIS department staff. They also may install your PC software, or it may be your responsibility or the responsibility of someone else in your department to install local software.

## The VAX As a Peripheral

The simplest way to go beyond terminal emulation is to use the VAX host as a large and flexible peripheral. Although high-capacity disk drives are becoming increasingly common on PCs, most VAXs still provide considerably more storage than you are likely to have on your desktop machine. In addition, the more storage you have available, the more difficult it is to maintain the information with adequate backups and archives. Information on a VAX hard drive, however, is backed up with the rest of the system, probably on a daily basis. This gives you automatic access to such facilities as 8mm tape, a low-cost option for a VAX installation but a very high-priced device from the PC perspective.

Printers for PCs don't cost as much as they once did, but getting high speed, letter quality, graphics support, and compatibility with such printing standards as PostScript is still a costly prospect for a PC user. At least one of this class probably is attached to your VAX, however, and with the proper software, your local workstation applications can access them as if they were attached directly to your machine.

Workstation software to provide these features can be loaded when you boot your system, so that the operation is transparent. For disk storage on the VAX, specify that files be sent to a drive as if it were a local device. The data is sent across the communications link to the VAX drive. For example, suppose you have a dual-diskette machine with one hard drive on your desk. These local drives are designated A:, B:, and C:. You can have one or more additional drives (D: and up) that actually specify storage locations on the VAX. So to store a file or program on your first available VAX partition, you use drive D:; to access the second partition use drive E:, and so on.

In the same way your workstation software can reroute print requests from the local port to a designated print queue on the VAX and in the process can handle whatever data conversion is required. In many cases you will not be required to modify your local applications software because the communications facility handles that chore for you. With such print drivers installed, when your local application sends anything to LPT1 or PRN, the local PC print devices, the communications software grabs these requests and routes them through the proper port to the VAX. Routines either at the PC or on the VAX scan the data and convert Epson printer data, for example, into LN03 print requests. You may have to use a setup routine when your software is installed to tell it which printers you have been using on the PC and which devices are available on the VAX, but otherwise the print process can be conducted automatically.

If all you really need is larger disk space and better print facilities, software that functions as just described will serve very well. Some PC packages go a little further and give you a somewhat tighter link into the VAX. For example, a small subset of VMS commands can be added at the PC to give you transparent access to VAX facilities, so you could type MAIL at the PC-/MS-DOS prompt and be connected automatically with VAX MAIL on the host without having to log on separately as a user.

Such features are useful for PC-oriented users who do not require regular access to VAX and who do not want to have to learn a new operating environment. You still will have to have a VAX user account to use such features, and a representative of your MIS department probably will have to install and set up such a package, but the operation is easy to learn, and the features help unify workstation users with the rest of the VAX user community.

The main limitation to software of this type is that it does not provide terminal users access to the data you are using on your PC and storing on the VAX. In fact, it is not uncommon for such software to store all of your PC-generated data in a single large VAX file. For example, if you have established a 20-MB remote disk as your VAX-based D: drive, you actually will be using a single 20-MB partition on one of the host drives. The host operating system sees the data as a single large file, and terminal users on the system have no way of determining what data may be stored there.

In many installations data sharing is not required, and additional features are not necessary. In other situations, however, it can be extremely useful for users to have at least directory-level access to workstation data. Some PC integration software supports the VMS directory format in such a way that as a PC user, you see the files in

MS-DOS format and VAX terminal users see the files in VMS directory format. At this level terminal users can list PC-generated files (assuming they have been given access rights to the directories where these files reside) and can access the data with standard VMS utilities. A text file created on a PC and stored in VMS format on the host, for example, probably can be edited with EDT or another VMS editor. Without additional data conversion, however, database or spreadsheet files probably won't be much use to terminal users. Perhaps they can type these files, and they may be able to see some of the data, but the information probably could not be incorporated into standard VAX applications.

There are applications that are more closely related to the VAX environment and that do provide this next level of sharing.

## The VAX as a Peer

With the rise in popularity of true distributed computing, we are seeing more and more applications that seamlessly bridge the gap between the workstation and the VAX. WordPerfect word processing software is one such package.

WordPerfect is a PC-based package that has evolved over the past few years to a highly functional, full-featured package with most of the features commercial users want. The company provides the software on a number of additional computing platforms, including the Apple Macintosh and the Digital VAX. Although these versions are not precisely identical, they are close enough so that an experienced PC WordPerfect user requires very little training to use the software on a VAX. The converse also is true, allowing VAX users to migrate easily to a workstation environment as necessary.

In addition, WordPerfect can use a variety of PC-to-VAX communications links to access VAX facilities from a PC. Once the WordPerfect file is stored on the VAX, users of the VAX version of the company's word processing software can access the file as if it were created directly on the VAX. WordPerfect conducts whatever file conversion is required between the dissimilar machines, permitting almost seamless integration of the two environments.

Such spreadsheet applications from Unipress and word processors from such companies as Marc Software perform similar integration, either because they run on multiple environments or because they are capable of performing the necessary format conversions to permit data access across different applications.

Remember, a communications package that can upload data or programs from your workstation to a VAX is not enough to ensure that VAX users can access them. An additional level of conversion must occur on the host or at the PC for this level of information sharing across a VAX network.

## PC Network-to-VAX

Many corporations are discovering that a tiered approach to VAX connectivity offers the best of both worlds by providing sophisticated departmental-level computing for PC users while affording access to a central host as required.

The popularity of PC LANs has risen sharply with the capabilities these systems offer. Products from such companies as 3Com and Novell, for example, provide a minicomputer-like environment for a group of PCs by establishing a PC server or host that attaches many user workstations. (See Figure 5-5.) Individual users retain the advantages of a desktop CPU while enjoying the convenience of shared access to central storage and other peripherals. The additional advantage of a PC LAN is that users and administrators already knowledgeable about PC hardware and software continue to operate in a familiar environment. No learning of host operating systems is required to achieve the advantages associated with host connections.

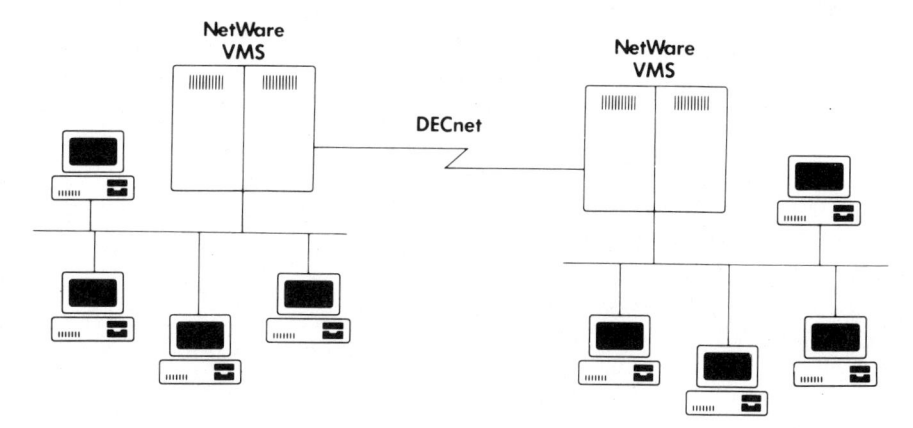

*Figure 5-5* **Novell Netware network with DECnet hosts. (Source: Novell, Inc.)**

In addition, PC LAN products are relatively inexpensive. Users within a department can link up for file sharing, electronic mail, and other applications without the expense of a minicomputer host. A PC, even a high-performance unit with hundreds of megabytes of storage, is considerably cheaper to buy and maintain than even the smallest VAX.

The next logical progression from the PC LAN environment is to full host sharing with a site- or company-level VAX. Because there are fewer attachments to the central host, the concept of distributed processing is carried even further. Individual workstation users talk first to their local host, in this case an inexpensive PC server; then the server or other communications gateway attaches to the host network as an entity. Routines can be established for file backup from the local server to the host and for downloading of information from the host to the server. Also, products such as Novell's Netware/VMS installed on the VAX can make LAN workstations full members of the VAX network by linking through the local server.

Such network-to-host environments potentially offer the greatest level of flexibility and growth potential because they can be used to separate users into logical clusters by application. Local server and workstation resources are used where possible, and the VAX host is accessed less frequently to handle higher-level operations, to share mail or data, or to provide laser printers, plotters, or other expensive resources to workstation users.

## CHAPTER SUMMARY

There are many aspects of PC-to-VAX connectivity: the hardware, or physical link; the software that makes the link work; and additional software that allows applications at both ends of the connection make use of the connection.

This chapter discusses the use of a VAX as a PC peripheral and introduces the concept of peer-to-peer communication between workstations and hosts. In addition, it shows how some software applications can share information between VAX and workstation users, either because the same application runs on both platforms or because a host or PC application can perform the necessary file conversions to make sharing possible.

Part of the selection process for PC-to-VAX connectivity solutions should involve a careful assessment of data sharing requirements in your application. Once that is determined, you can make an intelligent choice among the myriad of connectivity products available.

# 6
# Looking Down: The View from the VAX

If your computer experience has been solely or almost solely on a minicomputer or mainframe, learning to accept and to use efficiently the myriad hardware and software offerings for PCs can be difficult. In fact, you may have several levels of difficulty in moving to PCs, including accepting these small machines as capable and productive and learning the new system-level and applications software.

This chapter discusses PC-VAX communications from the VAX perspective and describes the major PC components. It should be useful as an introduction to PCs and as a summary and reference as you begin to work with personal computers.

## THE VAX PERSPECTIVE

As a VAX user, you may have mostly ignored the influx of desktop workstations into your operation, but you can not have been totally unaware of this change in the computing workplace. Individual PC users move desktop units into the office for some very good and defensible reasons.

In most minicomputer and mainframe shops, applications development constantly runs behind demand. One estimate we saw recently put the backlog at six months on the average. A knowledgeable computer user who can budget even $1,000 or $2,000 can purchase a desktop machine and the tools needed to produce the required application quickly.

Moreover, additional software for widely divergent tasks is relatively inexpensive compared with the same application on even a small VAX such as the MicroVAX II. If only two or three users require a given application, it can be difficult to justify adding it to the departmental- or company-level host when the price is several thousand dollars per user, as is frequently the case. However, a $500 software package is considered a costly item among PC users, and there are thousands of popular and highly functional packages available for under $100. Don't be misled. These two-digit software packages are not clumsy, limited toys. They run the gamut from word processing and utilities such as multitasking windowing programs all the way to sophisticated CAD/CAM design packages. For example, Microsoft Windows, one of the user interface standards among PC users, is available for about $80 from many suppliers. Digital sells third-party windowing tools for MicroVAX computers at prices ranging from $1,200 to $1,700 and for larger VAXs to $14,000. In the PC environment, however, user pressure and intense competition has forced companies that once marketed their PC software for thousands of dollars to cut the price to a tenth or less of the original price.

At these new reduced prices, you still receive professional documentation and agressive company telephone support in many cases.

The flat price of an application does not tell the whole story. You have to consider the number of users who require a given software package and whether it is important for many users to be able to share any data the program produces. If you have ten PC users who need Microsoft Windows, the price is $800 because you must purchase a separate license for each user. Where the number of users for a given application is small, however, it is hard to compete with PC prices in the minicomputer environment.

Another reason for turning to PCs for some computing tasks is the power they provide to individual users. Terminal users attached to a VAX share the power of the CPU with everybody else. Only a few years ago this wasn't a major problem because the minicomputer or mainframe host was so much more powerful than anything available in the PC world that even if you had to share it, the host CPU was a faster, more sophisticated machine.

Today the tables are turning. A Digital MicroVAX II, an extremely popular departmental-level minicomputer, can support thirty users or more from a hardware connectivity standpoint, yet the CPU is capable of only about 1 MIPS (million instructions per second). One of the newer 12-MHz 80286 PCs performs at about 2 MIPS, while the very latest PC technology, a 33-MHz 80386 machine, zips along at 8 MIPS. Although machines in this class can and do perform very well as LAN file servers, they also are being used as dedicated single-user workstations. Once you get used to driving this kind of power all by yourself, it seems limiting to share a 1-MIPS machine with anybody else, much less twenty or more users. If you had to give up your PC in favor of a terminal attachment into this computing environment, the result probably would be unacceptable.

Having PCs in key locations around the company can provide users a high-speed computing platform, and offload some tasks from the host. Properly designed and carefully placed PC systems are an efficient and cost-effective way to increase corporate computer resources.

An interesting sociological change is occurring. PC users are discovering the value of connectivity, of being able to share mail and data with other users around the enterprise. It is increasingly necessary and important for PC and host users to coexist, complementing each other, for the most efficient operation possible.

## ALL ABOUT PERSONAL COMPUTERS

*PC* has become a generic term for any personal computer, although the original PC was IBM's personal computer. Today hundreds of companies build PC workstations that are compatible with IBM's original BIOS (Basic Input/Output System) firmware, disk format, and display protocols. The third-party versions, however, generally are faster and have more features than IBM's original models.

In fact, IBM has all but abandoned this original open desktop architecture in favor of a new line designated the PS/2, for Personal System/2. There are several models in this family, and all of them surpass the original PCs in performance and features. The difference is that the PS/2 models use a new microchannel architecture that is basically incompatible with the original PC bus. Although IBM says the microchannel architecture provides better performance and a well-defined growth path to future operating systems and applications, one reason for moving away from the PC bus was to regain control of the desktop segment of the business.

So far, however, there has been no rising groundswell of support for the new systems, mainly because the new operating system, OS/2, has been so long delayed after the introduction of the hardware.

**Overview**

Since its introduction in 1981, the IBM PC has undergone many changes, and the original design has been cloned and copied by companies all over the world. The original PC used an Intel 8088 sixteen-bit microprocessor running at a clock speed of 4.77 MHz for its CPU. Although this chip handles sixteen bits internally, its interface to the outside world is over an eight-bit bus.

The standard PC (and there still are many thousands of the original IBM model on corporate desktops) consists of a horizontally mounted circuit board and up to five vertically mounted adapter cards, all enclosed in a metal case with a power supply and cooling fans. Rear-panel connectors are provided for AC power, a video display, and a Centronics parallel printer interface.

The main board, frequently called the motherboard (Figure 6-1), contains the microprocessor and its associated chips, including an optional math coprocessor, the BIOS and other firmware, an integral bus (backplane) with connectors to hold expansion modules, bus interface circuitry, and a real-time clock.

The motherboard is mounted in a case with fan, power supply, and room for up to two full-height 5.25-inch storage devices. The original PC contained dual diskette drives.

Subsequent models from IBM and from the many clone makers have modified this original design considerably, but the basic concept and underlying design remain the same. The IBM PC XT, for example, was supplied with a 10-MB hard drive as standard equipment and included eight expansion slots instead of five.

The clone makers have enhanced this basic design even further. They have increased the system clock speed and installed more modern versions of the basic CPU chip set, for one thing. Whereas the original PC XT used a system clock running at 4.77 MHz, clone makers

*Figure 6-1* **IBM-PC-class motherboard from the CompuAdd Turbo 10. (Reproduced with permission of CompuAdd Corporation)**

offer 10 MHz and faster systems. So-called Turbo clones of the XT are commonly sold by a number of vendors from the largest, well-known companies to little-known distributors who buy parts from offshore sources and assemble custom computers. Either way, the new PC XT is a more powerful, more flexible offering than the original, which is no longer available from IBM. The clones, however, continue to be sold.

Other enhancements include motherboard-mounted serial and parallel ports, integral disk controllers, and much larger hard drives.

IBM's next offering, sold for a while at the same time as the XT, was the IBM PC AT (for *Advanced Technology*). The AT remains the most popular in terms of unit sales. Originally priced far above the XT, AT-class models from the clone makers have fallen drastically in price, and IBM has discounted the AT. Both events have pushed the popularity of the PC AT.

The AT uses a newer chip, the 80286, that is compatible with earlier chips, but the 80286 is a sixteen-chip capable of twenty-four-bit external addressing. The AT shares physical similarities to earlier models, and consists of a motherboard (Figures 6-2 and 6-3) with room for eight plug-in adapters. The original AT motherboard was

*Figure 6-2* **PC AT-class motherboard from the CompuAdd 286 computer. (Reproduced with permission of CompuAdd Corporation)**

larger than that of the XT model, but many clone vendors offer a "baby" AT with a motherboard that is the same size as that of the XT. The smaller board fits inside a standard XT case, resulting in a smaller computer. Some of these smaller-format ATs have room for only five expansion modules, but this is not necessarily a limitation; whereas the XT design required that all system memory beyond the first 64 K reside on an expansion module, newer ATs can hold 4 MB or more of memory on the motherboard, a design that frees one or more expansion slots.

Early PC AT users welcomed the larger case of the AT design because hard disk drives of the time generally were full-height devices. With newer storage techynology capable of putting 40 MB and more in an extremely compact 3.5-inch container, smaller cases are acceptable and even desirable.

The next generation of PC-like machines uses a newer Intel chip design, the 80386. This is a 32-bit device, and its architecture allows true multiuser, multitasking systems. The 80386 chip forms the basis for IBM's new PC offerings in the PS/2 line and is the chip of choice among engineering and other power users who require multitasking, graphics, or multiuser operation. Versions of the 80386 chip can be

*Figure 6-3* **Assembled PC AT-class computer, the CompuAdd 286. (Reproduced with permission of CompuAdd Corporation)**

operated to 33 MHz, providing a desktop machine with performance that rivals many of Digital's VAX computers. Some of the newer 80386 machines, for example, have been benchmarked at 8 MIPS, while a MicroVAX II is rated as 0.9 MIPS. The newest Digital MicroVAX offerings, the 3000-family, range in performance from 2.4 MIPS to 2.7 MIPS.

A fully configured high-speed 80386 PC is available for around $7,000, about one-third the cost of even the least expensive MicroVAX. Why, then, would anyone choose a VAX instead of one of the new 80386-based PC machines? The major reason lies in the VAX operating system.

## Operating Systems

Digital's VMS is a well-established, mature and efficient multiuser, multitasking operating system. MS-DOS, the standard operating system on IBM-compatible machines (see chapter 8), was never designed for multiuser, multitasking applications. Recent extentions address some of the needs of networked users who share files and other system resources on a PC-based server, but the operating system isn't even close to VMS in power and flexibility.

IBM's new operating system, OS/2, is designed to replace MS-DOS on 80286 and later machines, but it is not fully implemented at this point. Even when all of its planned features are in place, it is not clear how well accepted the new software will be, at least initially. Here another dynamic is at work. Users of PC-class machines have developed thousands of efficient programs that work in a stand-alone or networked environment. Although multitasking would be a welcome addition to the PC's functions, users are hesitant to convert to a new and unknown operating system. Although OS/2 is designed to provide compatibility with MS-DOS, there may be problems with some software, and OS/2 at this point simply has not built a track record of performance, does not have an impressive library of applications, and is not widely used.

A recent study by International Data Corporation (IDC), a Framingham, MA, research firm, shows that while OS/2 sales should reach 7.5 million units by 1992, that will account for only twenty-five percent of the market. According to the study, one reason is that there are few applications available that will run under OS/2. (See chapter 8 for more information about OS/2 from the IDC study.)

A few companies are designing "UNIX boxes" around the 80386 chip, turning away from the more popular Motorola 68000-series chips common in UNIX workstations. Users of the 80386 chip say this line has a longer growth path because it is at the beginning of its development while the 68000 line (68010, 68020, 68030, 68040) is at the high end of its life cycle.

Although regular UNIX has not been implemented on strictly PC-class machines, a derivative called XENIX has enjoyed some acceptance, though its application is extremely limited compared with that of MS-DOS. One reason UNIX has not enjoyed acceptance on the low-cost PC boxes is that UNIX requires a lot of storage and memory. Although 80286 and later chips can address megabytes of memory, in some ways the basic PC design has tended to limit system-level and applications software development. The original PC was designed to use no more than 640 KB of RAM. As versatility and complexity of applications increase, the need for memory grows exponentially. However, in many PC systems, the 640 KB limit still must be worked around. The OS/2 operating system is designed to eliminate this restriction for 80286 and 80386 machines.

The problem, of course, is that while users want more powerful hardware, they want even more for the applications software they already have to be compatible with the new machines. Designers and manufacturers are hampered. New chip technology has the potential for opening up the desktop to extremely powerful multiuser, multi-tasking machines, but the requirement to remain compatible with older designs slows down development.

The UNIX operating system has the potential for gaining much broader acceptance if the new generation of desktop machines is designed for it. For now, however, MS-DOS and OS/2 remain the standards for PC-class computers.

## PERSONAL COMPUTER PRODUCTS

It is somewhat more difficult to summarize PC products than it is Digital's VAX offerings. There is no single vendor for these products, for one thing. It is true that IBM is the originator of the PC line, but the application of this original design goes beyond the boundaries of a single company's offerings.

IBM's strategic position says the 8088-based 4.77- MHz machines are outdated and have been replaced by newer designs. IBM no longer offers the PC or the PC XT. Hundreds of third-party vendors, on the other hand, still sell versions of these machines. In many cases, the motherboard is enhanced to hold more memory or provide other desirable features, but it is still the basic IBM design being offered.

Because of its broad acceptance among applications developers and users, this design has become a standard that transcends the originator. Many industry observers speculate that the XT- and AT-class designs will be enhanced and offered as basic desktop computing platforms for many more years.

Third-party developers are adopting the newest Intel CPUs, as well and incorporating them into MS-DOS- and OS/2-compatible machines. Although 80386 and 80486 machines are evolving with proprietary buses and individualized display systems, they are for the most part retaining compatible operating systems.

The IDC study mentioned above in connection with OS/2 predicts that computers based on the 80386 chip will support the majority of OS/2 sales through 1991, at which time 80486 processors will take over. "Developers are finding that OS/2 runs too slowly on 80286 processors to be of practical use to the end user," the study says.

A complete discussion of IBM PC-compatible computers would require much more space than is available in this book, and we acknowledge that this listing is not complete and probably is out of date by the time you read it. However, the following section will provide an annotated list of some of the available products. Although many companies provide enhanced and modified versions of these machines, we will discuss the standard offerings from IBM as a way of limiting the scope of coverage.

## The Original IBM PC

IBM's first personal computer started the revolution in desktop business computers and gave the industry the term PC for this class of system. Strange as it sounds today, this machine was configured with ROM-based BASIC, a cassette port for loading programs at 300 baud, and up to two 5.25-inch disk drives that stored 160 KB of information. Standard system memory was 64 KB, and five expansion slots were supported.

Thousands of these machines are still in use, though most probably have been upgraded with more memory and a hard drive. If you decide to use one of these old machines in a PC-VAX link, you probably will have to upgrade the system ROM BIOS, if this already has not been done. The original machine did not support hard drives, and this ancient ROM likely is incompatible with many communications programs.

## IBM PC XT

The PC XT added three expansion slots and a hard drive to the standard configuration of the PC. In addition, up to 256 KB of RAM could be placed on the system board without requiring an expansion card. For a while that was enough RAM to run most applications, but more memory was needed fairly quickly. Later models supplied 512 KB of RAM on the system board.

The standard PC XT was supplied with a 10-MB hard drive, and as late as 1985 a typical configuration would have cost close to $5,000. High-speed third-party clones of the XT are available today with more memory and storage at prices a fraction of the original.

## IBM PC AT

IBM's Advanced Technology PC, the PC AT, was the beginning of the next generation of PCs. Soon after the machine was released, Paul Somerson, a well-known writer in the PC marketplace, described the PC AT as "awesome." Compared to the available PC XT machines of the day, the advanced technology certainly was welcome. Using a sixteen-bit chip with an eight-bit I/O bus that includes twenty-four-bit addressing, the PC AT is capable of multiuser operation, using up to two serial ports and dumb terminals to support up to three users on a single machine. To support earlier expansion modules, the PC AT also includes some standard eight-bit expansion slots.

Although the multiuser aspects of the PC AT were highly touted when the machine was released, this capability never became particularly popular. The original 6-MHz clock speed did not really produce a machine powerful enough for multiuser applications.

The PC AT was supplied with a 20-MB hard disk and introduced the 1.2-MB high density diskette drive.

With the PC AT IBM also announced PC-DOS 3.0, a major upgrade of the operating system designed to support the personal computer line. Although version 3.0 and its later enhancements are backward-compatible with earlier hardware releases, earlier versions of DOS will not support the full features of the PC AT, especially the multiuser feature.

Although IBM has not released an 80386-based machine that retains the original PC bus architecture, many third-party manufacturers have done so. IBM's 80386 thirty-two-bit machines are designed around a new microchannel bus in the PS/2 line. (See discussion below.) Other manufacturers have chosen not to abandon the existing bus design, and consequently the industry has a plethora of thirty-two-bit bus configurations.

Most of the new machines include some AT-compatible expansion slots, so you can use existing peripherals and other expansion cards, as do IBM's PS/2 offerings.

## IBM PS/2

Early in 1987 IBM ended months of speculation about where it was taking its line of personal computers by announcing the first four members of its PS/2 line. It had been obvious for some time before the announcement that a change was in the offing. IBM started the popular PC line, then promptly lost control of its own market. By designing a machine with open architecture, IBM enabled a strong third-party market to offer compatible machines with more features at a fraction of the cost of its own products. The new PS/2 line was seen as an effort to bring the company's personal computers back into control.

At this writing, new models have been released and a few companies are talking about producing PS/2 clones. Still, the new line has not become a major market presence. Perhaps when the operating system designed to support the hardware, OS/2, is widely supported and users have enough experience to know precisely how OS/2 behaves, this will change. For now the PS/2 line remains an important industry offering because of who offers it and the fact that a significant number of major corporate PC users will adopt it, but it does not account for a large percentage of overall PC sales.

The four initial offerings were the PS/2 model 30, model 50, model 60, and model 80. Each machine also is available in multiple configurations. Interestingly, the new line uses an 8086 CPU at the low end, a midrange machine uses the 80286 CPU, and 80386 CPUs are used at the high end. The systems share some common features. All use the AT-style enhanced keyboard introduced in 1986. With the PS/2 line, IBM broke away from the 5.25-inch diskette drive in favor of 720-KB and 1.44-MB, 3.5-inch diskettes.

All members of the PS/2 line except the model 30 use IBM's new 32-bit *microchannel* bus, designed to provide the bandwidth necessary for new high-speed applications.

### PS/2 Model 30

The model 30 is the entry-level PS/2 machine. It uses the 8086 CPU running at 8 MHz and supports three AT-compatible expansion bus slots. Serial, parallel, and mouse ports are included on the motherboard. It is suplied with 640 KB of system RAM and available with dual 720-KB diskettes or one 720-KB diskette and a 20-MB hard drive. The integral video display is a superset of the CGA color display. This is an MS-DOS machine that is smaller and faster than the older XT, but it is not compatible with the OS/2.

### PS/2 Model 50

The model 50 uses a 10-MHz 80286 CPU and is available with a single 1.44-MB diskette and a 20-MB hard drive. It is supplied with 1 MB of RAM standard. A sixteen-bit version of the microchannel bus is provided in addition to three AT-compatible expansion slots. In addition, the model 50 introduces IBM's new display technology, the video graphics array (VGA). This is a high-resolution display that supports 640-by-480-dot resolution with up to sixteen simultaneous colors.

### PS/2 Model 60

The model 60 is an expanded model 50 and also uses a sixteen-bit microchannel bus with a 10-MHz 80286 CPU. Configured in a floor-mounted pedestal, the model 60 is supplied with either a 44-MB or 77-MB hard drive. One MB of RAM is standard, but that can be expanded up to 15 MB. The larger case of the model 60 also permits storage expansion with a second drive up to 115 MB.

### PS/2 Model 80

The model 80 also is supplied in a floor-standing pedestal and uses a 16-MHz 80386 processor. Standard configuration is 1 MB of RAM and a single 44- or 70-MB disk. Another model of the 80-line is configured with a 20-MHz 80386 chip and includes an 80387 math coprocessor, 2 MB of RAM, and a 115-MB hard disk.

Model 80 RAM can be expanded to 16 MB and can contain a second hard drive up to 115 MB. All model 80 configurations have a total of seven expansion slots, three thirty-two-bit slots and four sixteen-bit slots.

## CHAPTER SUMMARY

The material in this chapter is oriented toward the VAX user who is learning about PC-class computers. This chapter can serve as a reference section as you become accustomed to PCs.

This chapter covers some of the differences between the PC lines and Digital's MicroVAX offerings and provides a brief introduction to PC operating systems. See Chapter 8 for additional details on PC system software.

# 7

# Looking Up: The View from the Personal Computer

The user who looks at the computer world from the PC perspective has a very different view from that of the user who stands with his back to a VAX. Although many PC users resist integration into the MIS fold through links to a central host, the benefits of a well-designed heterogeneous network are significant. This chapter discusses PC-VAX communications from the PC perspective and describes the major VAX components. It should be useful as an introduction to the VAX world and as a summary and reference as you begin to work with Digital computers.

## THE PERSONAL COMPUTER PERSPECTIVE

If a PC is your only computer so far, you are used to commanding the full attention of your personal CPU. You can load and save programs at will; you can add new applications by inserting a new diskette and remove applications even more easily; your printer is probably beside your desk; you can turn your machine on and off whenever you want.

Although operation in a PC LAN environment is somewhat more restrictive, if your PC workstation includes local storage, especially if

95

it has a hard disk, you can continue to use it as before while enjoying the benefits of large central storage, and shared data, and peripherals.

Terminal users attached to a VAX, however, live in a different world. They share the power of the CPU with everybody else, for one thing. Only a few years ago this did not seem to present major problems because the host was so much more powerful than any PC available that even if you had to share it, the host CPU was faster and more sophisticated.

As a PC user, however, you don't need a terminal. You have one in the PC, so you can benefit from the services of the host while maintaining your dedicated CPU independence. The marriage of PCs to VAXs, distributing the processing power around a network so that the computing work can be done closest to the application, is the ultimate computing environment.

## ALL ABOUT VAXS

So what is this VAX beast? Digital Equipment Corp.'s VAX (Figure 7-1), introduced in 1977, is said to be the world's most successful single line of minicomputers.

VAX, which stands for virtual address extension, grew out of Digital's original line of minicomputers, the PDP (programmable data processor) family. The most advanced member of that series, the PDP-11, was built around a sixteen-bit processor that limited programmers to 64-KB memory segments.

**Overview of VAX**

The VAX, using a thirty-two-bit processor, can use up to four billion memory address spaces. But the VAX added another feature, virtual addressing. That means the machine can address (access) memory throughout the possible range, but the physical memory inside the computer does not have to be four billion bytes large. The architecture was intended to offer an essentially unlimited amount of memory for users. This is possible through memory management techniques. The VAX's memory management circuitry loads and stores programs in segments as they are needed and translates virtual memory addresses

*Figure 7-1* **The MicroVAX line is among Digital's most popular offerings. It ranges from the low-end MicroVAX 2000 to a surprisingly small but powerful 3600. (Reproduced with permission of Digital Equipment Corporation)**

to physical addresses. Because there may not be enough physical memory to run all of the programs being used at any one time, the VAX processor switches among processes very fast.

Each program appears to have the processor's full attention at any given time, but each process is halted periodically while the computer works on others. As a user or programmer, you don't notice this pause in processing unless things get very busy when a lot of people and programs all are vying for CPU service. During these times you may notice slower response times, but the functions remain, even though many users are sharing the CPU power and a limited amount of physical memory.

## VAX Operating Systems

In a move that may be at the heart of Digital's success, the company chose to standardize on a single operating system and to maintain hardware compatibility with that software across a developing line of VAX computers. Coupled with that is a consistent commitment to networking for the sharing of applications and data. Digital's core networking architecture is DECnet. (See Chapter 3.)

The preferred operating system for the VAX is VAX/VMS (virtual memory system). VMS is capable of time-sharing, batch-processing and real-time operations. (See chapter 9 for more details on VMS.)

A second operating system is ULTRIX, Digital's version of UNIX. ULTRIX is an implementation of AT&T's System V UNIX, extended with Berkeley 4.2 functions. UNIX, in its many versions from different computer manufacturers, is becoming a universal language of sorts, desirable in many applications because of the perception that it provides language compatibility and continuity across many product lines.

Like any standard, however, there are inconsistencies in the way it is implemented by various vendors. There has been a lot of discussion in Digital circles recently over ULTRIX and its place in the Digital product line. The company sells fewer ULTRIX systems than it does VMS systems, and some industry watchers have said that Digital does not want to support this operating system. Digital has stated publicly on numerous occasions, however, that ULTRIX and its associated applications are a definite part of the company's strategic planning and that it is fully supported inside and outside the company.

In fact, ULTRIX forms a significant portion of Digital's overall sales, and support for it in the user community is strong. Moreover, the importance of ULTRIX to Digital and its customers will increase with the popularity of UNIX, which today is gaining user acceptance as an operating system that provides programmer and user continuity across heterogeneous hardware lines.

At the same time, VMS, a proprietary operating system, is destined to remain the most popular operating system among VAX users. For one thing, the VAX and VMS were made for each other; they make a high-performance combination. As the Digital product line expands, VMS is expanding with it, making the proprietary solution more attractive. In addition, such developments as standards-based networking and DECwindows — a user interface that operates across VMS, ULTRIX, and MS-DOS — are narrowing the differences in operating systems at the application and development level. These advances probably will mean a further strengthening of proprietary operating systems from all vendors.

# VAX PRODUCT LINE

The VAX product line offers a wide-ranging choice of central processing power, communications facilities, software, and peripherals. VAX products can be grouped in a number of ways, but from the PC user's perspective, the most useful grouping is host and workstation. VAX host computers are designed to operate as servers on a network and are accessed through terminals or workstations operating as terminals. While a PC includes a keyboard and video display as part of its basic package, host VAX computers service only attached display devices.

VAX workstations are more like PCs in that they include a keyboard, display, display-driver hardware, windowing software, a mouse, and utility software. Although many workstations are capable of supporting multiple users, the general concept of a workstation is that it is a single-user device designed to be dedicated to only one user at a time. Digital's workstations are called VAXstations: VAXstation 2000, VAXstation II/GPX, and so on.

A complete discussion of each would require several books much larger than this one. However, this section offers a brief summary of the major VAX products.

## PCs by Digital

Digital is not known for its success in the personal computer arena. The Digital Rainbow and Professional lines have been around since the early 1980s, but neither has done well commercially. Digital's public policy calls for concentration on methods for permitting personal computers to have access to the Digital computing environment through networking tools instead of development of its own PC line. However, in the fall of 1988, Kenneth Olsen, president of Digital, stated publically that his company "will never make our own PC line. We may sell someone else's."

Digital has completed an agreement with Tandy Corporation for joint production of a line of PCs (Figure 7-2). Digital has specified some custom features for the existing high-end Tandy line and sells them under the Digital label. This is a way for Digital to get back into the PC marketplace without designing and building their own line.

*Figure 7-2* MS-DOS personal computers from Digital. Digital's family of personal computers is based on Intel Corporation's 80286 and 80386 chips; and these computers are designed to be full members of a DECnet/PCSA networking environment. From left (front to back): DECstation 316, DECstation 320, DECstation 210. The PCLAN Server 2000, based on the MicroVAX 2000 (back row), and all VAX/VMS services for MS-DOS-configured VAX systems support the DECstation personal computers. (Reproduced with permission of Digital Equipment Corporation)

## VAXmate

The VAXmate is Digital's IBM PC AT clone, oriented heavily to the Digital computing environment. The VAXmate uses an 8-MHz 80286 microprocessor, up to 3 MB of RAM, and 64 KB of system ROM for BIOS, diagnostics, and local boot. It is supplied with an Ethernet interface, and it uses the LK250 keyboard, Digital's standard keyboard on the VT series of terminals. The keyboard also carries standard IBM PC key labels. The dual-function keyboard provides function key support when running VAX-based applications and utilities and provides familiarity for PC users. The VAXmate can read and write Digital's RX50-format 400-KB diskettes in addition to the IBM PC AT 1.2 MB format and can read the PC XT's 360-KB diskettes.

The VAXmate is supplied with Microsoft Windows software and includes a DECnet/PCSA (personal computing systems architecture) software license. VAX/VMS Services for MS-DOS networking software provides virtual disk and VAX-host integration.

## Rainbow

The Rainbow is an older Digital PC offering with a brilliant concept, excellent design and execution, abysmal marketing, and lackluster industry acceptance. The Rainbow is a Digital MS-DOS–compatible machine that runs the 8088 microprocessor, the same CPU used in the original IBM PC and PC XT machines. It was designed to be everything to everybody. In the early 1980s, the industry still was trying to decide on standards, and the Rainbow, which runs both CP/M and MS-DOS, seemed like a good idea. Add a superior video display, VT-terminal emulation, an excellent keyboard, and the Digital name, and it looked like a sure success.

One of the first snags for Rainbow was a fairly rapid swing away from CP/M to MS-DOS. With CP/M out of the picture, the Rainbow's dual operating system was not particularly important. Moreover, Digital priced the Rainbow like an MIS department resource instead of a desktop machine, this when IBM PC clones were hitting the market at sharply reduced prices.

The Rainbow is still listed in Digital's systems summaries and catalogues, with prices only for accessories and subsystems. It is hard to imagine anyone purchasing any of these options, however. A 20-MB hard disk subsystem, the largest drive available for the Rainbow, is offered for $2,310. On today's PC systems a 20-MB drive is considered small and out of date and is priced with controller and cables for under $300 from most sources. For the price of the Rainbow disk subsystem alone, you can buy a complete, more powerful PC system with at least 60 MB of storage and other features not supplied with the Rainbow.

Although the Rainbow included hardware for VT-102 terminal emulation, an excellent display, and an expanded keyboard that was ahead of its time, the machine suffered from a lack of total compatibility with the IBM PC. This fact and its high price combined to kill the machine. It is useful to know about this Digital PC offering, but it is not currently considered a viable system.

### Professional 380

Digital classifies the Professional 380 as a workstation, not a PC. Where to draw that line always is a question, but we prefer to list the 380 with PCs.

The Professional 380 uses a PDP-11/70 sixteen-bit processor chip and provides desktop programming and system development for PDP-series machines. The professional series was released at roughly the same time as the Rainbow and has enjoyed more longevity, probably because of the continued popularity of the PDP line in industrial and engineering applications. The 380 provides an excellent development platform for these applications as well as for applications that traditionally fall into the PC category.

### DECmate III

The DECmate III is another nonsuccess. It is a microprocessor-based CP/M machine designed for dedicated word processing. Although communications and hard disk options are available, this machine cannot compete favorably with other PC workstation offerings that offer broader software support, better performance, and an almost unlimited range of hardware options.

## MicroVAXs

The Digital MicroVAX family offers a broad range of processing power and configurations for single users, work groups, and LAN servers. The MicroVAX CPUs provide compatibility with larger VAX applications, but they lack some of the instructions and are slower in performance than the big machines.

### P-VAX

Digital is moving back into the desktop arena with a series of VAX workstations. Although the industry called these machines "P-VAXs" prior to their release, Digital uses the VAXstation name. The VAXstation 3100 uses a 3000-series CPU in a desktop or deskside case and offers about three times the performance of the VAXstation 2000.

The VAXstation 3100 is priced competitively with high-end PCs and offers the advantage of the VMS operating system, VAX compatibility, and the Digital name. An MS-DOS software coprocessor offers

PC compatibility. It supports up to 32 MB of memory and handles disk drives up to 332 MB.

## MicroVAX 2000

The MicroVAX 2000 (Figure 7-3) is a desktop VAX, the low-end version of the MicroVAX II. It uses a MicroVAX II CPU, which is a subset of the full-sized VAX processor, and can support up to four interactive users. It offers an SCSI-like port for disk storage expansion and a built-in ThinWire Ethernet controller.

One of the main differences between the MicroVAX 2000 and the larger MicroVAX II is the 2000's lack of a bus. Standard MicroVAX expansion boards will not work with the small machine, limiting the amount of growth possible. On the other hand, the small size and relatively low price provide attractive alternatives to the MicroVAX II family for users who need thirty-two-bit VAX-compatible processors but not open-ended expansion.

## VAXstation 2000

This is the workstation version of the MicroVAX 2000. The VAXstation uses the same CPU, chassis, and case as the MicroVAX 2000, but a video display adapter and keyboard driver are added to make the VAXstation a stand-alone desktop computer. ThinWire Ethernet and other MicroVAX features are standard with the VAXstation. This machine is available in various configurations:

- Diskless monochrome system for use with a network. Includes 4-MB of memory and fifteen-inch or nineteen-inch monochrome monitor.
- Disk-based monochrome. Includes 44-MB disk.
- Diskless color system. Four MB of memory, fifteen-inch or nineteen-inch color monitor.
- Disk-based color system. With 44-MB or 159-MB disk.
- Diskless color system. Includes 14 MB of memory, four-plane graphics coprocessor, and fifteen-inch color monitor.
- Diskless eight-plane color system.

The diskless versions of the VAXstation are housed in a single small box that is almost a cube. To add disk or tape units, a second expansion box is added.

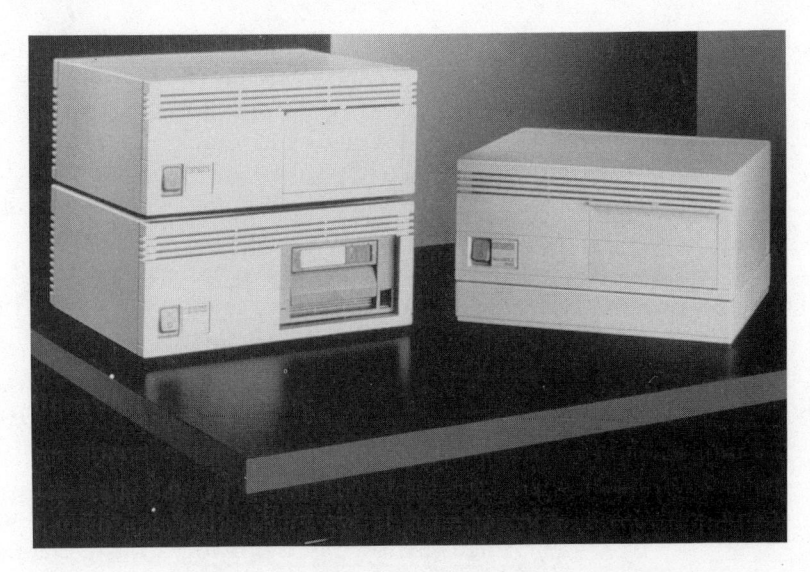

*Figure 7-3* **The MicroVAX 2000 is a desktop version of Digital's venerable MicroVAX II. In a workstation configuration, this machine becomes the VAXstation 2000. (Reproduced with permission of Digital Equipment Corporation)**

## MicroVAX II

Introduced in 1983, the MicroVAX II (Figure 7-4) brings about 1 MIPS to a single user or a shared system of as many as thirty users. (Digital officially specs the MicroVAX II at ninety percent of the performance of a VAX 11/780.) It uses Q-bus internal bus structure for storage and peripheral attachment and supports up to 16 MB of memory. Available in a variety of cabinets and configurations, it can be designed to fit under a desk. With a rack-mount cabinet, the MicroVAX II can provide up to 2.8 gigabytes (GB) of storage. Among Digital's new announcements is a UNIX-based desktop workstation (Figure 7-5).

## MicroVAX 3000 Family

The MicroVAX 3000 family is Digital's complementary metal oxide silicon (CMOS) line. It supports double the memory of the MicroVAX II — up to 32 MB — and according to Digital literature, is 2.6 times as fast as the earlier machine. Some third party vendors who have tested the machine, and sources inside Digital, say the 3000 series is actually a little faster than 3 MIPS for some operations.

The 3000-family processors likely will become a standard of sorts in the Digital world. It is fast enough and small enough (Figure 7-6) to fill a variety of growing computer needs. The company is expected to use the CMOS chip set in a variety of new machines over the next few years.

The 3000 series is available in four models, the 3300/3400 series and the 3500/3600 series. The 3300/3400 family (Figure 7-7) is the newest MicroVAX offering and includes an integrated CPU card with Ethernet controller, hard disk interface, and 4 MB of memory. The 3300 is shipped in a small six-slot cabinet, while the 3400 model comes in a full twelve-slot enclosure. Otherwise the two machines are identical. They use the same CPU and support the same peripherals.

A couple of unique features are part of this family. The line supports dual hosts that share up to six hard disks through Digital's digital storage systems interconnect (DSSI) bus. If one host should fail, users can switch automatically to the second host to access disk data. The DSSI bus is new with the 3300/3400 line, as is the RF series of disk drive that includes an integral intelligent controller. Digital calls these new drives integrated storage elements (ISE).

The 3300/3400 series is designed to replace the high-end MicroVAX II configurations and serve as an entry point to Digital's CMOS

*Figure 7-4* **The MicroVAX II was Digital's mainstay low-end system until the announcement of the 3300/3400 family. (Reproduced with permission of Digital Equipment Corporation)**

**106** □ LOOKING UP: THE VIEW FROM THE PERSONAL COMPUTER

3000-series chip set. It supports less memory than the 3500/3600 family and is slightly slower in performance than these larger machines.

The main difference between the 3500 and the 3600 is the 3600's larger cabinet, which allows it to support larger disk drives. The 3500 is designed for dual 280-MB disks and a 296-MB tape drive. The 3600 uses a 622-MB drive and the 296-MB tape drive.

The 3500 and 3600 are available as VAXstations. Like the VAXstation 2000 described above, they include keyboard and video

*Figure 7-5* The DECstation 3100 is Digital's RISC-based, high-performance workstation for UNIX-based applications. Based on the MIPS Computer Systems, Inc., chipset, the DECstation 3100 workstation delivers 14 MIPS on the Dhrystone benchmark. The same desktop package houses the VAXstation 3100, a CVAX-based workstation.

**Figure 7-6** The MicroVAX 3500 and 3600 are the high-end members of the 3000 family. This line is frequently referred to as the "C-VAX" family because of its use of CMOS technology in the CPU. The 3600 is shown here. (Reproduced with permission of Digital Equipment Corporation)

adapters and graphics support. These devices also can be configured as dedicated servers to support local work groups over a network.

## Midrange Systems

The usefulness of midrange systems is rising along with performance at other levels. Some of Digital's newest offerings, still classified as midrange systems, offer multiprocessor support and very good performance.

### VAX 6200 Family

Digital's 6200 family (Figure 7-8) is among the latest offerings in the VAX midrange. Four basic models are available, the 6210, 6220, 6230, and 6240. (Digital has released an enhanced version of this line called the 6300 Series.) The 6200 series is designed around multiprocessor architecture that supports one 6210-model processor up to four 6240-model CPUs and memory up to 256 MB. These are VAXBI, high-speed bus machines.

### VAX 8250

This entry-level VAXBI-based machine (Figure 7-9) is capable of approximately 1.2 MIPS. It supports Unibus peripherals to help users migrate from non-VAXBI machines and can be configured with up to 128 MB of physical memory.

### VAX 8350

This midrange VAX is about twice as powerful as the VAX 11/780, or approximately 2.3 MIPS. This is a dual-processor version of the 8250.

### VAX 8500 Series

These VAXBI-based machines are available in a variety of configurations that provide 4 MIPS to 6 MIPS of performance. The 4-MIPS 8530 model supports up to 320 MB of system memory. It can be field upgraded to the 8550, a 6-MIPS machine.

*Figure 7-7* The MicroVAX 3300 (left) and the 3400 (right) represent new disk and CPU technology built around the basic C-VAX chip set. (Reproduced with permission of Digital Equipment Corporation)

*Figure 7-8* The 6300 family began life as the "Calypso" or VAX 6200 inside Digital. The upgraded 6300 series offers enhanced performance and other expanded features over the original 6200 line. (Reproduced with permission of Digital Equipment Corporation)

## High-End Systems

Here is a very brief summary of some of Digital's high-end system offerings:

**VAX 8700.** 6 MIPS high-end machine, VAXBI
**VAX 8800.** Six to 22 MIPS, depending on number of processors. The 8810 is a uniprocessor machine, while the 8840 (Figure 7-10)

*Figure 7-9* The VAX 8250 (left) is an entry-level offering into the VAXBI and VAX cluster world of larger systems. The 8350 provides the same features with a larger bus. (Reproduced with permission of Digital Equipment Corporation)

runs four CPUs in symmetrical multiprocessing (SMP) mode. Includes VAXBI.

**VAX 8900.** A cluster of 8700 processors (Figure 7-11). The 8978, for example, joins eight processors for a resulting rating of 52 MIPS.

**VAXcluster.** A system from Digital to connect as many as sixteen VAXs and hierarchical storage controller (HSC) devices.

## Older VAXs

Although the more recent releases from Digital gain a lot of attention from users and the computer press, the company continues to supply a range of older equipment to enthusiastic users. The systems summarized

*Figure 7-10* **VAX 8840 is a high performance SMP machine. (Reproduced with permission of Digital Equipment Corporation)**

in this section are not as new as the ones described above, but they are being sold and already are in place in thousands of sites around the world.

**VAX 11/750.** A midrange early VAX, rated at about 0.6 MIPS.
**VAX 11/780.** Approximately 1 MIPS. Used as the benchmark in Digital's own VUP (VAX unit of processing) ranking.
**VAX 11/785.** An augmented 11/780, capable of approximately 1.5 MIPS.
**VAX 8600.** A 4-MIPS early VAX 8000 machine, lacking VAXBI.
**VAX 8650.** A 6-MIPS early VAX 8000 machine, lacking VAXBI.

## TERMINALS AND DIGITAL

We have just said that a PC-to-VAX link is the ultimate computing environment because it applies local processing in concert with the central CPU. However, terminals are a fact of life when you operate in

*Figure 7-11* **Clustered 8900-series machines provide performance up to 48 MIPS.** (Reproduced with permission of Digital Equipment Corporation)

a host environment. To get maximum use from host-based software, including operating system–level utilities, you must have a display that is compatible with the terminals commonly used with the host.

You can either use a separate terminal for applications that require strict display compatibility or run terminal emulation software on your PC, turning it into a host-compatible display. This section offers a very brief summary of VT-terminals. For details on the VT-series terminals from Digital, see Chapter 12 and Appendix D. Chapter 12 also offers more details on using PC workstations as terminals in the VAX environment.

**VT-Family Terminals**

Digital has put forth three major families of terminals over the lifetime of the VAX family—the VT100, VT200, and VT300 series. The VT-100 was the original VAX terminal and remains one of the most popular protocols in VAX-compatible computing. Because later terminal families are downward compatible, users of the older series still can access VAX hosts, although some display features of newer applications may not be available.

The VT220, introduced in 1983, sold over one million units from Digital alone, with almost as many additional VT220-compatible units sold by third-party manufacturers. The VT300 family, introduced in 1987, is expected to spawn another healthy market.

Why use a terminal? The cost is relatively low, and for users without need for local processing or storage, it can offer a simpler operating environment than a PC. In addition, a lot of terminals are in use simply because they have been around for a long time, they are paid for, and they are already installed.

## CHAPTER SUMMARY

This chapter is an introduction to Digital's VAX family of computers. It should serve as a reference section for PC-oriented users who are learning about Digital's minicomputer offerings.

A number of excellent publications about the company's VAX computers are available from Digital. A local Digital sales office can help you purchase the material you need.

# 8

# Personal Computer Operating Systems

The operating system is the computer's housekeeper; system-level software that is part of almost everything you do with the computer. Among the tasks handled by the operating system:

- Handling the movement of data between the computer and terminals or workstations
- Printing information
- Managing access to memory
- Moving data to and from external storage
- Trapping and reporting system errors
- Providing a platform and interface for applications (accounting, databases, word processing, spreadsheets)

Without the operating system it would be impossible to use the computer. (Some special-purpose computers, such as those involved in monitoring and controlling operations, actually function without a true operating system, but that's not the kind of system we are talking about here.)

This chapter will provide an overview of common PC-based operating systems, though it is in no way inclusive.

## OVERVIEW

Traditionally each computer vendor sells its own proprietary operating system. Diskettes and software from vendor A will not function with computers from vendor B without some additional work because of the differences among operating systems and hardware formats. The broad acceptance of the IBM PC standard has changed this tradition in this segment of the PC world.

Computers from such well-known vendors as AT&T, Digital Equipment Corporation, and Tandy have been offered with MS-DOS compatibility so they can use software written for the IBM PC.

MS-DOS was written for IBM by Microsoft, Inc. IBM's version, slightly modified, is sold as PC-DOS by IBM. Other vendors sell the generic version purchased from Microsoft for their machines.

XENIX, a Microsoft version of UNIX for PCs, is used by some PC-compatible machines. In addition, IBM's OS/2 is destined to become another standard for 80286-, 80386-, and 80486-based machines.

## MS-DOS

MS-DOS is the longest-running operating system on IBM-compatible personal computers. Beginning with version 1.0 when the IBM PC was first announced, the system has undergone a number of revisions and upgrades. The current version is 4.0.

### DOS versus VMS

If you are familiar with Digital's VMS operating system, the transition to DOS should go very smoothly. In some ways DOS is easier to learn and use because the directory and command structures are somewhat streamlined. DOS does not have the features of VMS; DOS is a single-user, single-task system, and it does not include Logon, Password, and other security features. There is no integral HELP facility within DOS. Although version 4.0 includes a DOS shell to make navigating around the system easier, you cannot ask for online descriptions in the same way as with VMS. Basically, however, from the end user's viewpoint, there are many similarities between the two systems. For more information on VMS, refer to Chapter 9 and Appendix A.

## Features and Commands of DOS

Like VMS, DOS is command-oriented system-level software, the interface to the hardware and a facilities manager. DOS operates in the background to handle such functions as disk I/O, screen displays, and printer output. In addition, a DOS command language (similar to DCL in VMS) provides the user interface to the system and its features.

It may appear that a computer speaks many different languages; in truth it speaks only one—the language of pulses of electricity representing one of two bits of information. This lowest of low-level languages is called *machine language*.

The designers of computers and operating systems have to deal with these binary codes, writing basic instructions in 0s and 1s to be placed directly in the computer's registers. Luckily, we users don't ordinarily have to come anywhere near this level. The typical user works several levels away.

When you interact with an operating system such as DOS, you use an intermediary language, usually called a command language. Command languages generally are similar to English and fairly intuitive. It takes some practice, however, to become familiar with all the aspects of a particular command language.

You can use DOS commands in two modes, interactive and batch. Interactive commands are issued directly from the keyboard, one command at a time. In batch mode you create a text file that contains a series of commands to be executed. DOS reads this file and carries out the commands in it.

There are two kinds of DOS commands, internal and external. Internal commands are memory-resident and can be executed from within any disk directory. External commands reside on a disk and must be loaded into memory like any other software before they can be executed. External commands must include a path prefix to point to the external file if the program is not stored in the default directory.

Commands are used to access the functions and features of the operating system. DOS commands display disk directories, execute DOS utility programs, change I/O or disk parameters, send information to a printer, set the date and time, and more. Most users ignore all but a small subset of the available DOS commands; others use most commands on a regular basis.

DOS commands are expressed in English-like syntax using verbs, compound modifiers, and objects or nouns.

Here are the names and positions of full DOS commands:

**C:\ PATH VERB PARAMETER /QUALIFIER**

Here are the elements of that command:

**C:\**  A DOS prompt. This symbol can be modified by the user. In this example "C:" designates which physical or logical drive is active. The backslash (\) shows that the root or first disk directory is selected.

**VERB**  A valid command name in the DOS dictionary. The verb can be a memory-resident command or the name of a disk-based file that will be loaded into memory and executed like any other program.

**PARAMETER**  The object of the action to be performed by DOS. There can be more than one parameter in a single command, but they must be separated by a space.

**QUALIFIER**  An element of the command that limits or modifies the action to be performed. For example, a qualifier can specify the size of elements associated with the command. More than one qualifier can be added to a command; they are separated from each other by slashes (/). Such qualifiers have rather limited use in DOS and are available with only a few commands.

## MS-DOS Files

All of the information and instructions that make up MS-DOS and that the system uses during operation are stored in files on a disk or diskette. DOS uses two basic kinds of files, program and data. Within these classifications there can be several types, usually identified by a specific three-character extension.

MS-DOS file names consist of an eight-character name, a period, and a three-character extension. Unlike some other operating systems, DOS does not allow you to change the allocation of these eleven characters. When you place a period in a DOS file name, the system allows only three more characters to follow. Commonly used extensions in operating system files:

.BAT  A batch file. Consists of a series of DOS commands in ASCII (text) format.
.COM  A compiled program file. An executable file.
.EXE  An executable program file.
.SYS  A system file, used by the operating system. Usually, the operating system loads system code as needed.

Other conventions include the following:

.ASC  A text file. See .DOC below.
.BAK  A backup file, usually a duplicate of another file with the same name but a different extension.
.DBF  Used by some database programs to designate the main data file.
.DOC  A document file, usually in a format that can be read, displayed, and printed directly from the operating system, as opposed to special files used by some word processors.
.HLP  A help file. Usually text used with a separate program to display help.
.IDX  Used by some database programs to identify a data file's index pointer file.
.TXT  See .DOC above.

## MS-DOS Devices

MS-DOS supports a number of standard devices and peripherals. A keyboard, a display, and several disk drives are the most obvious devices. The system also supports printer ports and communications ports. These devices are given internal names that can be used from DOS to specify where output will be presented. Device names are listed below.

AUX      The first serial port.
CON      The console keyboard and screen.
COM1     The first serial port. See AUX.
COM2-4   Serial ports 2 through 4. Used for serial printers, modems, direct links to other computers, or other serial (RS-232) applications.

| | |
|---|---|
| LPT1-3 | Parallel ports. Most commonly used for Centronics-compatible printers. |
| NUL | A nonexistent device that can be specified to hide output. When specified as an input device, an end-of-file marker is generated. |

## MS-DOS Directories

Information is stored on DOS disks in a series of directories and subdirectories. Although everything on a disk can be stored in one large directory, it is more convenient to separate programs and data according to application. DOS supports a hierarchical directory. The first, or main directory is called the root. Subordinate directories branch from the root. Figure 8-1 shows a typical hard-disk directory structure.

This sample directory does not show what files are stored in each of the directories; it shows only the name of the directories and the relationship among the directories. This sample is a relatively simple structure. Large disk systems can have hundreds of directories with many more layers. The only limit on your directory design is the number of files allocated to each directory, usually 128 on a hard disk, and a DOS-imposed 64-character limit on any directory path name.

Note that the same directory name can be used more than once as long as it appears under different parent directories.

You specify files and directories by separating each directory name with a backslash (\). To run a program called *SPEED* in the Utility directory, for example, enter the following command:

`\DOS\Utility\Speed`

This command assumes that you have set the disk drive where this directory is stored as the active disk. The first backslash in this command line stands for the root or main disk directory. The second backslash separates the two subdirectory names Freeware and Utility. Likewise, the final backslash separates the directory name from the

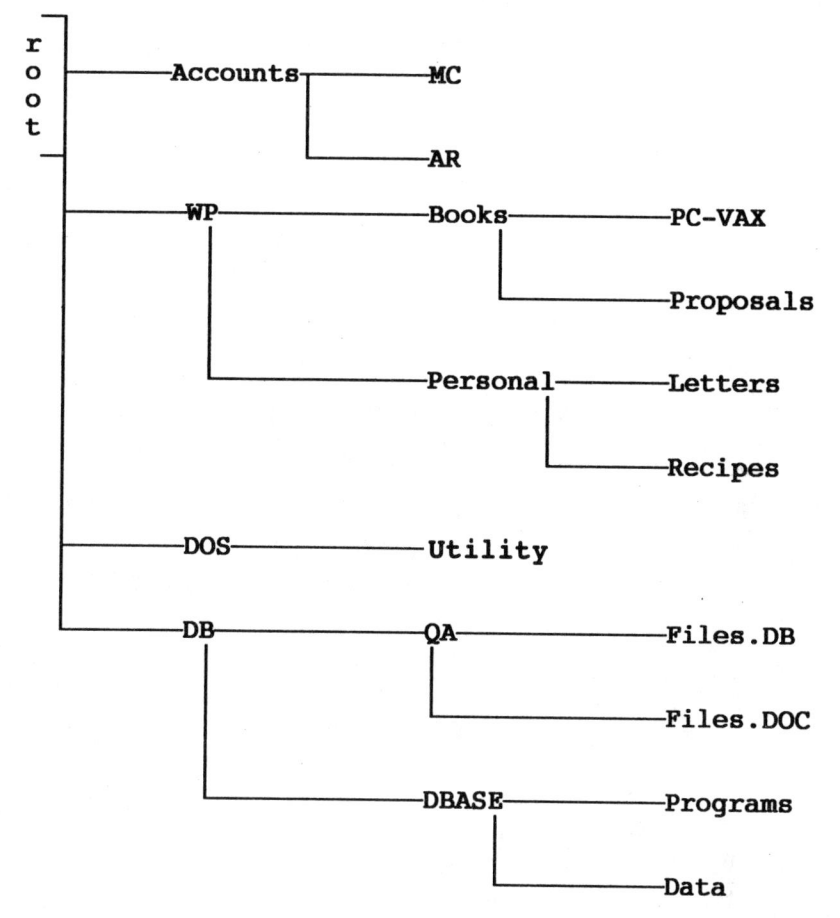

```
root
 ├──Accounts──┬──MC
 │            └──AR
 ├──WP────────┬──Books────┬──PC-VAX
 │            │           └──Proposals
 │            └──Personal─┬──Letters
 │                        └──Recipes
 ├──DOS───────────Utility
 └──DB────────┬──QA───────┬──Files.DB
              │           └──Files.DOC
              └──DBASE────┬──Programs
                          └──Data
```

*Figure 8-1* **Typical-hard disk directory structure**

name of the program you want to run. DOS scans the command line, stepping through the directories until the end of the line is reached and the specified file is found.

If this directory were stored on a disk other than the active drive, you could add a drive designator in front of the command line:

```
D:\DOS\Utility\Speed
```

DOS supports up to six local devices, identified by the letters A through F. The colon is part of the drive identifier. A networked PC, such as one attached to a VAX, can have a total of twenty-six drives if the network software supports this number.

## Other Features

Compared to UNIX, VMS and other system software for larger computers, MS-DOS includes a relatively limited list of integral utilities and features, but some additional features should be mentioned.

The MS-DOS batch programming facility is fairly sophisticated, although it is somewhat cumbersome to use. At the simplest level, you can place standard DOS commands in a text file in the order you want them executed, and when you execute the file, the commands are carried out as if they had been typed from the keyboard.

You can go beyond this simple sequence, however. The batch command language supports parameter passing, looping, error detection and messaging, GOTO, and the IF comparison. Using just these simple programming constructs, you can build batch programs to support inexperienced users in conducting system backup, starting and ending programs, installing software systems, creating directory structures, and more. Even experienced users find the batch capability a way to save time and to help you make maximum use of all of the features of DOS. For example, the switches and options of infrequently used commands may be difficult to remember. By studying the procedure and writing a batch file once, you can use the nuances of a command without having to refer to the manual each time.

A line-oriented text editor, *EDLIN*, is included with DOS. Although this program can be used to create and edit text files in DOS, hardly anyone ever tries to master it. EDLIN is old-fashioned, arcane, and difficult to use. If you need a look at computing in the dark ages, load EDLIN and try to create and edit a simple five-line file. You will quickly turn to a low-cost or no-cost full-screen editor.

DOS includes support for many foreign-language keyboards in addition to English. A Country file can be used to configure the keyboard for the desired language. The external command COUNTRY is used to specify the keyboard, date, time, collating sequence, and capitalization of a given country. The information displayed on your computer screen and data sent to the printer conform to the standards of the selected country. Note, however, that error messages and other DOS information are not translated into the language of the chosen country.

# OS/2

OS/2 is designed to provide the new standard in operating systems for IBM's new 80286 and 80386 lines of computers. OS/2 addresses many of the weaknesses in MS-DOS, including the lack of multiuser and multitasking support, the arcane user interface, and memory limitations. OS/2, like operating systems for much bigger computers, includes database, communications, and other facilities that cost extra with MS-DOS. OS/2 runs about ten times as much as MS-DOS, but neither is expensive when compared with the cost of the machines they run. MS-DOS now costs less than $100, and OS/2 is under $1,000.

## Features of OS/2

Announced with the PS/2 computers, OS/2 ultimately will include an integral windowing interface, (the presentation manager) as well as support for communications and database. In its programming announcement of the enhanced version of OS/2, IBM announced the following functions of OS/2:

**Support for 16 MB addressable random access memory.** This feature allows developers to take full advantage of memory beyond the previous 640-KB limit for applications and data. Removing that limit can open the door for richer, more user-friendly applications. In addition, OS/2 segment swapping implements virtual memory, allowing an application program to be larger than available real memory. In operation, memory segments are swapped out to disk and recalled as required.

**Concurrent processing of multiple applications.** Applications written to take advantage of new OS/2 features can run concurrently, and users can switch among applications as required. Without concurrent applications you have to stop one application, exit, load another, and start it. With concurrent applications, you use a pointer such as a mouse to select which windowed application you want in the foreground, leaving others to run unattended in the background. The OS/2 standard is expected to allow development of concurrent applications without requiring individual developers to know which applications will coexist.

**High-level programming interface.** This feature will help program developers keep their products compatible with enhancements to OS/2. The new operating system's high-level CALL interface provides a link between applications and the operating system at a level that can remain consistent even as the underlying operating system is changed and enhanced. System facilities at this level also provide for a high level of device independence, permitting them to run on a variety of existing computers and machines that will be designed in the future.

**Enhanced ease-of-use facilities.** Among the ease-of-use facilities is a comprehensive HELP system, designed to help novice users learn the system and to serve as a memory jogger to experienced users. A software tutorial helps you get started with OS/2, while context-sensitive online HELP answers specific questions while you use the system. A menulike command interface makes it easier to access all the power of the operating system. OS/2 is more interactive than MS-DOS, which is completely command-driven, requiring you to remember the commands you want to use.

**Compatibility with MS-DOS.** The enhancements available in OS/2 may be desirable, but if you have spent years developing MS-DOS-based applications, you may be slow to make the switch to the new operating system. OS/2 will support many MS-DOS applications unchanged, but the transition will not be entirely painless. Some programs—communications, real time, hardware-specific routines such as device drivers, and network-dependent applications—probably won't run with OS/2.

IBM claims the transition to OS/2 should be fairly easy, however, because many of the same commands are used. The experienced DOS user need only learn the OS/2 commands associated with the new system's enhanced features. Further, MS-DOS 3.3 files are compatible with OS/2 and can be interchanged without modification. Users of earlier versions of DOS may have to make some conversions.

**Communications manager.** The communications facility includes support for emulation of IBM 3270 synchronous and IBM 3101 and Digital VT100 asynchronous terminals as well as IBM strategic SNA protocols, including 3270 data stream and advanced program-to-program communications (APPC), also known as Logical Unit 6.2 (LU 6.2). LU 6.2 is particularly important to users on a multisystem network in the IBM environment. As heterogeneous networks (networks that include computers from multiple vendors) become more common, other vendors may also support LU 6.2, permitting communications with other systems while you run applications on the local machine.

**Presentation manager.** The presentation manager (PM) supports windowing and graphics in addition to applications development. Its roots are in Microsoft Windows. The PM lets you view several applications on the screen simultaneously, and each application can support several windows. A clipboard lets you extract data from one window and move it to another window or from one application to another. You can use this facility interactively, or it can be invoked from within applications.

**Database manager.** Large-computer operating systems frequently include a database. Because the database file and command structure is a part of the operating system, these facilities tend to set standards for applications development. The database manager in OS/2 mirrors the big operating systems, and according to IBM, the OS/2 database management system will be compatible with DB2 and IBM SQL/DS, IBM's big-machine database standards. The OS/2 database uses SQL for definition, update, and retrieval of data. Data is organized in rows (records) and columns (fields).

Tools for the creation of high-level applications give inexperienced users access to the database. Features such as a query manager, report generator, forms and menu tools, make this database manager a fully functional and powerful system.

An optional RPG II tool kit permits OS/2 to run many applications written for the IBM System/36 minicomputers. One estimate shows that about three-quarters of System/36 software was developed in RPG II (Report Program Generator). This holds the potential for opening a broad selection of high-order business programs such as inventory, order entry, and vertical applications in such industries as construction and medicine.

## Positioning of OS/2

Despite all the enhancements in OS/2, the industry is not united behind the new operating system. A recent study by analysts at International Data Corporation (IDC), the Framingham, Massachusetts research firm, concludes that OS/2 "will penetrate only twenty-five percent of the personal computer marketplace by 1992." One of the reasons, the study shows, is the lack of broad-based applications support. "There are few applications currently available that will run under OS/2 and there are several other barriers to market entry for OS/2 which will inhibit its growth for the next five years," the study continues. Data from the same study, however, reveals something about the size of the overall PC marketplace. IDC predicts that "worldwide OS/2 shipments will grow from 334,200 in 1988 to 7.5 million by 1992," accounting for the twenty-five percent penetration into the PC market.

"However, OS/2 has a minimum hardware requirement of an Intel 80286 processor and 1.5 MB of memory. This requirement currently rules out the bulk of the installed base of the personal computer marketplace. This will inhibit OS/2's ability to emerge as an operating systems standard in the short term," according to the IDC report. In addition, the company's predictions about who will sell OS/2 also predicts the course of the associated hardware marketplace. Until 1992, IDC says, most OS/2 operating system sales will come from IBM, but a turnaround is expected by 1992, when third-party PS/2-compatible machines will take on an increasingly important role in the marketplace.

Another study, by Forrester Research, an office automation consulting firm in Cambridge, Massachusetts, investigates how LAN servers will be used in the future. The Forrester analysts predict that by 1992 OS/2 and UNIX together will have ninety percent of the server software market. According to this study, fifty-five percent of servers will be running OS/2 by 1992, and UNIX-based systems will account for thirty-six percent. Applications for OS/2 will be primarily low-end file and print server systems, while UNIX will be handling sophisticated database and fault-tolerant computers. Forrester predicts that users will turn away from proprietary systems, including VAX/VMS, turning to open systems such as OS/2 and UNIX.

Microcomputer users need a true multitasking, multiuser operating system to take full advantage of the power already available in the new hardware. Whether this new system is destined to be OS/2 or something else such as UNIX has yet to be decided. Probably OS/2, UNIX, MS-DOS and perhaps other systems will run desktop computers.

## XENIX

XENIX is UNIX for microcomputers. XENIX is not the only UNIX for PCs, but it is the best known. So far it has not received wide acceptance, though the potential for very wide use certainly is there. UNIX is an extremely popular operating system, particularly among scientific and educational users. It supports multiuser operation; it is extremely portable, meaning it can run on a wide variety of hardware platforms; and thousands of applications are available for it. In addition, UNIX is enriched with a number of utilities that generally are supplied as part of the operating system. These include communications programs, editors, and graphics and formatting utilities, making XENIX a richer operating environment in general than MS-DOS. It is true that the full operating system requires a lot of storage, but in exchange you get a system that provides many of the features you have to add to MS-DOS with third-party utilities. The visual editor, for example, is an integral part of all XENIX and UNIX systems. This useful screen-oriented editor is closer to a word processor than the simple line-oriented editor supplied with MS-DOS.

One major drawback for PC users, at least until recently, has been the size of the operating system and its system overhead requirements. Just to install the basic operating system can require 10 MB or more of storage. Although 10-MB hard drives for PCs have been around for several years, only recently have very large disks become available at reasonable prices.

Newer PCs also have more powerful CPUs and larger RAM; both features could open up the PC world to XENIX. Indeed, if OS/2 does not prove its promise, XENIX and other versions of UNIX for the PC may take on increased importance.

## XENIX Commands

PC users familiar with other UNIX systems will feel very comfortable with XENIX. If your experience comes from VMS or MS-DOS, however, the arcane nature of XENIX can be intimidating. The MS-DOS command COPY, for example, becomes "cp" in XENIX; to rename a file, XENIX uses "mv"; and DEL from MS-DOS becomes "rm" in XENIX.

File-naming conventions in XENIX are more flexible than in MS-DOS. While MS-DOS is limited to eight-character file names, XENIX supports fourteen-character names. With MS-DOS you can use a three-character extension, a period, and an eight-character file name. In XENIX, however, the fourteen-character name can be broken up in about any way as long as you do not include spaces in the name.

You could use a fourteen-character name with no extension, for example, or a three-character name with a nine-character extension.

Although XENIX commands are different from those of MS-DOS, the way commands are given is similar. In addition, the XENIX file structure with subdirectories is similar to MS-DOS. The main difference is that in XENIX you use the solidus (/) to separate the parts of a path command, whereas in MS-DOS the backslash (\) is used. Generally, however, if you are making the transition from DOS to XENIX, the first hurdle is to become accustomed to the shortened command structure. Thereafter the learning process should go rather quickly.

Moreover, recent versions of XENIX include menu systems. There are predefined user front ends available for most XENIX and UNIX systems, and XENIX's utilities *menusys* and *digest* help you create custom menus.

## CHAPTER SUMMARY

The operating system is the heart of any computer. In many cases the operating system is the only interface the user has with the system. An understanding of the basic features of the operating system can help you use the computer more effectively. This chapter discusses common PC operating systems, summarizing the major features and providing a summary of MS-DOS commands.

# 9

# The VMS Operating System

V<sub>MS</sub>, for Virtual Memory System, is Digital's most popular operating system for VAX computers. Although in the strictest sense you, as an end user, never actually interact with the operating system, by convention we generally refer to the lowest level of user interaction with the computer as the operating system. When you log on to a VAX running VMS, unless your account is set up to run some other application automatically, you will be talking to the computer at this lowest level.

The following sections introduce you to the basics of VMS and of DCL, Digital Command Language, which allows you to send instructions directly to the operating system. For more detailed information on how to use VMS and its associated utilities and features, refer to appendix A.

## GETTING TO KNOW VMS

Accessing a VAX (and generally any minicomputer) requires some extra steps, compared with using an MS-DOS machine. Unless the PC uses special software in addition to the operating system, when the system is started, you are sent directly to the operating system. Once the system software is loaded, the MS-DOS operating system prompt appears.

The process of making yourself known to the VMS operating system, however, is a little like entering a speakeasy or private club. You knock on the door, give your name or other identification, and supply a password. Only then is the door into the front room opened. Depending on how well you are known to the operating system—your level of security clearance—you may spend your entire time in the front room. If you have system-level privileges, usually reserved for one or two system managers, you can go all the way upstairs and talk to the boss. Your authorization to use the system probably lies somewhere between these two extremes.

This introductory process is called logging in, logging on, or signing in. Once you are in the front room you are involved in a session. There are two basic things to understand before you undertake your first session: first, it is almost impossible to damage the computer itself by any action you might call for from the keyboard of the terminal; second, you must be careful not to damage the programs and data. Among your privileges as a user is the right to erase or change files. Learn about what you have to do before you plunge into your first session.

## Logging In

Your first task as a user is to connect your terminal to the computer. Turn on your terminal or workstation. Most terminals have a green or red pilot light on the front to indicate that the power is on; workstations have various lights and indicators on the display and the main CPU enclosure. Screens typically take fifteen to thirty seconds to warm up.

If you are using a direct-connect terminal, you are ready to log on as soon as the screen wakes up. If you are using a workstation, you must load its local operating system and invoke terminal emulation before you can log on to the VAX. You may also have to dial up the computer before you can log in.

When the terminal or workstation is ready, press the return key, which is on the right-hand side of the standard typewriterlike keyboard. On a VT terminal, the standard terminal for VAX computers, there is both a return key and an enter key. The enter key is used in certain applications and is generally not the same thing as return. Although the return and enter keys are in roughly the same place on

PC keyboards, both of these keys may be labeled enter. With your terminal-emulating software running, these keys should function as they do on a standard VT-series terminal. The enter key to the right of the central section of the keyboard is the return key; the key on the far right that is part of the numeric keypad is the enter key.

Press the return key, and you should be greeted by the sign-on message. Remember that almost everything you do at the terminal end is merely notetaking until you press the return key and send the message on down the cable to the computer. If you get no response, try typing Ctrl-C or Ctrl-Y by using the control key as a shift key.

You should now see,

Username:

The computer is asking you for the name of the account you have established; you have just knocked on the door, and someone is peeping out, trying to find out who you are. This is part of the security system. Only persons with a valid account and password are given access to the computer. (Even after you log on, you may meet further levels of restriction designed to protect vital files from unauthorized access.)

Type in your account name and press Return. In most systems your account name will be your last name or some combination of your first name or initial and your last name. If you share an account with other users, the account name may be the name of your department or job function. When you are assigned a user ID and granted access to the host, the system manager will tell you what name to use at this prompt.

If you don't see **Username:** but you do receive some other message from the computer, you are attached to a *terminal server* or other intermediary device. A terminal server is a remote hub that accepts attachments from many terminals or workstations, then attaches to the host computer through a single wire or network link. The terminal server is like a small computer and can route your request for computer services to more than one host. Try entering a **C** and Return at the terminal server prompt. If there is only one host in your system, you will then receive the prompt **Username:**. If multiple hosts can be accessed from this terminal device, you will be asked for the name of the host. If you have difficulty making the attachment at this level, consult your system manager.

Next the computer will prompt

```
Password:
```

Type in your password and press the return key. Note that the characters you type are not printed on the screen. This is to prevent an onlooker from seeing your password.

The computer will compare your account name and password with the secret list it maintains. If the password or account name is not on the list, you will receive this message:

```
User authorization failure
```

Depending upon the system, you may be granted additional attempts to sign on or the terminal connection may shut down for a while as part of a security system to prevent unauthorized access.

If your entry is accepted by the system, you will see a "welcome" message. Here is a typical successful login sequence:

```
Username: BADGETT

Password: password

Welcome to EDEN-CORP's VAX/VMS V5.0 System

Last interactive login on Monday, 19-SEP-88 06:01

Last noninteractive login on 10-JUL-87

You have 2 new mail message(s)

$
```

That last dollar sign is not your bill—it is the standard prompt of the DCL interpreter. A prompt is a request for a command.

### Remote Logins

This login is typical of a session in which the user is communicating with a local computer or one linked directly over a network such as DECnet.

It is also possible that you will be communicating from a remote location, using a modem. Your system manager will provide instructions on how to dial up the access port on your computer.

Once you have phone contact with the VAX, you will be greeted with the same or similar sign-on process as with a local connection. On some systems modem users will face an additional level of security. One such system uses a *callback modem*. This device queries the user for a password and disconnects the link. It then calls back to a predetermined phone number to open communications. This arrangement adds two levels of protection to the system—even if a password is compromised, the computer will make connection only to a specific location. Consult your system manager to determine if there are any special security requirements for your system.

Another form of remote login involves a connection from a local node to another system across interconnected networks. In such a situation the user must sign on to the local system and then change hosts. In many cases using the next host will require an additional login.

## Passwords

Why bother with passwords? Are you absolutely convinced there is no chance any person will ever attempt to read your confidential files or to change them without your authorization? Are you certain that no untrained person will ever accidentally erase or change or damage your critical files? Yes? Would you please invite the rest of us over to your place—we've never seen such perfection.

The best policy is to use passwords, make them difficult or impossible to guess, and change them regularly. Although your job may not involve government contracts or secret operations, the work you do with the computer is yours, and other people don't have any right to see or change it. How many hours have you spent preparing the word processing, database, or spreadsheet files you have stored on your system? Do you want to do it all over again? Worse, what if some of the information gets changed, but the file appears all right? This is worse than losing an entire file.

Here's a fact to keep in mind: the majority of file damage in most organizations is not caused by some nefarious hacker getting unauthorized access to your computer; it is caused by a well-meaning employee who thought he or she was doing the right thing. Save yourself from this kind of help by establishing good security practices.

The proper strategy for picking a password is not to have an obvious pattern. Don't use your nickname. Don't use your husband's or wife's name. Don't use your telephone extension. These have all been tried before, and a clever hacker will try them first. Reach for a word or a combination of numbers that is outside of your public persona.

Try to retain the password in your head rather than writing it down. If you must write it down, don't tape it to the side of the terminal or the underside of the keyboard, and don't leave it on a slip of paper in your desk drawer or your Rolodex. Trust us, that's a bit obvious.

You might try writing it down in code — scramble it by adding letters or numbers, for example. Keep the paper in your wallet or purse.

Make the habit of changing your password every few weeks or months. Use the command SET PASSWORD and enter first the old password and then the new one.

Finally, you should log off your terminal any time you are going to be away from it for a length of time. An unattended, logged-on terminal is an open door to your files.

This is all a bit of trouble, but so is locking the front door of your house when you go away. And the importance is about equal.

## THE DIGITAL COMMAND LANGUAGE

The Digital Command Language (DCL) lets you communicate with the VAX/VMS operating system and through it with the computer itself. DCL lets you develop and run programs; work with files, disks, and other storage media; obtain information about the system; and modify the work environment for a custom fit between machine and user.

DCL has two modes, interactive and noninteractive. The computer accepts interactive DCL commands directly from the terminal. In noninteractive mode VAX/VMS executes a set of DCL commands that are part of a batch job or another process.

Security aside, the login procedure is partly procedural, to make sure that each user is able to work with his or her own set of files and programs. When the system lets a user log in, it creates an environment from which the user can issue commands — referred to as a *process*. The computer consults its user authorization file, set up by the system manager, to determine the allowable characteristics for each process. Such characteristics include

- The user's account name and identification code
- The default disk drive and directory name to help the system find the user's files
- The privileges and quotas assigned to the user on the system

A DCL command is made up of English-like syntax using verbs, compound modifiers, and objects, or nouns.

Here is a full DCL command, using the names of its elements:

```
$ LABEL: VERB PARAMETER /QUALIFIER   ! A COMMENT
```

Here are the elements of that command:

| | |
|---|---|
| **$** | The default DCL prompt. This symbol can be modified by the user. |
| **LABEL** | An optional element of the command. The label assigns a name or gives an explanation but is not acted upon by the computer. VMS distinguishes the label by the colon that follows it. A label is useful in writing a multiline program of DCL commands. |
| **VERB** | A valid command in the DCL dictionary. |
| **PARAMETER** | The object of the action to be performed by VMS. There can be more than one parameter in a single command, but they must be separated by a space or tab. |
| **QUALIFIER** | An element of the command that limits or modifies the action to be performed. For example, a qualifier can call for a full or a brief display of the result of a command. More than one qualifier can be added to a command; they are separated from each other by a slash (/). |
| **COMMENT** | Preceded by an exclamation point, the comment can be used as a reminder of the purpose of a command or information about other commands or procedures. Comments are ignored by the system. |

Generally the commands you use in DCL are much simpler than that. You can get a list of the files stored in your personal directory, for example, simply by typing

**DIR**

Additions (such as parameters) to the command DIR can provide more information about your files.

To list only those files with a *.DOC* extension, for example, add the parameter *\*.DOC* to DIR:

**DIR \*.DOC**

Refer to Appendix A for additional information.

## Logging Out

Logging out is the final act of any session. Why log out? The most important reason is to preserve the security of the data and programs on your system. Once a session is logged out, it can be reactivated only with a password-protected login procedure. A secondary reason, but not unimportant, is that it frees up system resources for other users.

The logout is a simple process. Just enter:

**$ LOGOUT**

or

**$ LO**

If you'd like to obtain more information about your session, use the following command:

**$ LOGOUT/FULL**

to yield such data as total time logged on to the account, total CPU time used and other information.

Here is an example of a full logout:

# THE DIGITAL COMMAND LANGUAGE □ 137

```
$ LOGOUT/FULL
```

BADGETT  logged out at 23-OCT-1988 10:30:53.25

Accounting information:
Buffered I/O count:            694     Peak working set size:       929
Direct I/O count:              270     Peak page file size:        1421
Page faults:                  2384     Mounted volumes:               0
Charged CPU time: 0 00:00:35.11   Elapsed time: 0 00:08:22.27

## VMS HELP

No matter where you are in a DCL session, in most applications programs you are just a keystroke away from help at all times. The command

```
$ HELP
```

or the F15 key on a VT-200, VT-300, or compatible keyboard will bring up a menu of help topics. Select the subject you need by typing the full name of the displayed subject or as many characters as are needed to make your choice obvious to the computer. For example, to seek information on the CONNECT command, you have to enter at least CONN to avoid confusion with CONTINUE and CONVERT.

Here is an example of a request for help on RENAME:

Topic? RENAME

RENAME

   Changes all or part of a file specification(s).

Format

      RENAME input-file-spec,... output-file-spec

Additional information available:

## 138 □ THE VMS OPERATING SYSTEM

```
                    Parameters Qualifiers

/BACKUP /BEFORE[=time] /BY_OWNER[=uic] /CONFIRM /CREATED (default) /EXCLUDE
(=file-spec, ...) /EXPIRED /LOG /MODIFIED /NEW VERSION (default) /SINCE[=time]
```

At this point the computer asks if the user requires any assistance on subtopics of the command.

```
RENAME Subtopic?
```

If you enter the name of one of the subtopics listed and press return, you will be given additional information:

```
RENAME Subtopic? /BACKUP

RENAME

  /BACKUP
  /CREATED (default)
  /EXPIRED
  /MODIFIED
```

This selects files for RENAME according to the date of the most recent backup, the creation date, the expiration date, or the date of the last modifications. Relevant only with the qualifiers /BEFORE and /SINCE.

Here is a list of the help topics on a typical VMS system:

Additional information available:

| | | | | | | |
|---|---|---|---|---|---|---|
| 20-20 | 2020 | ACCOUNTING | ALLOCATE | ANALYZE | APPEND | ASCII |
| ASSIGN | ATTACH | BACKUP | BASIC | CALL | CANCEL | CLOSE |
| Command_procedure | | CONNECT | CONTINUE | CONVERT | COPY | CREATE |
| CTRAIN | DEALLOCATE | DEASSIGN | DEBUG | DECK | DEFINE | DELETE |
| DEPOSIT | DIFFERENCES | | DIRECTORY | DISCONNECT | DISMOUNT | DSCALC |
| DUMP | .EDIT | EOD | EXAMINE | EXIT | Expressions | |
| File spec | FMS | GKS | GOSUB | GOTO | HELP | Hints |
| IF | IMPRINT | INITIALIZE | INQUIRE | Instructions | | Kermit |
| Lexicals | LIBRARY | LINK | LOGOUT | MAIL | MERGE | MESSAGE |
| MF | MOUNT | New_Features_V44 | | Numbers | ON | OPEN |
| PRINT | Privileges | Procedures | Protection | PURGE | READ | RECALL |
| RENAME | REPLY | REQUEST | RETURN | RUN | RUNOFF | SEARCH |
| SET | SHOW | SORT | SPAWN | START | STOP | Strings |
| SUBMIT | Symbol_assignment | | SYNCHRONIZE | | TEX | THEN |
| Time | TYPE | UNLOCK | WAIT | WP | WPSPLUS | WRITE |

Here are some of the general navigational tools of the HELP command under DCL. Enter a Return after each one.

| | |
|---|---|
| PROCEDURES | Information on commonly peformed tasks. |
| HINTS | If you are not sure of the name of the command or topic for which you need help. |
| INSTRUCTIONS | Detailed instructions on how to use HELP. |
| QUESTION MARK (?) | Redisplays the most recently requested text. |

Press the return key one or more times to exit from HELP.

You can skip past the display of help topics by directly querying the help library. Just enter HELP followed by a topic or command:

```
$ HELP LOGIN
```

With such a direct query, you can also enter the subtopic and even a sub-subtopic from the command line:

```
$ HELP RENAME/BACKUP/CREATED
```

### Help within Applications

Consult the instruction manual for the application to determine the amount and nature of help available. Or press the help key and see what happens.

A number of special programs such as word processors and VT emulation packages include on-screen displays of the keyboard to help locate any special command keys and to show how a PC keyboard has been adapted to emulate keys on the LK201 keyboard.

# VMS FILES AND DIRECTORIES

At the heart of the way a computer goes about its business is the way it organizes information into files. Each job is indexed and stored like a folder in a filing cabinet.

The nature of the data in the file folder is of no importance to the system—it may be text, numeric information, graphics, or a combination.

The file folders may be automatically opened, updated and closed by a program such as a word processor, or the folders may be created and managed under the direct command of the user. Depending upon the version of the operating system in use, the type of storage media used, and the limits placed on the user by the system operator, each user can have many hundreds or even thousands of readily accessible files.

If you think of these files as residing in a large box, mixed in with the thousands of other files from other users and from the system itself, you can see the importance of having a logical and uniform identification and storage scheme.

On a VMS system, the identification system is called a file specification and can include as many as six elements. Here is a specification for a word processing file from Holstein Industries:

```
NODE_NAME:DEVICE_NAME:[DIRECTORY]FILE_ NAME.EXTENSION;VERSION
```

- *Node name*. If the system is part of a network of other computer systems, it operates as a network node and uses a node name. Depending upon the privileges granted your system and each user, you may be able to access files from other systems on the network.

    If your system is not part of a network, the VAX will not expect a node name. If your system is part of a network but you do not specify a node name, the computer will assume the file to be located within your own node.

- *Device name*. This is the physical location of the file, usually on a disk drive but possibly on a tape drive, a cartridge drive, or other device. The name itself consists of four letters or numbers to identify the type of device and the controller hardware involved.

    If you do not specify a device name, the system will look on the default device as defined for your account or as modified in a DCL command since the last sign-on.

- *Directory*. Within the hardware storage device, this is the name of the directory or subdirectory where the file is stored.

    If no directory is specified, the system will look in the default directory as indicated at sign-on or as modified in a DCL command since the last sign-on.

- *File name.* This is the actual title of the file. You can use as many as thirty-nine letters or numbers as the file name. Certain programs automatically create file names, while others have some specific limitations on names or alphanumeric characters employed.

## File Names

The following characters can be used in file names and file types:

- A through Z
- a through z
- 0 through 9
- Underscore
- Hyphen

The dollar sign can also be used, although Digital has reserved this character for special purposes. The system will interpret lowercase letters the same as uppercase; TESTFILE.TXT is the same as testfile.txt or Testfile.Txt.

No two files can carry the exact same file specifications, although there can be thousands of files with the same name but with different version numbers.

- *File type.* Also called a file name extension, this code of up to thirty-nine alphanumeric characters indicates the type of file. Typical extensions include .TXT for text, .DTA for data, .COM for a command procedure and .TMP for a temporary file. Some programs assign their own file types to file names. If you do not specify a file type, the computer will assume that the file name has no extension.
- *Version number.* Each time a file is changed or another version created, the file version number is increased by one. The highest number indicates the most recent edition.

  The user can edit any existing version of a file. A file can have any version number up to five digits.

### Style Conventions for File Names

You can use any standard alphanumeric character in naming a file. Several punctuation marks and special characters serve other purposes.

No blank spaces are accepted as part of a file name. However, the user can substitute an underscore for a space for the same effect:

`DAILY_FEED_FIGURES.DTA`

Each element of the file name has a size limit:

| | |
|---|---|
| Node: | up to 6 characters |
| Device: | 4 characters |
| Directory: | up to 9 characters |
| Subdirectory: | up to 9 characters |
| File name: | up to 39 characters |
| File type: | up to 39 characters |
| Version number: | any number from 1 to 32,767. |

## Defaults in File Specifications

VMS does not require the user to enter all of the file specifications each time a file is called for. If the file is in the primary directory and stored on the expected hardware, all the computer requires is the file name and extension, the operating system will fill in the blanks with the default information of directory and disk.

Left to itself, the operating system will always choose the latest version of a file. For example, to read the seventh and latest version of the file "DAILYFEED.DTA", enter:

`$ TYPE DAILYFEED.DTA`

To read the sixth version, you could enter DAILYFEED.DTA;6 or use a negative number version number, which makes the computer count backward from the latest version. For example,

`$ TYPE DAILYFEED.DTA;-1`

would yield the next to the last version on file.

## Global Characters

One shortcut to many VMS operations involves the use of the asterisk and percent sign to apply a single DCL command to a set of files rather than a single file.

The asterisk tells the computer to accept any alphanumeric characters from the position of the asterisk to the right end of a particular element of the file specification. Suppose we have the following files in our default directory:

```
HOLSTEIN.DTA;1
GUERNSEY.DTA;1
GUERNSEY.DTA;2
DAILY_FEED.DTA;1
DAILY_FEED.DTA;2
DAILY_FEED.DTA;3
DAILY_EXPENSES.SPD;1
DAILY_REVENUES.SPD;1
DAILY_REVENUES.SPD;2
SUPPLIES_ORDER.TXT;1
MAILING_LIST_CUSTOMERS.LIS;1
```

If you were to ask for the following directory:

```
$ DIR DAILY_FEED.DTA
```

you would receive a listing of all three of the versions with that name in the directory.

If you want a list of the files that begin with the word "daily," you enter the following instruction:

```
$ DIR DAILY*.*
```

This produces a listing of all files that begin with "daily" and have anything else in the file name. The use of the second asterisk extends the definition to any file name extension. This would be your yield:

```
DAILY_FEED.DTA;1
DAILY_FEED.DTA;2
DAILY_FEED.DTA;3
DAILY_EXPENSES.SPD;1
DAILY_REVENUES.SPD;1
DAILY_REVENUES.SPD;2
```

Suppose you just want a list of spreadsheet files beginning with "daily." The instruction

```
$ DIR DAILY*.SPD
```

would yield

```
DAILY_EXPENSES.SPD;1
DAILY_REVENUES.SPD;1
DAILY_REVENUES.SPD;2
```

To see the names of all files ending in the extension .DTA, enter

```
$ DIR *.DTA
```

This yields

```
HOLSTEIN.DTA;1
GUERNSEY.DTA;1
GUERNSEY.DTA;2
DAILY_FEED.DTA;1
DAILY_FEED.DTA;2
DAILY_FEED.DTA;3
```

The global characters can be used in many DCL operations, including DIRECTORY, PRINT, COPY, RENAME, and DELETE. You should handle a global delete command with great respect — it is quite easy to make a minor mistake in a DCL DELETE command and end up with a major headache.

You'll find that as you become more adept at using global characters you may add your own file-naming conventions to make it easier to retrieve and manipulate particular types of files. For example, a dairy might name all of the files dealing with specific breeds to begin with B, all daily feed reports with an F, and all reports on income and expenses with an A, for accounting. The new subdirectory would include

```
A-DAILY_EXPENSES.SPD;1
A-DAILY_REVENUES.SPD;1
A-DAILY_REVENUES.SPD;2
A-SUPPLY_ORDER.TXT;1
A-MAILING_LIST_CUSTOMERS.LIS;1
B-HOLSTEIN.DTA;1
B-GUERNSEY.DTA;1
B-GUERNSEY.DTA;2
F-DAILY_FEED.DTA;1
```

```
F-DAILY_FEED.DTA;2
F-DAILY_FEED.DTA;3
```

Then, to look at all accounting files, no matter what the file name extension, enter this instruction:

```
$ DIR A-*.*
```

To find just the A- files with a spreadsheet extension, enter

```
$ DIR A-*.SPD
```

Suppose you want to look at all daily files. The percent sign comes into play, identifying a single position as a wild-card spot.
The instruction

```
$ DIR %-DAILY*.*
```

tells the computer to look for any file in the default directory that has any character in the first position of its name, a hyphen in the second position, the word "daily" in the third through seventh spot, anything else from that point in the file name on, and with any file name extension. Here is the yield from our sample directory:

```
A-DAILY_EXPENSES.SPD;1
A-DAILY_REVENUES.SPD;1
A-DAILY_REVENUES.SPD;2
F-DAILY_FEED.DTA;1
F-DAILY_FEED.DTA;2
F-DAILY_FEED.DTA;3
```

The possible permutations of searches using wild cards include all of the various elements of the file name and specifications.

## File Manipulation

You can manipulate these files in other ways. Special DCL commands APPEND, COPY, DELETE, RENAME and others help you maintain your disk directories and control files. Refer to Appendix A for details on these and other useful file manipulation features of VMS.

## VMS UTILITIES

VMS includes a number of utilities for end users. The following section provides a brief summary of utility programs for mail and phone. For additional details on the operation of these utilities, refer to Appendix B and Appendix C.

### VMS MAIL

MAIL lets you exchange electronic messages with other users on the network. You can use this facility to send quick notes to local or remote users, to send word processing files to other users for review, or to broadcast letters and memos to everyone on the network or to groups of users.

To access MAIL from the VMS prompt, simply enter the command

```
$ MAIL
```

The system executes and gives you a special prompt:

```
MAIL>
```

#### Sending Mail

To send a message to someone else, type SEND at the mail prompt. The mail system responds with:

```
To:
```

Enter the name of the recipient's account. If you type an account name that is not registered in the system, an error message will be displayed. If the name you enter is valid, MAIL asks for a subject. You can enter a short description of your message or simply press return.

```
To: WHITED
    Subject: Lunch Tomorrow?
```

Next MAIL prompts you to enter your message:

```
Enter your message below. Press CTRL/Z when
complete, or CTRL/C to quit:
```

The system then puts you into a line editor. You can type in text and edit each line before pressing Return. After you press Return, however, you cannot return to a previous line.

As a workstation user, you can upload a file at this prompt instead of using the MAIL editor. That way you have the use of a screen or page editor that you probably are more familiar with than the VMS editor.

When you have finished typing in your message or after the file has been transferred, enter Ctrl-Z to tell MAIL you are at the end of the message.

## Reading Mail

If someone sends you mail while you are logged on to the system, you will get a message on the screen on top of whatever else you are doing:

```
New mail on node HOLSTEIN from JORDAN
```

If you don't want to interrupt what you are doing, ignore that message. Although the message overrides some of the previous display, it does not affect your work.

When you are ready to read your mail, use the MAIL command at the VMS prompt. When you receive the mail prompt, you can read the first message in your mailbox by simply pressing Return. If you have a number of messages, you may want to display a list of messages and read them selectively. Use DIR to list your mail messages:

```
MAIL> DIR
```

MAIL shows you who the messages are from and the subject of each one if the sender entered it.

| # | From | Date | Subject |
|---|------|------|---------|
| 1 | SANDLER | 6-OCT-88 | Travel plans |
| 2 | RECEPTION | 6-OCT-88 | Telephone messages |
| 3 | WHITED | 7-OCT-88 | Budget reconciliation |
| 4 | JORDAN | 8-OCT-88 | Holstein futures |

Read the first message by pressing Return. Read specific messages with the Read command:

```
MAIL> READ 3
```

### Exiting the Program

When you are finished reading or sending mail, return to VMS by typing EXIT or by entering Ctrl-Z at the mail prompt:

```
MAIL> EXIT
```

VMS MAIL is a rich utility with many more capabilities and commands. For more detail refer to Appendix B.

## The Utility PHONE

You also can use the network and host facilities to talk directly to another user via PHONE.

### Calling with PHONE

To enter the phone utility, type PHONE at the VMS prompt:

```
$ PHONE
```

The screen will clear and the split PHONE screen will be displayed:

```
     VAX/VMS Phone Facility                          1-OCT-1988
%
----------------------------------------------------------------
                      HOLSTEIN::BADGETT



----------------------------------------------------------------
```

PHONE commands are entered at the **%** prompt. The screen is split, so what you type appears at the top of the screen and replies from the person you called appear in the bottom half of the screen. The message

```
HOLSTEIN::BADGETT
```

below the first dividing line shows the name of the node (Holstein) and the user ID (Badgett).

To call another user, simply enter the required ID at the **%** prompt. If that user is logged on to the system, a message will appear on his or her screen saying that you are phoning from node HOLSTEIN.

### Answering Phone Messages

To answer PHONE, exit what you are doing and type PHONE at the VMS prompt.

### Exiting PHONE

To leave PHONE and return to VMS, type EXIT at the **%** prompt or use Ctrl-Z.

There are several other features of PHONE and a number of other commands. If you need more detail, refer to Appendix C.

# CHAPTER SUMMARY

You don't have to be an expert in VMS or its associated DCL command language to conduct useful work with a VAX host. However, an understanding of the basic features of this system-level software is essential for successful operation.

This chapter introduces the VMS operating system and provides a brief tour of its major features and utilities, including the Phone and MAIL systems. By studying the portion of this chapter on file naming conventions and subdirectories, particularly, you can have a better understanding of where your data resides on the host and how to access it when you need to.

# 10

# Terminal Emulation

Until the past few years, when desktop workstations and personal computers started moving into the corporate computing environment, almost everybody who used a computer also used a so-called dumb terminal. These input/output devices differ greatly from mainframe terminals, which frequently were front ends to the main CPU, complete with their own processor, memory, disk drive, and printer.

Both types of device have changed over the years; the terms we use to describe them have changed also. Still, they coexist, terminals looking more like computers and desktop computers making themselves function like terminals to gain access to the expanded resources and processing power available on host computers.

The process of turning a PC into a terminal is called terminal emulation. It is usually achieved with software that runs on the PC, although the host may also have software. Some hardware is sometimes used at the workstation to improve performance and increase compliance. A plug-in PC board can be used to enhance the screen display, for example, or to provide host graphics compatibility.

This chapter describes common terminals in the VAX computing environment and discusses various options for terminal emulation.

## WHAT IS A TERMINAL?

For most computer users today, *terminal* means a keyboard and screen that communicate with the host through a serial port or network connection such as Ethernet. (See chapter 2.) These are no longer dumb terminals; they frequently include powerful microprocessors, memory, graphics processing routines, calendar and math management utilities, printer ports, and other local processing capabilities. But they don't have local disk storage and they still require a host to perform much useful work. When you type on the keyboard of a terminal, data is sent out the terminal port, across a communications line or network, and into the host's communications port. The circuit may also contain other devices such as terminal servers, multiplexers, and network repeaters. The received characters are processed by the computer and sent back to the terminal across the communications link for display on the screen (Figure 10-1).

*Figure 10-1* Digital's VT-300-series Terminals, typical of terminal devices used in the VAX computing environment. (Reproduced with permission of Digital Equipment Corporation)

## WHAT IS A WORKSTATION?

The terms *workstation* and *personal computer* are merging as PCs become more powerful and increasingly common. We will use that convention in this book, although some purists may disagree with us. A workstation (PC) is a stand-alone computer that includes a powerful microprocessor, memory, storage, a keyboard and display, and a myriad of other facilities (Figure 10-2). Even though some workstations can support more than one user, the consensus in the industry is that a workstation is a single-user device. When you type on the keyboard of a workstation, you are entering data directly into a parallel input port of the computer; information displayed on a workstation screen comes directly from the computer's display interface.

As you can see, terminals and workstations behave differently. One is a communications device that provides input and output to a separate computer; the other is a stand-alone computer that communicates directly with the keyboard and display. Even though workstations are increasingly common, some applications still require terminal services.

The next section discusses how conventional terminals comunicate with host computers. Later parts of this chapter describe in detail some of the terminals common to VAX and how workstations can be made to emulate them.

## TERMINAL-TO-HOST COMMUNICATIONS

The host computer and the terminal are separated by a length of cable. A critical need, then, is for the computer to match its transmission of information to the ability of the terminal to accept data. At the same time, the terminal has to be assured that when it sends data to the host, the host can accept it and understand it.

One of the first steps to accomplish this task is establishing the baud rate, or the speed of characters moving over the line, and selecting the convention used to describe individual characters (typically a seven- or eight-bit ASCII code).

The computer's internal code—the so-called machine language—can be based on any vocabulary and rules of grammar the designers choose, for this code is resident within the machine for its own purposes only and goes nowhere else. However, if one computer

154 ▫ TERMINAL EMULATION

*Figure 10-2* **PC-AT-class machine, the CompuAdd 286. Millions of personal computers are in use as standalone computers as well as windows into a larger computing environment. (Reproduced with permission of CompuAdd Corporation)**

is to communicate instructions or results or data to another, there must be a shared language. It doesn't matter whether the code says that a value of 65 is an A or a J, or whether 128 equals an instruction to lift up a steel beam or drop it down—all that matters is that the code is reliable and reproducible between man and computer, computer and computer, computer and machine.

One of the most commonly used codes in computers is ASCII (American Standard Code for Information Interchange), which uses seven-bit binary representation for characters. In this set of 128 codes are numerical values for all 52 lowercase and uppercase letters, numbers from 0 to 9, a set of punctuation and mathematical symbols, and 32 special computer control commands for such things as escapes, carriage returns, and line feeds.

Remember that ASCII represents characters only and therefore is not limited to English words. The same code can be used for any language that shares the characters.

The next level of cooperation between host and terminal is called data flow control. This is accomplished through the use of a character input buffer and an XON/XOFF handshaking communication scheme.

You can think of the character input buffer as a bucket of data with a pipe bringing information in at the top and a spigot dispensing data at the bottom. In the computer model, the pipe at the top is automatically shut off when the bucket is near to overflowing. The spigot at the bottom dispenses the information that has been in the bucket for the longest time first. Playing off a common manufacturing term, this buffer is called a first-in, first-out (FIFO) buffer.

XON and XOFF are control codes that tell the computer or terminal to resume or stop sending information. XOFF is control code DC3, the same as Ctrl-S. You can enter this code from the terminal keyboard when you are displaying information that scrolls too rapidly off of the screen. When you hold down the Ctrl key and push S, screen scrolling stops. To resume data flow, press Ctrl-Q. This is the XON, or DC1, code. Computers and terminals exchange these codes automatically to control information flow and to avoid buffer overflow.

The user can turn off the XON/XOFF handshaking protocol from the setup menus. However, if this option is chosen, there is no way to ensure that data will not be lost in transmission.

The host computer uses XOFF to tell the terminal to stop sending data. The keyboard has a data buffer of its own. If that buffer overflows, the keyboard will lock and not accept further keystrokes until it receives an XON message from the host. When the keyboard is locked, the Wait indicator on the Digital terminal keyboards will illuminate.

## WORKSTATION TERMINALS

The desktop or deskside workstation is a fact of corporate life. Increasingly host computer users are turning to individual workstations to replace aging terminals and to supply new users. Today's

PC marketplace enables the prudent buyer to purchase a reasonably powerful workstation for about the same cost as a medium-priced display terminal. For applications that can benefit from local processing and storage, a low-end PC is an excellent bargain today.

Not every application lends itself to desktop processing, of course, but some do. One benefit of desktop computers is the variety of low-cost software available for them. High-performance software packages for a variety of disciplines are available for under $100 per user. For $500 or less, a PC user can install about any conceivable application. Particularly when users don't need to share data, software for the PC should be considered.

In addition, desktop applications offload some duties from the central host and provide the individual user with the power of a dedicated CPU. When twenty or more users share the facilities of a MicroVAX, a 0.9 MIPS machine, response times can be sluggish to frustratingly slow. Having your own 0.5 MIPS to 2.0 MIPS processor on your desk can be an enlightening experience if you are accustomed to waiting for a shared host.

Among the applications that adapt well to workstation platforms:

- Word processing
- Spreadsheets
- Personal databases such as sales tracking and contacts lists
- Graphics and publishing
- Personal utilities such as to do lists, calendars, and calculators

If you are using a PC and your company also has VAX computers, you certainly should consider installing terminal emulation equipment to allow you access to the host machine. If you are about to be added to the host network, consider installing a workstation with terminal emulation instead of a standard serial or network terminal. The initial cost will be only slightly higher, and flexibility and functionality will be much greater.

For example, with the proper software, your workstation can perform all of the functions of a standard VT-series terminal as well as download information from the host for local storage and processing. You can upload data from your workstation to the host to benefit from the storage and backup facilities of the host or to share information with other users.

The following section discusses various options for terminal emulation and describes how to install a workstation with terminal emulation capability.

# TERMINAL-EMULATING WORKSTATIONS

Any workstation of the class discussed in chapter 6 can operate in emulation mode with the proper configuration. All you need is a communications link to the host and software to make the workstation function as a terminal instead of a dedicated computer.

If you are using a network interface instead of a serial interface, you will need additional software to access the network port and to use the attached network facilities. This software is sometimes called a network driver or network interface driver. If you are using a dial-up link instead of a direct connection, you will need a modem in addition to the serial port (or an internal modem that combines serial port and modem functions), and additional software to handle dialing and other modem functions. This usually is part of the terminal emulation package.

For more details on making the physical connection to the host, refer to chapter 5.

## Configuring the Workstation

One of the first steps in setting up a workstation as a terminal emulator is to decide how your use of the machine will be weighted. Will you spend most of your time using VAX facilities, or is the PC your primary computing platform with occasional need to access the host? Will you be running VAX-based software from the PC—and how frequently and how many different packages—or will you use the host only for file storage and to communicate with other network members? The answers to these questions affect how you choose terminal emulating facilities.

You can use relatively limited emulation software if you access the VAX only occasionally, but if most of your time is spent running host applications, you will need sophisticated software that precisely matches the VT-series terminal. Likewise, you may want to consider a special keyboard for your PC if you spend most of your time attached to a host. The following sections discuss various keyboards and programs.

### The Keyboard Question

The keyboard is part of your intuitive and natural interface with the computer. After you have spent a few hours with a particular keyboard, it seems like an old friend, and someone else's terminal or workstation—even if the same make and model as your own—can seem foreign and cumbersome.

This fact alone causes one of the major problems associated with using PCs with the VAX. If, after considerable experience on a PC, you switch to a VT-series keyboard, you will be frustrated by the keyboard's unfamiliar feel and configuration. The same is true of people who are accustomed to using a VAX with a terminal. When they change to a workstation, the keyboard seems awkward and difficult to use.

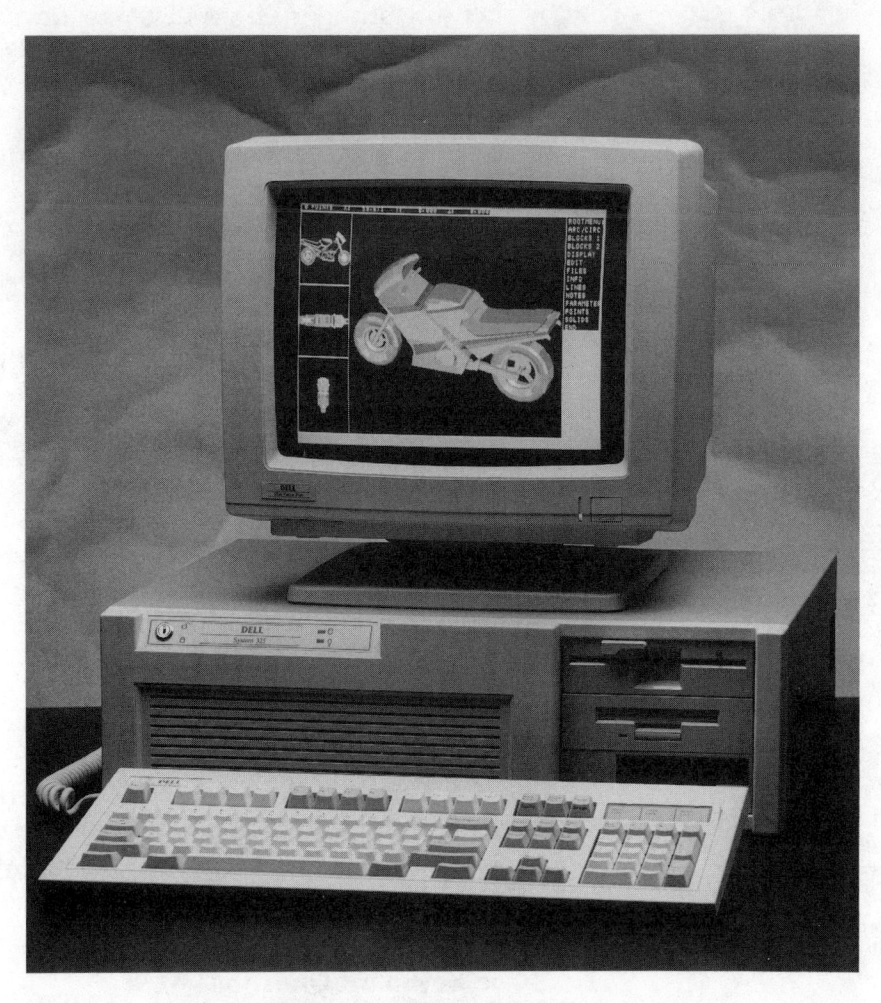

*Figure 10-3* **Enhanced PC keyboard shown with Dell System 325. (Reproduced with permission of Dell Computer Corporation)**

*Figure 10-4* **VT-family standard keyboard
(Reproduced with permission of Digital
Equipment Corporation)**

Each has special keyboard functions that make your life easier if you are familiar with the environment you are using. Figures 10-3 and 10-4 illustrate the difference between the PC keyboard and the VT-series terminal keyboard.

Many terminal emulation software packages include keyboard templates or quick-reference charts that help you make the transition. Still, there's no substitute for the real thing, and you must compromise at one or the other end of the emulation operation.

If the majority of your computing time is to be spent with PC-based applications and you need the host only for data storage and communications, you will want a standard PC keyboard and relatively simple terminal emulating software. However, if the PC is the secondary device, you should consider installing a Digital or Digital-compatible keyboard and rather more sophisticated emulation software to take full advantage of host-based applications.

At least two companies supply terminal emulation packages that include a Digital keyboard for your PC. The Powerstation from KEA Systems, for example, includes a Digital LK-series keyboard and software that emulates Digital VT-240, VT-220, and VT-100 terminals.[2] You can select either the standard keyboard or one with special keytops marked for WPS-Plus word processing. The DCS EM220 package is similar to the KEA offering and includes terminal emulation software with a Digital keyboard.[3]

The advantage to packages such as these, of course, is that you use a familiar Digital keyboard for VAX-based applications, so you don't have to bother with paste-on templates, quick-reference cards, or other methods to convert from the PC keyboard to the Digital keyboard. The disadvantage is that when you use PC-based software with the Digital keyboard, you have the reverse problem. The Digital keyboard is foreign to the PC environment, and you may have difficulty making the transition.

Depending on your use patterns, you may want to swap keyboards when you change computing environments. Workstations are relatively easy to reconfigure, and it is a simple matter to unplug one keyboard and replace it with the one you want to use next. To make this sort of transition easy, purchase a short keyboard extension cable that plugs into the PC's keyboard port, route the cable to a convenient and accessible location, and plug in the keyboard. Now, when you want to switch keyboards, you don't have to lean over the top of the unit or crawl under the desk to reach a rear-mounted keyboard connector.

Once you have decided the physical questions of terminal emulation—the physical connection to the host and which keyboard to use—you must answer some questions and make some decisions about software. The following section discusses consideratioins for choosing terminal emulation software.

## Terminal Emulation Software

Terminal emulation software for PCs covers a broad range of capabilities. In fact, the term itself means different things to different users and software providers. Basically, however, "terminal emulation" means two things.

### Host Communications Functions

At the first level it is software that will use the serial port— or other communications port such as a network adapter—to send characters between the workstation keyboard and the host.

This is a significant level because the PC is a self-contained device. When you type on the keyboard, data is entered through a parallel keyboard port directly into the local machine, and the display screen likewise presents information directly from the PC. Any calculations and other CPU operations are conducted locally. A terminal, on the other hand, depends on the host for any computing.

In effect the software converts your stand-alone workstation into a terminal that uses a communications link and the facilities of a remote computer. The local CPU does not work very hard in this configuration because it is only running the emulation software and handling the screen and keyboard. The actual application you are running—electronic mail, database, spreadsheet, word processing—is operating at the host. Your input to the application and the displayed results go through your local PC, but the calculations are conducted somewhere else.

Software for this process is readily available. It may even be free or cost so little as to be considered free. IBM at one time distributed a simple terminal emulation package with PC-DOS. This software, written in BASIC, was very limited, but it demonstrated how the serial port could be accessed for remote computing, and it did allow access to host computers.

There are popular freeware offerings that offer a broad range of capability. Freeware is software that is distributed free of charge through electronic bulletin boards, computer clubs, and user organizations. Usually the supplier requests a royalty of $25 to $50 if you decide to use the software, but the payment is strictly voluntary. Sometimes such software is distributed as user-supported instead of freeware. The procedure is generally the same: you receive the software from an electronic bulletin board or other source, install it, and operate it for a period, then send the writer a payment. The difference is that user-supported software may be fully registered and copyrighted, restricting distribution and payment requirements. Both types of software are inexpensive compared with some commercial offerings; they offer surprising versatility and ease of use; and generally they include complete and detailed documentation on disk. You can load the manual into your word processor or text editor and print it to produce an indexed, cross-referenced reference manual.

One of the long-standing and very popular freeware terminal emulation packages is PC-Talk III from The Headlands Press.[4] This full-featured package includes a dialing directory, script language (see

```
                          ┤ TERMINAL SETUP ├

    1) Terminal emulation ... VT-100        10) Break Length (ms) .... 350

    2) Duplex ............... FULL          11) Enquiry (CTRL-E) ..... OFF

    3) Flow control ......... XON/XOFF

    4) CR translation (in) .. CR

    5) CR translation (out) . CR

    6) BS translation ....... NON-DEST

    7) BS key definition .... BS

    8) Line wrap ............ OFF

    9) Scroll ............... ON
```

OPTION ⇒ 1                                                      ESC▶ Exit

TERMINAL EMULATION ⇒ VT-100
Terminal type to emulate.

*Figure 10-5* A set-up screen from the Procomm communications software, showing support for the VT-100 terminal protocols. (Reproduced with permission from Datastorm Technologies, Inc., Columbia, MD.)

programming discussion below), file transfer support, emulation of the VT-100 series terminals, and other useful features.

A package that shares many features with PC-Talk III but offers a much better user interface and some additional functions is *Procomm* (Figure 10-5) from Datastorm Technologies, Inc.[5] Procomm is an example of how successful freeware can be. First offered with a voluntary payment of $25, the company now has an enhanced version for sale at a very low price. You can still get the original software from bulletin boards or friends and pay only the $25 royalty if you wish.

However, the commercial version includes a printed manual, company support, and additional functions.

Other such packages include Telix,[6] Qmodem,[7] and BitCom.[8] Some of them have gained additional status by being selected for inclusion with modems or other software from commercial companies. Bitcom, and a professional spiral-bound manual are supplied with the Everex line of modems.[9]

There are dozens, maybe even hundreds, of similar packages that can be obtained from a variety of sources. This book is not designed to provide a comprehensive buyer's guide; rather we hope to introduce you to enough types of products to get you started on research of your own. There is one caveat in using freeware or user-supported software. You should obtain such packages only from sources you know you can trust. Computer-borne viruses that attack your data or the computer itself are a fact of life. If you install software from an unknown source, it may be infected, and the virus could be transmitted to your host or to other workstations on the network. By exercising reasonable caution, however, you can secure extremely useful communications software at very reasonable prices.

Remember, this important but relatively limited level of functionality is sufficient only if most of your work is conducted on a PC and you need access to a VAX only occasionally. Most user-supported software includes limited emulation of the VT-100 or other popular terminal. Likewise, many dial-up services and host computers can support the VT family at least superficially. This is all that is necessary for occasional and simple functions.

These packages, however, rarely make any effort to emulate the look and feel of a Digital terminal. The Digital setup function, for example, probably won't be supported, nor are other terminal-specific features such as function keys likely to be available. For these reasons, if you expect to require more frequent use of the VAX host, and especially if you are running a variety of VAX-based software, you will need a higher level of terminal support, and you probably will want compatibility with the VT-220 or newer terminal to support the applications you will run. For complete terminal compatibility, you will require software designed to support Digital's line of terminals. The next section discusses some of the important considerations in selecting such software and mentions some actual products to help you begin your research.

### Emulating a Specific Terminal

As you might have guessed from the previous section, there are multiple levels of Digital terminal emulation support. (See Appendix C for a discussion of the major features of Digital VT-series terminals.) These terminals use a number of special keys for various functions. Most of the user-supported and freeware communications packages provide little if any support for these special keys.

At the most basic level, software support for Digital terminals provides compatibility with the terminal's screen addressing and other control codes. That means that when the host sends your workstation-turned-terminal the standard Digital command to clear the screen, the screen is cleared; if codes to move the cursor to position 10,20 on the screen are received, the cursor goes to that location. Similarly, you may be able to erase to end of line; move cursor left, right, up, and down; and perhaps control such display attributes as reverse video. Support for these attributes depends heavily on the target audience of your software package.

Commercial software designed to support the serious VAX user has a decided advantage over user-supported software. Many of these packages attempt to duplicate the VT environment precisely, even enhance it. Some emulator packages, for example, display a bottom-of-screen prompt that shows the operation of function keys, how to use application-specific keys, and other continuous help.

These commercial-grade packages include setup features that duplicate the target terminal and generally add more detailed functions. In addition to the terminal's characteristics, emulator software may include settings for programmable or user-defined keys, file transfer parameters, display enhancements, I/O port selection, and other features that address specific software capabilities.

### Enhanced Features

Chapter 2 shows that an intelligent workstation attached to a VAX provides some advantages over a standard terminal. Among the advantages you might find in a PC emulator package:

- Distributed applications
- Wide variety of PC software at reasonable prices
- File transfer and host data storage
- Programmable keys

- Programming or script languages
- Dual sessions — PC and VAX simultaneously

With distributed applications you can offload some of the processing from the host to the local CPU. A PC offers a rich platform for personal and departmental software applications that may not be available for a VAX or that cost much more than the PC's hardware and sofware combined. Other features let you transfer files, use the VAX as a very large, remote disk, and enjoy the benefits of an improved user interface.

Some emulator packages not only match the VT-series terminal as closely as is possible, given the difference in architecture between the two devices, but also offer graphics or object-oriented user interfaces, extensive online help, color screen (even on a VT-100 or VT-220), and other extensions to the native environment.

For file transfer many packages support Kermit, Xmodem, or another error correction protocol. (See chapter 11 for more information on file transfer).

Programming or script languages are another plus with terminal emulation software on a PC. Full-featured emulators allow you to write simple programs or even save keystrokes in a command file so you can dial a host, log on, check your mail, upload messages, transfer files, and log off without typing any commands.

With some of these packages, you can even program the system to make automatic calls at a specified time — or log on to a local system — after hours or in a background mode. Such a feature can be useful for backing up your local PC disk drive to the the VAX, for example, or helping make sure you don't miss important electronic mail.

## Terminal Emulation Hardware

A relatively few companies have solved the terminal emulation problem with hardware. The theory is that the basic PC has certain display and performance limitations that cannot be corrected with software. The VT-series terminals, for example, can display 132 columns with reasonably good resolution. The PC's EGA monitor is not designed for 132 columns, and software emulation is not always satisfactory. In modes that require continuous graphics output, the speed of the PC pseudoterminal can be unacceptably slow.

These hardware solutions take at least three forms: display enhancement, expansion board, complete hardware solutions. KEA Systems, for one, supplies an optional module to attach to the PC's EGA expansion port to produce better 132-column displays. DataMedia Corporation[10] produces a series of 80286- and 80386-based PCs that include hardware-based VT-series and Tektronix 4208 terminal emulation and support for DOS-and-VAX sessions. The advantage of Datamedia's approach is that you have full use of the PC portion of the system without concerns over software compatibility, RAM-resident memory usage, and the like, while maintaining a continuous connection to the VAX. The Datamedia systems are acceptable PCs in their own right, showing innovative design and good performance, and the terminal emulation and VAX compatibility they provide is above average.

A slightly different solution is provided by Novell, Inc.[11], the PC LAN company, with the custom PC that includes Ethernet hardware as part of the motherboard. With this arrangement you can load the networking software over Ethernet, eliminating the need for a local disk drive. This computer does not include integral VT-terminal emulation, however.

We likely will see other hardware solutions as the need for PC connectivity grows in corporations.

## CHAPTER SUMMARY

Terminal emulation is an important part of any PC-to-VAX interaction. The question of terminal emulation goes beyond simple compatibility with a few display features. There are questions of multiple session support, keyboard compatibility, and the physical connection between the PC and the VAX.

This chapter suggests definitions for "workstation" and "terminal" and describes the PC-to-host connection with the associated terminal emulation requirements. Chapter 5 provides more information on the physical link between workstations and hosts. Chapter 11 shows how to use connectivity and terminal emulation to exchange information between a PC and a VAX.

# 11

# Transferring Files

One of the major reasons for connecting your PC to a VAX is to exchange information. You may want to use the VAX to store large data files; you may want to share spreadsheet or database information with users on the VAX, or you may need access to data normally stored on the VAX.

These scenarios involve moving file data across the communications link. This chapter examines some of the concepts of communications, showing how in many instances human models have been applied to the high-speed world of computers. This chapter is concerned with the physical aspects of getting information from point A to point B.

## SOFTWARE PROTOCOLS

How do we English speakers know that an electronic data processing device is called a computer or that a mass of stony material is called a rock? We know these things because they are part of a language that has been developed and passed from generation to generation to represent thoughts and physical objects. If you and I were to grow up in total isolation from society, you might call a rock a googie, and I might refer to it with a particular type of grunt. There are thousands of languages and dialects on this planet, and almost all of them contain the elements to describe events and feelings.

By contrast almost all computers speak only one language: a binary code consisting only of 0s and 1s expressed by a series of bipolar gates.

Using just 0s and 1s, the binary counting system can represent any finite number, and computer words can represent the characters, words, symbols, and commands of any human or machine language. (See chapter 4 for more information on how the computer handles these internal on and off states.)

## The Human Model

Let's assume I am German and you are Yugoslavian. I don't speak a single word of Serbian, and you are equally limited in German. However, we both know enough simple phrases in English to attempt a conversation. If we were to meet on a street corner in New York, I might begin a conversation in German, and you might attempt to respond in Serbian; you might start in English while I stayed in German; I might greet you in English and you might respond in Serbian. Thus far we have three situations in which there is no meaningful communication. The only situation in which we manage to exchange some understanding would come when we both spoke English. We call that language compatibility.

Now, let's assume that we will both speak English. What would happen if we both blurted out our greetings at the same instant and paused for the same period for a response before together beginning again? The chances are we would blot each other's message out. What we need is some sort of agreed-upon timing compatibility. I need to signal to you that I want to speak; your acknowledgment to me is the indication to begin. When I complete my communication, I am signaling to you that you may respond.

### Representing Human Language

These various human protocols—those officially incorporated into culture or language, and those intuitively determined and conveyed in social intercourse—have their counterparts in computer-to-computer communications.

IBM, in the design of its PC family of microcomputers, added a second 128 ASCII characters for graphics purposes, calling its eight-bit binary set Extended ASCII. A character code in common use on mainframe computers is IBM's EBCDIC (Extended Binary Coded Decimal Interchange Code). This eight-bit set is used mostly in bisynchronous communications. (An earlier version was Binary Coded Decimal, which used six bits and was limited to uppercase and numeric values.)

Even older is Baudot, a five-bit code in use since 1875. It was first used on some early teleprinters and is still used in some unupdated teletype systems. Its five bits can represent values only in the range from 0 to 31, and the system is therefore necessarily limited to uppercase letters only. A five-level code is also used for the control of certain laboratory devices, such as data monitoring and capture equipment, chemical analysis devices, and the like.

### Diplomatic Protocols

When humans converse face to face, they are able to look for visual cues to help them know when it is their turn to talk and to listen. When we speak over the telephone, we have to make our decisions strictly on the basis of the content and context of what is being said. We can notice a pause, or the rising inflection of a question, and determine that it is our turn to respond.

Communicating computers also need to know the rules of the game: Will conversation be in one direction only? In two directions but not at the same time? In two directions with transmitting and receiving channels open simultaneously?

The computer needs to know what kind of language is to be employed, how many bits will make up each word, and how to figure out where one word ends and the next one begins.

**Synchronicity**

There are three types of transmission protocols in common use: asynchronous, synchronous, and bisynchronous.

Asynchronous is the simplest and cheapest protocol to implement and is the most common system for personal computers. Characters and numbers are defined in a binary code such as ASCII. Each character is framed by a start bit and one or more stop bits and each bit of data is of equal duration as it is transmitted. These elements allow the computer to send bits and words as they are ready—there is no need for special timing between bits or words.

Synchronous communication depends on precisely timed bits and characters. This more complex and more expensive protocol is used in large computers, where it can allow significantly faster transmission. Data is broken up into blocks or groups of characters and collected in buffers before transmission. It is then sent as a continuous stream of bits. One of the computers or modems generates a timing signal that puts both devices in synch. The computers or modems are also responsible for sending synch characters between each data block to keep sending and receiving devices occupied, and help to maintain proper timing.

Synchronous communication follows the same general assignment of functions as an asynchronous signal does on an RS-232C cable, but with the added function of clocking. Unlike asynch, in which each byte is independent and can be separated from the next byte by any period of time, synchronous communication requires that the next byte be transmitted on a certain click of the clock. The synchronous clockbeats can be supplied by the modem and transmitted on pin 15, or the timing pulse can be sent out by the computer, in which case pin 24 is used. The modem receives a clock signal on pin 17.

In addition to the possibility of running synchronous communication at faster raw speeds such as 9,600 or 19,200 baud, the net speed of synchronous communication is usually faster than that of asynchronous communication when both are rated at the same number of bits per second. Since asynchronous communication must give over two or three framing start or stop bits for each character, it has a twenty percent to twenty-seven percent overhead that does not convey information.

Bisynchronous transmission, IBM's version of synchronous transmission, is used in its 3270 terminal protocols. It is similar to synchronous communication except that both modems send synchronization signals. Transmission speeds of 2,400 baud are typical, and IBM offers excellent error detection and recovery. You probably will not encounter this protocol in the Digital VAX or PC environment, unless you are working with a very specialized system such as a heterogeneous network that attaches to both Digital and IBM equipment.

## Starting and Stopping Computer Words

How does the computer know where one word ends and the next begins? When the words are distributed within RAM, the computer keeps track of what is where by means of their physical location—in one of the memory addresses that make up the computer's electronic postal system. But what happens when the bits are strung one after another as they move down a serial communications line or out of a modem and over a telephone line? The answer is that framing bits demark the beginning and end of each computer word.

Let's look at a simple wake-up message, "Hello!" in standard seven-bit ASCII code. In the individual memory addresses would be the following:

1001000    H
1100101    E
1101100    L
1101100    L
1101111    O
0100001    !

Sent out unaltered down the serial line, the message would read 100100011001011101100110110011011110100001, almost as confusing to a computer as it is to a person.

Instead, the serial port controller for the computer frames each individual word with start and stop bits. The computer is told when serial communication begins, and it is quite capable of keeping count of the stream of bits passing by.

We can take the capital H and add a 0 start bit and a 1 stop bit, making the word as follows:
0 1 0 0 1 0 0 0 1

The start bit alerts the terminal, and the stop bit says, "That's all."

When sending to certain slow terminals, usually operating below 300 bits per second, the protocol may call for two stop bits.

In your specifications to the software that will control the serial port hardware, you can choose almost any word length. This uses a seven-bit ASCII code, which is used most often in microcomputers for text purposes. However, some applications, including some word processors and graphics programs, use eight-bit codes.

If you specify eight-bit computer words, with most microcomputer systems you will also have to choose no parity, since the eighth bit is not available for that purpose. We'll discuss parity in greater detail later.

## Traffic Control

The next issue in acceptance of a protocol for communication involves the direction of traffic. There are a number of choices:

| | |
|---|---|
| Simplex | One-way transmission only. Simplex systems include radio and television broadcasting, most cable television systems, and security monitoring circuits. |
| Half duplex | Two-way transmission over a single channel, but not at the same moment. The transmitting station must give over the channel to the receiver to allow a response. Examples include citizens band radio and push-to-talk intercoms. Designers sometimes call the process "turning the line around." A half-duplex system may be the solution to dealing with noisy telephone lines. |
| Full duplex | Simultaneous two-way transmissions. This is usually accomplished by having two frequencies on the same wire. The standard voice telephone system operates in this manner. |
| Echoplex | A variety of full-duplex transmission in which the transmitted character is echoed by the receiver to be displayed on the transmitter's screen. This serves as a form of manual error detection: If a character is lost, it won't show up on the transmitter's screen. If a character is distorted, it will show up as a different character. |

**Shaking Hands Properly**

When I stick out my right hand in greeting and you do the same, we shake hands. This is a prearranged signal; some anthropologists and sociologists say that the handshaking ritual was derived to signify to a stranger that you were carrying no weapons in your hand.

The handshaking protocol in telecommunications is a way to send control and acknowledgment signals back and forth between the two parties to a circuit.

Elements of software handshaking protocols include null characters, line feeds, and XON/XOFF characters.

Though two microcomputers may be nominally communicating at 1,200 baud, it is possible for one side or the other to become bogged down in other tasks and be unable to maintain that speed of transmission or reception. This is a fairly common condition with mainframe computers and with personal computers engaged in multitasking or multiuser operations.

In such a situation, the software is often able to pad out the communications link to buy time. Devices to do this include

| | |
|---|---|
| Null characters | The ASCII character 0 is called a null and can be used as a delay. |
| Character delays | Though each byte may zip along at high speed, the software can be told to insert timing delays between transmission of each character, thereby cutting down on the effective speed of transmission. |
| Timed delay loops | These are flow controls determined by the modem. |

The line feed character tells a terminal or printer to go to the next line before printing more text. This is a holdover from the days of very dumb terminals, which couldn't automatically wrap characters that extended past the end of a displayed line. If your computer or printer requires use of line-feed characters, most applications software will allow automatic insertion of the codes.

## Filling the Bucket

The XON and XOFF are an essential part of the control of the data stream. The speed of the transmission link is often different from the ability of either computer to send or receive data. In one scenario computer A may be able to pump out data at 9,600 baud, while the communications link can only move the information at 1,200 baud. At the other end of the line, computer B may only be able to accept new data at 4,800 baud.

The key to control is handshaking. With software handshaking, the two computers exchange control characters as part of the data. The ASCII characters DC1 and DC3 represent XON and XOFF, or send and pause. On many computers these signals can also be sent directly from the keyboard as Ctrl-Q and Ctrl-S.

In hardware handshaking the CTS (clear to send) and RTS (request to send) pins of the RS-232C cable are used to start and stop the data stream. Incoming data is usually collected in a buffer in RAM and let out to storage, a printer, or other destination as needed. When hardware shakes hands, the computer shuts off the flow of incoming data by dropping the voltage level on the CTS pin. When the buffer is clear, a CTS signal goes out. This is sometimes called RTS/CTS handshaking.

This, then, is the way computers use handshaking to communicate:

COMPUTER A: "Computer B, are you ready to receive?"

COMPUTER B: "Yes, I am."

COMPUTER A: "Look out, here it comes."

COMPUTER B: "Got it. Want me to read it back to you?"

And so on.

## PROTOCOLS

A protocol used in certain communications schemes with mainframe computers is called the send-lines protocol. This system breaks up data into individual lines, each terminated with an end-of-line character. The receiver sends an acknowledgment character when it has successfully accepted the line of data and is ready for another.

Some expressions of this protocol have the computer send out new lines of data after a predetermined period; other systems use manual timing, with the operator pressing a key to send each new line; and finally, some implementations have the transmitting computer dependent upon receipt of a start character from the receiver before the next line is sent.

### High-Tech Microcomputer Protocols

X.PC extends the X.25 network to the personal computer. This error checking and correction protocol is backed by the Tymnet network but has been placed in the public domain for any manufacturer or user to adopt.

X.PC claims error-free data transmission and the ability to conduct simultaneous sessions to several hosts on the same network at the same time. The X.PC protocol is just beginning to become available in microcomputer software—Microsoft's Access package includes an implementation of the system for use with the IBM PC and compatible machines.

A competitive protocol is Microcom's networking protocol, MNP. Offered by Microcom, Inc., a modem manufacturer, MNP is available to other manufacturers for a low licensing fee.

The X.25 standard is one of the few areas of international accord in telecommunications. This standard defines an interface to the packet networks (like Tymnet and Telenet and their European equivalents). It was put into effect by the CCITT in 1976 and modified in 1980. X.25 defines the logical interface between host computers and the network. At its base X.25 is nearly identical to IBM's SNA/SDLC protocol for mainframe communication. Its electrical standard is an improvement upon the RS-232C protocol.

X.25 can support data rates as fast as 100,000 baud, with 56,000 baud a typical speed limit.

The packet assembler and disassembler (PAD) sits at the gateway to the network to break up outgoing data into packets and to reassemble packets from inbound communication. X.25 uses several packet types: The call-request packet initiates communication between any two points on the network; the standard will support as many as 4,096 simultaneous communications along the network. The data packet carries the actual blocks of information. Other types of packets contain information about network conditions and errors, baud rate of incoming messages, and other control information.

## Data Compression

Modem makers have sought ways to wring out more speed from a communications session without increasing the physical transfer rate for bits. One such scheme is data compression. Various algorithms are employed, including the substitution of single characters for whole words, or elimination of spaces between words by adding a particular value to the last character of each word.

As with error correction protocols, it is necessary for sending and receiving modems to employ the same data compression system.

## Error Checking

We've all played the children's game of telephone, in which a whispered message starts at one end of the circle and comes out completely different at the other end. Each repeater in the circle is forced to pass along what he has perceived to be the message without any means to check the information.

When the conductor on a commuter train announces "All aboard," the microprocessor that is the human brain is able to figure out that he is telling everyone to get on the train. The listeners know that he isn't telling them to make a hole in a piece of wood ("awl a board") or saying that all are bored, because these messages make no sense in the context.

Later, when the conductor announces over the distorted, squealing public address system, "Frangum Setter," the passengers make the translation into the station stop Framingham Center because they have been there before and it makes sense in the context of other station stops.

But if the conductor is on the telephone and needs to convey the exact spelling of the town, he might say, "That's Framingham, *F* as in 'fancy,' *R* as in 'regular,' " and so on. For even greater assurance, he might ask the listener to read back the information.

Obviously, some data is more important than others: information from a heart monitoring machine being sent across the country to a doctor or the space shuttle launch control circuit or your company's payroll records cannot be allowed to include random errors. Other data though, such as a word processing file that will be checked at the recipient's end before being used, may be sent as is.

The incidence of errors is usually related to the quality of the line and the speed of transmission over that line. With an average-quality line, some experts estimate, the average error rate at 150-baud communication is less than 1.5 characters in 10,000; at 1,200 baud, the error rate increases to an average of about 6.5 errors per 10,000 characters.

Remember that your risk is greater at high speed transmission—a one-second outage or disturbance on a 300-baud line should affect just 30 characters or so; a one-second problem on a 1,200-baud line, about 120 characters.

One of the key things to remember about any error checking protocol is that both ends of the communication circuit must use the same protocol for the system to work.

## Parity Checking

The simplest means of error checking in common use by microcomputers is parity checking. This system will catch many simple errors in communications. Under a parity-checking scheme, the hardware and software work together to analyze each outgoing word and count the number of 1s in the computer word. If the agreed-upon method is even parity, every word must have an even number of 1s. If the protocol is odd parity, there must be an odd number of 1s.

The parity protocol adds an eighth bit to standard seven-bit ASCII code. This parity bit indicates the even or odd status of the word being transmitted.

Let's assume we have specified even parity and are sending the letter W over a communications link. Here's the seven-bit ASCII code (87) for the letter:

**1 0 1 0 1 1 1**

This character has an odd number of 1s, and so the parity protocol will make it even by inserting another 1 before the stop bit. The new computer word, including a single start and stop bit, is:

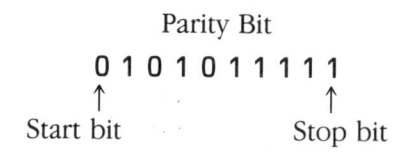

Parity Bit
**0 1 0 1 0 1 1 1 1 1**
↑                 ↑
Start bit      Stop bit

If the 1-count is even, putting in a 0 for the parity bit keeps it that way.

Now, it should be apparent that the parity-checking method has a large flaw to it: it will work just fine if one, three, five, or seven of the bits of a seven-bit word change from one indicator to another. However, if an even number of bits change from 0 to 1 or 1 to 0, the parity sum will remain unchanged even though the character is now incorrect.

In general, though, unless the data is of such critical importance that a single undetected error will cause serious problems in operation or validity, parity checking is a reasonable entry level of error checking—many estimates say that under ordinary circumstances data sent with parity checking can be expected to be accurate with ninety-nine percent certainty.

The other disadvantage of parity checking as a means of error detection—and this becomes more important as the amount of necessary communication increases—is the large amount of overhead—and corresponding drop in throughput—such a scheme creates.

More accurate and less demanding of transmission time is application of an algorithm to a block of data. Some of these means of error checking:

**CRC,** or cyclical redundancy checking
**LRC,** or longitudinal redundancy checking
**VRC,** or vertical redundancy checking

These methods, employed in one or another advanced error checking and correction formula, can advance the confidence level to 99.9 percent. Each works by having the modems at each end of the circuit perform a mathematical calculation based on the data in a particular block of information. For example, the code could be as simple as counting up the ASCII values of all of the characters in the block and transmitting that number along with the data; the receiving modem does the same calculation and compares its result with the number sent it by the transmitter. If the two values do not match, a change has occurred somewhere in the block of data, and the transmitting modem will be instructed to resend the information.

## Xmodem

Xmodem is one of the more widely used error-checking protocols on microcomputers. Developed for CP/M bulletin board systems, the protocol is in the public domain and has been incorporated into many commercial communications programs.

Xmodem is a cyclic redundancy check (CRC) error-checking protocol. Each 128-byte block of data ends with a CRC character that is the result of a calculation called a checksum performed by the computers on the ASCII values of the characters being transmitted.

Xmodem uses software flow control and error checking codes that rely on ASCII codes. The on or off signal for transmission of blocks uses acknowledge (ACK) and negative acknowledge (NAK), ASCII codes 6 and 21. Once the signal to begin communication has been received, the transmitting computer begins with a start-of-header (SOH) character, ASCII code 1. The next element of the packet of information is a pair of block numbers to identify the block of data. After the 128 bytes have been sent, a checksum character is sent.

At the receiving end, the computer calculates its own checksum for each block of data and compares it with the value sent by the transmitting computer. If the two values are the same, the receiving computer sends an ACK, and the next block of data is transmitted. If the two values differ, the receiving computer sends a NAK, and the block is retransmitted. The retransmission is repeated as many as nine times before the software declares the link inadequate for its purposes.

The final code for a successful transfer of data is the end-of-transmission (EOT) character, ASCII code 4.

## Kermit

Another popular protocol that is almost sure to be available on the host computer and supported by most terminal emulation software (see chapter 10) is Kermit, also in the public domain.

Like Xmodem, Kermit is undergoing constant revision and improvement. Among the features of Kermit are data compression, passing of file attributes, and support for sliding-window data exchange. The sliding window is a full-duplex protocol that enables Kermit to send and receive data at the same time. This ability improves efficiency, saving time during data transfers.

## Hardware-based Error Checking

There are several protocols for error-checking by the modems themselves, although a scheme from modem maker Microcom is among the most popular.

MNP works like many of the other schemes that use checksum calculations, with the added wrinkle of variable-size data blocks called adaptive data block sizes. If MNP detects none or just a few errors, it will allow use of large blocks of data. On the other hand, if MNP detects multiple or recurring errors, it instructs the transmitting modem to send smaller blocks until the line quality improves.

MNP devices operate at different levels called classes:

| | |
|---|---|
| Class 2 | Uses standard asynchronous framing techniques. Because of overhead, on a 2,400-baud modem it will allow transmission of slightly less than 2,400 bits per second. |
| Class 3 | Modifies the scheme slightly to allow transmission of about 2,600 bits per second. |
| Class 4 | Adds adaptive data block sizes, transmitting about 2,900 bits per second. |
| Classes 5,6 | Include data compression in addition to error correction, increasing the speed again. |

Microcom has released the simplest levels of its scheme to the public domain, holding classes four through six for its own use and that of licensed manufacturers.

Hayes has put forth its own hardware-based protocol, called LAP-B, for use with its V-series modems.

## CHAPTER SUMMARY

This chapter summarizes data communication, comparing human and computer models. Software and hardware handshaking as well as error-correcting protocols were covered. Data format is addressed in Chapter 13.

# 12

# Other Communications Environments

This book is not designed as a hardware- or software-specific book except for coverage of the VMS and MS-DOS operating systems. Rather, we intend to introduce you to the concepts of PC-to-VAX connectivity so that you will be familiar with the general terms and concepts as you move into this environment either from the VAX or the PC.

However, certain products are key to this marketplace because they demonstrate the concepts we have introduced and are classics, well known and popular.

This chapter discusses briefly some of these classic products. There are hundreds of other products that function well for these and other applications. However, the computer marketplace, especially in the communications area, is changing so rapidly that it would be impossible to publish a timely list of available products. You should be aware, moreover, that this discussion of even these classic and fairly stable products probably will be out of date by the time this book is published. This discussion is to introduce you to some of the well-known products and to give you a better idea of how actual products in the marketplace function.

## OVERVIEW

You will recall from our initial discussions of PC-to-VAX connectivity that many desktop-to-minicomputer communications systems consist of two components. One is software that runs on the host; the other is software for the desktop. What functions are provided depends on the individual products, but the general design of PC-to-VAX products remains the same. In addition to host and PC software, some products include hardware that resides inside the PC as a plug-in bus attachment, or there may be an external box that facilitates the network interface. The latter class of product usually is designed to bridge incompatible network protocols, as from AppleTalk to DECnet.

## DIGITAL'S VAX/VMS SERVICES FOR MS-DOS AND DECNET/PCSA

This is Digital's classic PC-to-VAX connection. VAX/VMS Services for MS-DOS is the VAX-based, or server, component of the system and DECnet/PCSA is the PC-based, or client, component.

### General Features

VMS Services allows any VAX to function as an application, data, and resource server to a large group of personal computers. DECnet/PCSA (personal computing systems architecture) provides DECnet support for the PC in conjunction with a Digital or third-party Ethernet interface. PC users attached to DECnet with DECnet/PCSA are treated as peers with other systems on the network. That means the PC user can store and retrieve files from designated VAX servers, can use the system's printers, and can even run PC-based applications directly from networked servers. PC users can communicate with each other or users of local and remote servers anywhere on the network.

This PC-to-VAX architecture is becoming increasingly common as PCs move up in importance in the corporate environment. Some earlier solutions support only a local VAX as a server, and remote machines must be accessed through network bridges or communications servers. VMS Services more fully integrates the power of the desktop with the networked hosts.

## Client Software

The client portion of this system includes Microsoft's MS-Windows user interface, network management tools, terminal emulators, and other utilities. The server component provides the interface between the VAX and the PC.

After the host and PC components are loaded, the PC user accesses one or more VAXs in the system as if they were local disk drives. MS-DOS generally allocates up to five drive designator letters, A through F, as local drives. The remaining letters of the alphabet can be assigned to remote devices. With VMS services, for example, you could access one VAX system by specifying drive G:. This VAX may hold MS-DOS and other utilities, H: could store one class of application, I: another group of applications or data services, and so on. These are virtual drives, which actually represent portions of VAX-based disk drives. Each virtual drive can reside on a separate VAX host, or several virtual drives can be mapped to a single host. How the system is configured depends on the network and the applications.

In addition, PC users can use the DECnet to log on to any of the networked hosts in the conventional ways. Terminal emulation software included as part of DECnet/PCSA supports VT-220 functionality from the PCs on the network. Of course, to run VAX-based applications, the PC users must be assigned appropriate user rights. The emulator support permits each PC user to establish multiple-host sessions either via Ethernet or through the PCs serial ports.

## Data Sharing

Because data files and programs are stored on one or more central servers, PC users can share these files simply by specifying the appropriate virtual drive. Assuming the software is designed for multiuser applications, more than one user can execute the same application, stored on the same host virtual drive, simultaneously. Likewise, users can simultaneously access the associated data files if the application software supports this level of file sharing.

MS-DOS files on a VAX host are stored as RMS streams or sequential fixed-length records, each 512 KB long. When a PC user requests one of these files, the resident software makes the necessary conversion to PC format. VAX-based users, however, can access these files directly because they are stored in native VAX format. This is not necessarily as useful a feature as it may seem, because even though a VAX user can access the physical file, the information may not be in a useful form. A database file, for example, could be typed or edited, perhaps, with a VAX-based editor, but it is doubtful whether you could access the database as a data file from a VAX database application.

Increasingly there are products that operate on both the VAX and PC, so this type of data and application sharing may become more useful. Products such as WordPerfect word processing, for example, operate on the PC or the VAX, and files created in either environment can be accessed and used on the other system as if they had been created there.

Virtual disks created under DECnet on a PC can be sized from 360 KB (equivalent to a standard double-sided, 5.25-inch PC diskette) to 32 MB (the largest disk that can be accessed by MS-DOS prior to Version 4.0). Management of this disk space can be conducted from the PC or from a terminal on the host.

## Remote Boot Support

Among the interesting features of Digital's solution is the remote boot capability. If the networked PCs are equipped with Digital's own DECnet interface for PCs (a DEPCA board), diskless PCs can be used as network members. When the PC is turned on, MS-DOS software is automatically downloaded over the network. The advantage to this system is that you save the expense of disk drives for individual PCs. The disadvantage is that every remote-boot PC is totally dependent on the integrity of the network and at least one attached host. If the host should be down for maintenance or any other reason, the local PC will not function. Another disadvantage is that all applications and data must be stored on a host drive and transferred over the network anytime it is accessed. This approach increases overall network traffic and can slow down the speed of execution at the PC. This is particularly true if the application regularly transfers data during operation.

## DATABILITY'S REMOTE ACCESS FACILITY (RAF)

Datability Software Systems, Inc. is among the third-party vendors, offering systems similar to Digital's DECnet/PCSA software.[12] The RAF software takes a somewhat different approach to the PC-to-VAX solution and offers additional functions over Digital's product.

## General Features

RAF consists of two basic software components, one for the host, the other for the PC. A RAF host can be any VAX or DECSYSTEM-20. The PC software runs on the IBM PC, PC XT, PC AT or any close compatible.

The host installation requires about a hundred units of memory for the basic installation, but memory requirements vary with the level of remote access. The more remote facilities attached to the host, the more memory is required.

A minimum PC installation requires approximately 60 KB of RAM for asynchronous operation and around 100 KB for an Ethernet connection. RAF is a RAM-resident facility; once installed, it is instantly available through user-defined hot keys. It must be loaded from a CONFIG.SYS file when the PC is booted.

The PC installation also uses about 4 KB of RAM for each session screen defined. Users can configure RAF for any number of host sessions and one MS-DOS session. However, memory considerations put some restraints on the number of sessions that is practical.

## Utilities and Other Functions

In addition to the basic RAF software, a number of separate PC-based utilities provide added features. REMOTE, for example, handles host printer assignments and other features of the link, and DUMPER offers easy data backup to the host disk.

RAF handles communications between workstations and the host under a LAT-compatible (local area transport) protocol that essentially causes the PC to function as an Ethernet terminal server.

RAF also includes VT-100 and VT-220 terminal emulation over an asynch or Ethernet link. RAF gives the remote PC user virtually transparent access to a DEC host computer by assigning host facilities to PC disk drive letters in the way described above under DECnet/PCSA. This makes accessing a file or subdirectory on a VAX as simple as selecting the appropriate PC disk drive.

Moreover, RAF supports remote procedure calls to host subroutines from BASIC, C, FORTRAN, and Pascal. Ethernet users can link their PCs so that anything entered or displayed on one PC also appears on the other. This feature is valuable during software or procedural training, for joint document preparation, and other dual tasks. PC users can print to host-attached printers, and with release 2.0, a PC-attached printer can serve as a host printer.

## Applications

Applications for the features of RAF are varied. Because it is a relatively compact program, requiring very little local disk storage, diskette-based PCs can use RAF to access greatly expanded storage and printer facilities. PC applications software and data files can reside on the host for general access by many PC users. In this mode the host machine functions as a network file server for PC users.

One desirable feature of RAF, according to a number of users we interviewed, is that it operates as a single process on the VAX. With this configuration, as additional PCs are added to the network, the load on host resources should not change. Some users report hundreds of PCs in RAF networks with little or no host degradation.

Function keys and commands drive the basic RAF software, and there is little need for menus or other user aids because of the transparency of the product. The PC software automatically assigns up to sixteen additional drive letters, which can be mapped to separate host facilities.

In terminal mode, status-line feedback is excellent, including such information as type of terminal being emulated, keypad status, and print status. If a print command has been issued to a printer that is not online or not ready, the PRINT indicator on the status line blinks continuously.

During installation the user can assign certain tasks to special key combinations. The default configuration uses Left-shift+ Ctrl+ <Key> for selected functions. During terminal emulation, PC keys frequently are assigned to terminal programmable function keys. A separate utility permits versatile keyboard assignments for use with specific software packages. An assignment configuration for Word-Perfect is supplied with the RAF software.

In the event of a communications or software error, complete error messages show the location of the error (host or workstation), a diagnosis, the current RAF state and how the error was handled. Context-sensitive help is available during many RAF operations.

## Performance

RAF communicates at speeds up to 100 KBytes over Ethernet and up to 19.2 KBits asynchronously. Although you can use a dial-up link by entering the terminal mode and sending manual dial commands to an attached modem, or by constructing a conversation file for automatic log-in, this is comparatively cumbersome. A direct-connect asynch link is preferable to a dial-up connection, and the most impressive and useful configuration is in Ethernet, where the program's high-speed communication becomes most evident.

RAF stores PC data in the host format, performing any necessary format conversions transparently as information is transferred. To the PC user the host functions as a large, flexible disk drive where applications software and data can be stored as if on a local drive.

RAF conducts syntax conversion as well as file format conversion. For example, a PC user attached to VAX can create host subdirectories by issuing the MS-DOS command "MD <directory>," where "<directory>" is the name of the desired directory. The appropriate VMS command is issued, and the VAX directory is created.

In addition, host facilities such as MAIL are available directly at the workstation. Even when actively involved in a PC session, as long as a host session is active in the background, the user is notified immediately when new mail is available. Mail and other host-system messages appear in a pop-up window on top of the PC application.

REMOTE constructs PC-based .COM files that issue host commands. This facility gives users access to the host while keeping them in the MS-DOS environment. When a REMOTE command file completes execution, the user is returned to MS-DOS instead of the host native environment. A USERS.COM file on the PC disk, for example, could issue the command SHOW USERS to the host and display the result without leaving MS-DOS.

RAF uses a sliding-window communications protocol, transferring data in continuous, numbered packets and responding to transfer errors as they occur. A lost or garbled packet is retransmitted in the midst of other packets, eliminating send-confirm delays. This technique helps maintain high speed.

## LAT Support

Datability is among the few non-DEC companies that use LAT-compatible protocols. This feature greatly expands RAF's flexibility and versatility. For example, even without an active host session, a PC user can display Ethernet traffic to determine active hosts and other information. In essence, each RAF workstation appears to the host to be a terminal server that supports a listing of available services and connections to specified systems. Users familiar with terminal server interaction will find RAF's local command language easy to learn. To connect an Ethernet service, for example, you type CONNECT plus the name of the service, just as you would on a terminal server link.

The terminal server emulation also permits the PC to support sophisticated printer services. The host system can route PC-based software requests for the local printer to a host-attached printer, for example. In addition, with optional software, host-level print requests can be routed to a workstation where the local printer is used as if it were attached directly to a standard terminal server, making the PC act like a printer server for the host.

Several sessions can run concurrently on the PC. As each process is accessed, the inactive screens are saved. When a previous session is reactivated, unlike a terminal server connection, which presents only the last prompt, the RAF PC user sees the full screen as it appeared when the session was terminated. An active PC session can be maintained in addition to multiple host sessions.

RAF uses an efficient host configuration to maintain fast system throughput and to support large numbers of PC users. Under RAF, each workstation is established as a separate host process that lies dormant until it is accessed. Programs that use a single host process to service all attached PC workstations tend to run more slowly and can generally support fewer practical attachments.

RAF's programming language supports sophisticated features, including remote file access and execution of subroutines that reside on the host. A host number crunching routine in FORTRAN could be called through RAF from a compiled PC BASIC program, for example, to use the speed of the host with the convenience of the PC. RAF handles all the interaction between the PC and the host, including passing of parameters, so the calling PC program need never know about the big computer assistance. A library of subroutines can be compiled and linked to one of the supported languages, giving your applications access to RAF facilities.

## TECHNOLOGY CONCEPTS' COMMUNITY-DOS

Digital Equipment Corporation's DECnet is becoming a standard, and more companies are supporting it with their own hardware and software. Among the DECnet offerings that are gaining user acceptance is CommUnity-DOS from Technology Concepts, Inc. (TCI).[13]

## General Features

CommUnity-DOS is a software package for the IBM PC and compatibles. It uses Ethernet controllers on the PC to access DECnet running on VMS, ULTRIX, and RSX-11M hosts. According to the company, the product is a full implementation of Digital's network architecture and is compatible with DECnet phase IV running under VMS. CommUnity-DOS comes with a number of applications, including file server, remote file access, virtual terminal, network management, and VAX/VMS MAIL support.

"We were the first company to clone DECnet phase IV and make it available to non-Digital systems," Howard Sholkin, marketing communications manager at TCI told us. "We started with UNIX and MS-DOS in 1986 and added Mac this year." Community-Mac, for Macintosh users, is similar to CommUnity-DOS.

Stuart Wecker and Michael Begun, former employees of Digital, founded TCI in 1981. Instrumental in designing DECnet, they developed a DECnet clone to link hospital intensive-care equipment to a host on a UNIX network.

"We felt that by putting a commercially viable networking package on UNIX, we would be in a leadership role in the UNIX environment. That's not what happened," Michael Begun, TCI vice president for technology, recalled. "By 1986 Digital had started to develop a dominant role as a computer vendor—which they didn't have back in 1981—so all these UNIX vendors came to us because they needed connectivity into Digital because they wanted to be able to sell their boxes into Digital shops."

## Network Access

The present version of CommUnity-DOS supports Ethernet controllers on the PC from Excelan (EXOS 205E or 205T), or Ungermann-Bass (Personal-NIU). These controllers, in conjunction with CommUnity-DOS, set up your PC as an end node on Ethernet. In addition to one of these controllers, CommUnity-DOS requires at least 512 KB of memory, 1 MB of disk storage space, and MS-DOS 3.1 or later version. Using CommUnity-DOS, you can communicate with any system that supports the DECnet protocol.

The package provides functions similar to those of Digital's PCSA, including remote access to files on a VMS node; support for virtual disks; creation, renaming, and deletion of files from remote nodes; transfer of files with remote nodes; and the ability to logon to remote nodes. In addition, CommUnity-DOS includes a task-to-task interface that lets you write programs that communicate with programs on other computers. This facility uses the same network services that CommUnity-DOS uses for virtual terminal, file transfer, and other network directory operations. Network links at this level usually are set up by system developers who understand the inside operation of their applications and who can link existing code with the appropriate assembly-language code to conduct network access.

Like most communications facilities of this class, CommUnity-DOS lets you use the host in two ways. You can run programs on your PC and access remote files stored on the host, or you can use the PC as a terminal emulator to execute programs and access resources on one or more host nodes. In most applications you probably will want to use both of these capabilities at different times.

## NOVELL'S NETWARE/VMS

Novell, Inc. is among the premier suppliers of PC-based local area network software and hardware servers. Novell's NetWare software has become a LAN standard and is supported by the majority of network hardware suppliers. Even companies that supply their own network software frequently also support Novell's NetWare.

### General Features

Early in 1988 Novell announced NetWare/VMS, software that runs on a VAX host and opens up NetWare-based PC LANs to the VAX. NetWare/VMS permits single PCs or PC networks to access VAX hosts as network servers. Once into the VAX environment through the Novell network, PC users also can access other system resources, such as high-speed printers and plotters, and even remote VAXs connected to the primary server with DECnet.

When you sit at a PC attached to Ethernet, with VAXs and PC servers on the other end, NetWare brings remote resources to the local workstation with almost the speed of a direct connection.

You can access files and network services noticeably faster from a Novell PC host than from a VAX—maybe twice as fast—but operation is of VAX-based netware still rapid enough to appeal to users of, say, a 9,600-baud serial link.

## System Requirements

At the PC end, NetWare is installed as a 50-KB RAM-resident program that works through virtually any Ethernet card to attach to a departmental LAN or directly to the backbone. NetWare VMS runs as a single VAX process and requires a minimum of 2 MB of memory and about a thousand blocks of storage. It can use any Digital or Digital-compatible Ethernet controller for the network link. NetWare VMS can reside with other network protocols such as LAT or DECnet, though it does not directly use them.

The company positions NetWare as a PC-centric product, designed to provide PC users nearly transparent access to a VAX. In operation NetWare turns the VAX host into a very large disk drive for the PC and through a terminal emulation service gives PC users access to traditional VAX services over the network. With these facilities VAX and PC users can easily exchange mail and share files across a variety of network topologies. In addition, transferring files is as simple as entering an MS-DOS copy command.

After the PC is configured, users access the VAX as if it were another local disk drive. Different host subdirectories can be assigned different PC disk drive letters. Netware supports up to twenty-six disk drive volume assignments. Host-based NetWare files are stored in VMS format and converted to PC format as they are accessed by workstations. Both VAX users and PC users have access to files generated under NetWare. A software package such as WordPerfect that can run on both the PC and the VAX provides users full data sharing across the Novell network.

More than one VAX network can be accessed from a single workstation if there is a DECnet link between the two VAX installations and if NetWare VMS is running on both hosts. All security operations remain under the control of the VAX system manager, including account management, file access, queue control, and passwords.

## Product Positioning

Novell's VAX-based NetWare will certainly appeal to the PC user who has become frustrated over not being a part of the departmental network. It provides the best of both worlds, the user-friendly workstation as well as the large disk, high-speed printers, electronic mail and other services of the VAX.

Because VAX system personnel tend to stand with their back to the VAX and look out at the rest of the world, they may be a little slower to accept NetWare. If Novell's specifications are accurate, however, there should be little hesitancy. NetWare VMS is described as a "multithreaded, event-driven process optimized for file service" and is active only when users ask for file service operations.

Obvious advantages from the VAX end are the coordination of PC resources and automatic file backup with the main system. According to Novell, a NetWare-based system can actually support more users than a stand-alone VAX. Novell's stated goal is to maintain leadership in network operating systems and to support evolving workstation standards while remaining independent of any specific hardware.

## TERMINAL EMULATOR SOFTWARE

We have already described the general operation of terminal emulators in chapter 10. This section will provide some additional details on selected terminal emulation packages.

### EM220

Diversified Computer Systems offers a noticeable twist with its EM220 terminal emulation package: it includes a standard-issue Digital LK-250 keyboard. When you plug this keyboard in to your PC and load up the emulator, for all practical purposes you are using a VT-220 terminal, except you have the additional capability of downloading files and doing local processing with your PC.

EM220 includes a DECNET software interface that works with an optional PC-based Ethernet interface card, auto dialer, script files, and file transfer protocols, allowing easy access to VAX systems. Fancy features in the printer setup and reverse scrolling screens add a polished touch to the package.

EM220 can be purchased without the LK-250 keyboard, and there is an optional EGA Expander, manufactured by Quadtel Systems, that provides true 132-column display on screen.

### PowerStation 240

Another emulator with Digital keyboard is the PowerStation 240 from KEA Systems. PowerStation 240 provides excellent VT compatibility by focusing on three key points of emulation: I/O, video, and keyboard compatibility. It also includes bells and whistles such as multisession LAT support and file transfer.

The KEA package includes an optional LK keyboard look-alike in standard or WPS-Plus configuration and KEA's ZSTEMpc Smart Terminal Emulator software for either VT-240 or VT-220. An optional EGA enhancement card plugs into the expansion socket of an EGA display card to produce clear 132-column displays.

PowerStation is a graphics-based emulator that supports true ReGIS (remote graphics instruction set) and Tektronix graphics. ReGIS colors can be altered with a setup menu, a useful option, since monochrome displays often distort some colors. Pointing devices such as the mouse are supported, but only in Tektronix mode. Pointing in ReGIS mode is done with the cursor keys.

If you use RAM-resident software extensively, you should test the operation of the ZSTEMpc software with these packages. Some users have reported conflicts between the terminal emulator and pop-up programs. This is common with graphics-driven products and generally does not present a problem as long as you understand where the conflicts lie so they can be avoided.

## SmarTerm 240

SmarTerm 240 from Persoft is another popular entry in the terminal emulation field.[14] SmarTerm supports VT-series emulation through the VT-241, Tektronix 4010 and 4014 emulation, and ASCII as well as protocol-protected file transfers. SmarTerm supports ReGIS and Sixel graphics.

A keyboard mapping menu helps you specify how the PC keyboard will function in the VT terminal environment, and you can program soft keys to conduct multiple operations with a single keystroke. A macro command language is supported, but this is somewhat more limited than the full command structure you will find in other products such as PolyStar.

SmarTerm supports Persoft's proprietary file transfer protocol in addition to the popular Xmodem and Kermit protocols.

## PolyStar/240

PolyStar/240 from Polygon[15] has achieved a relatively high degree of popularity among terminal emulator users. PolyStar/240 supports the full VT terminal series through the VT-241, including ReGIS graphics.

This is a menu-driven product; that makes for easy navigation through its features, but it also includes a robust programming language so you can customize operation and automate many processes. The command language has full access to the menu structure, so that anything you can do from the menus you can control from the command language. This language even supports IF/THEN/ELSE and DO/WHILE constructs. PolyStar also supports user-defined soft keys, so you can make a single keystroke carry out a series of commands.

Polygon has included support for multiple VAX sessions so that if your PC system has more than one I/O port (multiple serial ports, for example, or a serial port and an Ethernet adapter) you can conduct more than one session simultaneously and switch easily among the various sessions.

Digital's LAT protocol is supported for Ethernet connections, but PolyStar uses a proprietary file transfer protocol.

## Reflection 4 Plus

Walker, Richer & Quinn[15] offers VT-340 emulation in addition to support for the earlier VT terminals. Reflection 4 Plus provides complete VT-241 emulation and supports all of the ReGIS graphics features of the VT-340. It does not, however, provide the VT-340's split-screen or multisession features.

Reflection 4 supports sixteen-color ReGIS, scaling the 800-×-480-pixel ReGIS image to fit on a 640-×-350-pixel PC screen. This requires the use of an EGA- or VGA-compatible video display card that supports PC graphics mode 16. Graphics mode 16 implies 256 KB of RAM onboard the EGA or VGA graphics board. This much memory is not standard on all EGA cards, and older PC monitors may not support the 640 × 350 resolution.

Reflection 4 also allows use of a standard text editor to create sets of commands on the PC. Such commands permit manipulation down to the level of single pixels, and a single command can create or fill arcs, circles, and polygons.

In addition, the package handles emulation of the Tektronix 4014 graphics terminal as well as VT-241 graphics emulation. Support is provided for VAX/VMS, UNIX, Kermit, Xmodem, and PC-to-PC file transfers. File transfers to VMS require that a special utility (VAXLINK), which comes with Reflection, be installed.

A LAT command interpreter supports the creation of multiple, interruptible LAT sessions on your LAN with a single Reflection session. For instance, you can log on to your host, start a process, uninstall Reflection, use your PC for another task, restart Reflection, and pick up where you left off in the host session. Using LAT involves setting up both command interpreter (CI) sessions and LAT sessions. The CI session establishes the connection between the LAT command interpreter and Reflection 4, while the LAT session provides connectivity to a LAT service such as a DECserver on the LAN. More than one LAT session can be set up for each CI session.

Reflection's script language gives users the facilities of a communications-oriented programming language. It supports variables and conditional execution. Script programs can accept interactive input into script variables, handle command time-outs, and transfer files using Xmodem and Kermit in addition to the normal protocol used with a VAX. In this language you can write command scripts that hide from the user most of the details of connecting to a host computer, transferring a file, and initiating an application.

Reflection 4 also includes a pop-up terminal emulation feature. Hot keys allow Reflection to alternate between foreground and background modes. In foreground mode you interact normally with the package. In background mode the DOS prompt reappears and another application can be run while Reflection continues a file transfer, printing, terminal operations, or command file execution in the background.

## CHAPTER SUMMARY

As with many specialty markets, the PC-to-VAX arena has its classic performers, products that set the standards with which the hundreds of other successful, well-designed products frequently are compared. This chapter discusses some of the well-known PC-to-VAX products to familiarize you with these standards. This is not an attempt to endorse any particular product or concept; rather, the material in this chapter should help you understand some of the various approaches to PC-to-VAX connectivity. These companies, and the products they supply, can provide an excellent beginning point from which to begin your research into PC-to-VAX connectivity solutions.

# Appendix A

# DCL Command Notebook

Chapter 9 introduces VMS and discusses operating systems. The Digital command language is introduced, but some of the command details and hints on usage are reserved for this appendix.

This section shows you how to issue abbreviated DCL commands to reduce typing and speed up command entry. Later sections of this appendix detail some of the major DCL commands. Use this appendix to learn about DCL in general and as a continuing reference as you use VMS.

## ABBREVIATED FORMS

Commands do not need to be spelled out completely. The computer only needs to know enough to distinguish between similar commands. For example, if you were to type

    $ SHOW PR

the computer would not know whether you wanted to know about the PRinter, the PRocess or the PRotection level. Type

$ SHOW PRO

and it is narrowed down to PROcess or PROtection, but the computer is still uncertain. Add one more character and the command is suitably unique.

$ SHOW PROC

can only mean SHOW PROCESS in DCL terminology.

## SELF-PROMPTING COMMANDS

Although it is often easier and more direct to enter a compound sentence as an order to the computer, many of the commands in DCL will ask the user for information if not enough is supplied at first.
For example

```
$ COPY FILE_NAME
    $_From: FILE_NAME

$_To: FILE_NAME
```

Here is an example of a message you may see appear on your screen when you use the print command:

```
$ PRINT FILENAME.EXTENSION

Job FILENAME (queue LPA0, entry 246) started on
SYS$PRINT

$
```

In this case the system is notifying you of the completion of a printing job it was given earlier. The computer names the job, using the file name as source, tells which queue the job has been assigned to, gives the job a number for tracking, and confirms the name of the printer where the work will be performed.

A number of DCL commands, including PRINT, will accept as a modifier the request /NOTIFY. This will cause the system to send a message to the user when a job has been completed. It will help in your own scheduling. In the case of a print job, this will tell you when the job has been dispatched from the computer to the queue waiting for the printer's attention—it does not necessarily indicate that the printing itself has been completed.

Here is the form for /NOTIFY using PRINT:

```
$ PRINT FILE_NAME/NOTIFY
```

## A FEW HOUSEKEEPING ESSENTIALS

You should understand a few housekeeping details to help in the orderly management of your account on the computer.

Following are some basic commands. Like any environment, a computer benefits from orderliness, including the discarding of unnecessary files, proper identification of needed files and a logical system of organization.

### APPEND

Another housekeeping chore might be the merging of one or more files into another. For example, daily price lists might be merged into a weekly list. The command to merge files is called APPEND, since it appends one file to the end of another.

Here is how the command works:

```
$ APPEND input-file-spec output-file-spec
```

In use, the specified input file or files are placed at the end of the specified output file. The input file is named first, and the name of the output file is used for the merged file.

If you use *APPEND* without any file specifications, VMS will query for the information it needs:

```
$ APPEND
From: A-DAILY_REVENUES.SPD;1
To: A-DAILY_EXPENSES.SPD;1
```

This will yield a new file with the same file name, A-Daily_Expenses. Spd;1, containing the original contents of that file followed by the contents of Revenues.

It is important to note two things about this command:

1. APPEND does not erase the file that is copied onto the tail of the new file, and
2. The command does not create a new version of the appended file, but instead merges the two files and keeps the same file name and version number.

## COPY

Suppose you want an extra copy of one of your files, either as a backup or to be modified for another purpose while retaining the original. The solution comes with the use of the command COPY. Enter the following:

    $ COPY original-filename new-filename

The computer will assume that the source, or input, file is in the present directory and will write the destination, or output, file to the standard storage area for your account.

It is possible to copy a file from your directory into a subdirectory of your account or into the directory or subdirectory of another user — if you have been granted the right to make such a transfer. Here is an example of how such a copy and transfer operation is performed:

    $ COPY [BADGETT]PRICES.TXT;3 [EDEN]PRICE_LIST.TXT

In this case we are asking the computer to copy version three of the file PRICES.TXT and place the new copy in the directory of another user named Eden. That new file will be given the name Price_List.Txt. Since no version number is specified and there is no other copy of a file with the same name in Eden's directory, the new file will be version one.

As with almost every other DCL command, you can use global characters to perform multiple operations. Assume a directory with the following files:

    A-DAILY_EXPENSES.SPD;1
    A-DAILY_REVENUES.SPD;1
    A-DAILY_REVENUES.SPD;2

```
A-MAILING_LIST_CUSTOMERS.LIS;1
B-HOLSTEIN.DTA;1
B-GUERNSEY.DTA;1
B-GUERNSEY.DTA;2
F-DAILY_FEED.DTA;1
F-DAILY_FEED.DTA;2
F-DAILY_FEED.DTA;3
```

The command

```
$ COPY %-DAILY*.* [ARCHIVE]*.ARCHIVE
```

instructs the computer to make a copy from the default directory of all files beginning with any letter plus a hypen followed by the word "Daily." The second half of the command says that the new files are to be placed in the subdirectory Archive and will be given the same file names with a new extension, "Archive."

The command selects the files

```
A-DAILY_EXPENSES.SPD;1
A-DAILY_REVENUES.SPD;1
A-DAILY_REVENUES.SPD;2
F-DAILY_FEED.DTA;1
F-DAILY_FEED.DTA;2
F-DAILY_FEED.DTA;3
```

and creates the following new files in the Archive subdirectory:

```
[ARCHIVE]A-DAILY_EXPENSES.ARCHIVE;1
[ARCHIVE]A-DAILY_REVENUES.ARCHIVE;1
[ARCHIVE]A-DAILY_REVENUES.ARCHIVE;2
[ARCHIVE]C-DAILY_FEED.ARCHIVE;1
[ARCHIVE]C-DAILY_FEED.ARCHIVE;2
[ARCHIVE]C-DAILY_FEED.ARCHIVE;3
```

## DELETE

Did you see any files in the directory that you no longer need? To remove a file from your account, use the command DELETE plus the name of the file to be removed.

```
$ DELETE filename(s)
```

If no location is given, the system assumes the file is in the default directory. It is necessary to indicate the version number.

If we were to issue the command

$ DELETE A-DAILY_REVENUES.SPD;1

that file would be removed, but version 2 of that same file would not be erased.

You can use a global command with a delete instruction, but please exercise great care. A slip of the finger could remove many or even all of the files in your directory. Here are two delete commands using global characters:

$ DELETE *.SPD.*

$ DELETE %-*.L*;2

The first command deletes all versions of all files with the extension .Spd. The following files, then, would be deleted:

A-DAILY_EXPENSES.SPD;1
A-DAILY_REVENUES.SPD;1
A-DAILY_REVENUES.SPD;2

The second command is more complex. You could state it as: Delete any file that begins with any letter plus a hyphen followed by any other letters or words, with a file extension that begins with the letter "L," but only with version two. In this case, the computer will sight in on the following file:

A-MAILING_LIST_CUSTOMERS.LIS;1

but will not erase that file, since it is not version two.

## DIRECTORY

Let's start with the organization. After you have signed on to your account, examine the catalogue of files assigned to your name. This is done with the command DIRECTORY. Type in

$ DIRECTORY

You will be greeted by a listing of files together with some of the attributes of those files.

## PRINT

Ordinarily the process of printing a file from within DCL is very simple, although you should consult with your system manager to learn about the printers and default queues in use on your system. The command is the verb PRINT:

```
$ PRINT filename
```

This will send the specified file to the default printer.

Your system may have logical names assigned to various printing devices, in which case the command may be

```
$ LASER filename
```

for a laser printer or

```
$ LINEPRINT filename
```

for output to a line printer.

Command qualifiers help you specify your needs to the computer. These include /COPIES=n to request more than one printout and /NOTIFY, which asks the system to send you a message when the job has been completed.

Within an applications program such as a word processor, database, or spreadsheet, the commands and procedures for printing may vary.

## PURGE

In the directory of files you may have seen more than one version of the same file:

```
SAMPLE.TXT;3
SAMPLE.TXT;2
SAMPLE.TXT;1
```

This is the result of one of the VMS operating system's automatic protection schemes. Every time you add to or update a previously created file, the system will create a new version of the file and add one to the version number, which is the final element of the file name. The previous version of the file is kept in your directory in case you need it. You may decide that the changes you have made were not correct or not needed; you may decide that you need the version of a file in effect on a previous day. Until you delete previous versions of files, they are kept by the operating system.

Obviously, most times it is not necessary to keep all of the older versions of your files.

Stop and think before you try this: If you require only the latest version of your files (the latest version is the file with the highest version number) use the following command:

```
$ PURGE
```

This command will automatically remove all of the extra files from your account, leaving only the most recent version.

If you need to purge a few files while retaining early versions of others, you can use PURGE with the file name. Enter the following command:

```
$ PURGE FILE_NAME
```

or

```
$ PURGE A-DAILY_REVENUES.SPREADSHEET;1
```

If you want to delete some but not all versions of files, you might find it useful to use the qualifier /KEEP:

```
$ PURGE/KEEP=3
```

This command will purge all files in the directory except the most recent three versions.

```
$ PURGE/KEEP=3 A-D*.*.*
```

This command will do the same for any file beginning with "A-D."

After you have carefully considered whether there are any earlier versions of files you need to retain, you should purge your directory of unneeded files to free up disk space.

## RENAME

There may be times when you want to rename a file. For example, you may choose to maintain a regular log of activities or a price list in your directory at all times, always using the same name for the current version. In this case you will rename outdated versions from time to time.

```
$ RENAME input-file-spec output-file-spec
```

Input is the present name and specification and output is the new name and specification. If directories are not included in either the input and output elements of the command, or both, the computer will assume the unadorned file names are in the default directory of the user.

Here's a shortcut if you want to move a file from your directory to your subdirectory or another user's directory, renaming it in the process: Rename the file and designate the new directory as part of the output file's specification.

```
$ RENAME [BADGETT]PRICES.TXT;3
[EDEN]PRICE_LIST.TXT
```

In this instance the file Prices.Txt;3 has been renamed Price_List.Txt, and made part of the directory Eden. It no longer exists in the directory Badgett.

RENAME can also be used with global characters:

```
$ RENAME *.SPD *.SPREADSHEET
```

renames all files having the extension. Spd with the new extension Spreadsheet. Otherwise the files keep their original names:

```
A-DAILY_EXPENSES.SPREADSHEET;1
A-DAILY_REVENUES.SPREADSHEET;1
A-DAILY_REVENUES.SPREADSHEET;2
```

## TYPE

If you want to examine a file, there are several routes. One is to load the file from within a word processor or through use of the VMS program EDT.

A more direct way is to type a file from the VMS prompt. The command uses TYPE as a verb followed by the file name, as in:

$ TYPE A-DAILY_EXPENSES.SPREADSHEET

VMS displays the file contents on the screen.

## DIRECTORIES AND SUBDIRECTORIES

Over the course of time—probably a lot sooner than you expect—you will end up with a large collection of files. Although the system will automatically list those files in alphabetical order, it is still quite easy to end up with an overwhelming collection of several hundred files, which are difficult to manage.

The solution to this information overload is to subdivide into smaller, more specific lists. The central file is called your directory, also called a root or top-level directory; secondary divisions are called subdirectories.

VMS allows as many as seven levels of subdirectories beneath the root directory. The presence of a subdirectory is indicated in the directory above it by a directory file. The name of the subdirectory is the file name and .DIR is the extension.

To create a subdirectory, use the command *CREATE*, specify */DIRECTORY*, and enclose the name of the subdirectory in [brackets].

Assume we are in our root directory, HOLSTEIN, and we want to create a subdirectory called ARCHIVE in which we will keep archive copies of our revenue and expense reports. To create the file:

$ CREATE/DIRECTORY [.ARCHIVE]

To move into the subdirectory, use SET to change the default:

$ SET DEFAULT [.ARCHIVE]

Once inside the subdirectory, deeper levels of directories can be created with CREATE/DIRECTORY. Here is a command for a 1988 subdivision within the subdirectory Archive:

$ CREATE/DIRECTORY [.1988]

If you issue a DIR command, you will obtain the listing of files of the directory or subdirectory in which you are working.

An alternate way to examine the contents of a subdirectory is to include the directory and subdirectory names in the command, as in:

```
$ DIR [HOLSTEIN.ARCHIVE.1988]
```

Finally, you can ask for a directory that includes all of your files, wherever they are. Use ellipsis points within brackets:

```
$ DIR [...]
```

# Appendix B

# VMS MAIL Notebook

Neither rain nor snow nor time of day nor location of user can slow VMS MAIL, an extremely useful utility that links VMS users for the purposes of exchanging messages, text files, and data.

Every user has an account for sending mail and a mailbox to receive incoming information. The name on the mailbox is generally that of the account user. Messages can be created and sent from within MAIL or prepared beforehand using any VMS application, including a word processor, and transmitted as mail.

If there is new mail waiting for you, you will see a notice when you sign on to the system:

> You have 2 new messages.

If someone sends you a message while you are signed on to VMS, a note will appear on screen:

> New mail on node BLUEFISH from TESSA

or

> New mail from TESSA

## READING YOUR MAIL

You must enter the program MAIL to read and respond to your mail:

`$ MAIL`

The program will respond with its own prompt:

`MAIL>`

If there are any messages in your account that you have not yet read, you will see a message such as

`You have 4 new messages.`

To read the messages in FIFO order (oldest messages first), simply press the return key or type

`READ`

You can then step through the messages one by one by using the return key or by typing

`NEXT`

## CONSULTING THE DIRECTORY

To learn something about the messages in your mailbox before you read them, examine the MAIL directory first. The command follows the format:

`$ DIRECTORY [folder_name]`

This lists the messages in the mail file, including the sender's name, the date the message was sent, a subject line if used by the sender, and a message number.

If no folder name is included in the command, VMS Mail will assume the user seeks information about the currently selected folder and will display a directory of messages in that folder. If there is no currently selected folder, MAIL displays a directory of the NEWMAIL folder (if there are any unread messages) or the MAIL folder for previously read mail.

Here is an example of a directory command and response:

```
MAIL> DIRECTORY
```

| # | From | Date | Subject |
|---|------|------|---------|
| 1 | TESSA | 6-JUL-87 | Travel plans |
| 2 | RECEPTION | 6-JUL-87 | Telephone messages |
| 3 | JANICE | 7-JUL-87 | Budget reconciliation |
| 4 | TESSA | 8-JUL-87 | Bluefish futures |

At this point you can choose to read all of your messages by typing the return key or READ, or you can select individual messages:

```
MAIL> READ 3
```

This command will call up message number three. If you type a return key or the command NEXT after reading message three, you move on to the fourth message.

You can also select a message by merely typing its directory number:

```
MAIL> 3
```

There are a number of parameters and qualifiers that can be used to make the directory command more specific. The parameter

```
DIRECTORY Folder_Name
```

will yield a listing of the messages in a particular folder, which is a subdirectory of messages within MAIL.

Qualifiers of DIRECTORY include

```
MAIL> DIRECTORY/BEFORE=date
```

in the form

```
MAIL> DIRECTORY/BEFORE=6-JUL
```

to display mail messages received before the specified date.

> MAIL> DIRECTORY/FOLDER

displays a listing of all of the folders in the current mail file.

> MAIL> DIRECTORY/FULL

yields a listing of mail messages that will tell you the number of records in each message and whether you have replied to each message.

> MAIL> DIRECTORY/NEW

yields a display of any new or unread messages in the current folder.

> MAIL> DIRECTORY/SINCE=date

in the form

> MAIL> DIRECTORY/SINCE=6-JUL

displays a listing of all messages received since the specified date.

> MAIL> DIRECTORY/START=start

serves as a wild card to specify a directory listing of messages that begin with the number or letter specified.
You can stack the wild card with /FOLDER:

> MAIL> DIRECTORY/FOLDER/START=A

The directory will list folders with names that begin with the letter A.

## USING FOLDERS TO ORGANIZE YOUR MAIL

MAIL can subdivide your mail messages into folders, much as VMS uses subdirectories.

When you first begin using your mail account, you will have a folder called MAIL. As soon as you receive an incoming message, the system will create a folder called NEWMAIL. New and unread messages are automatically routed into NEWMAIL; once read, they are automatically moved into MAIL. When the contents of NEWMAIL have been read, that folder is removed until it is needed again.

If you delete a message, it is placed in a folder called WASTEBASKET, which is cleaned out when you exit from the program or issue a PURGE command from within MAIL. If you accidentally delete a mail message, you can retrieve it if you have not yet exited from MAIL or purged your mail account. Set the folder to WASTEBASKET, obtain a directory, and then use FORWARD or SEND to transfer the deleted message to another folder.

There is no real limit on the number of folders that can be created. When you enter a READ or DIRECTORY command, the system will display the name of the current folder at the top right corner of the screen. The command DIRECTORY/FOLDER will yield a display of the folders in the mail file.

A folder is automatically removed when all of the messages in it have been deleted or moved.

The creation of a folder is automatic when you direct MAIL to file or move a message.

## The Hierarchy of Mail Folders

Your Mail account is organized by VMS as follows:

```
                    Personal Mail Utility (MAIL)
     mail file      { [+ + + + +]  [+ + + + +]  [+ + + + +] }
        folder                     [+ + + + +]
         message                       +
```

Most accounts have just one mail file and multiple folders with multiple messages in each folder.

# MOVING MESSAGES

After you read a message about the budget reconciliation, you move it from Newmail to a folder called Budget:

MAIL> MOVE BUDGET

or

MAIL> FILE BUDGET

If you attempt to move or file a message to a nonexistent folder, the system will query you to see if you want to create a folder with that name. Here is an example of such a conversation, in this case using the self-prompting feature of VMS:

```
MAIL> MOVE
_Folder:BUDGET
_File:

Folder BUDGET does not exist.

Do you want to create it (Y/N, default is N)? Y

%MAIL-I-NEWFOLDER, folder BUDGET created
```

A command qualifier can be added to eliminate the query about new folders. In such usage the system will automatically create a new folder if the specified one does not exist:

MAIL> MOVE BUDGET/NOCONFIRM

When you move or file a mail message, that message is deleted from its previous folder.

If you enter the MOVE command, supply a folder name, and then decide that you do not want to move the message, enter Ctrl-Z to abort the operation and keep you within MAIL.

## COPYING A FILE

To send a copy of a mail message to another folder while keeping the original, use COPY:

MAIL> COPY foldername

If the folder name as specified does not exist, the system will create the new folder and copy the currently displayed mail message to it.

If you need to copy a message to a sequential file outside of MAIL, such as an EDT file for editing, use EXTRACT.

If you enter COPY, supply a folder name, and then decide that you do not want to copy the message, enter Ctrl-Z to abort the operation and keep you within MAIL.

# SENDING A LETTER

At the heart of MAIL, of course, is the ability to send a message. There are two interchangeable commands: MAIL and SEND.

If you enter only the command SEND or MAIL, the system will prompt you for the name of the user or users to receive the message. If the user is within your local network, just enter the account name. Otherwise it will be necessary to enter a node name for transfer to connected systems. You can also use a distribution list of names, which will be explained later.

Here is the form for mailing addresses:

[[nodename::]username,. . .] [,] [@listname]

For example,

**HOLSTEIN::JONES**

or

**HOLSTEIN::@ EMPLOYEES**

The text file EMPLOYEES in this example contains a list of names of those to receive the mail.

MAIL will next ask for the subject of the mail. If you want to skip that prompt, specify the /SUBJECT qualifier with the MAIL command.

You can include a file specification with the MAIL command, with the text in that file sent to the specified user or group of users. If no file is specified, MAIL will prompt the user for the text of a message.

At this point you have access to a line-by-line editor. Messages created within MAIL itself will wrap at the end of the line; or you can hit the return key somewhere before the 80th character position on the screen (or the 132nd if you are in 132-column mode.) Once a new line is started, there is no way to get back to that line to edit it.

When you have entered your message, press Ctrl-Z to transmit it. If you decide to abandon a message before it has been sent but want to stay within MAIL, type Ctrl-C. To abandon a message and exit from MAIL, type Ctrl-Y.

## SENDING A FILE BY MAIL

You can use MAIL to send a copy of a file from one user to another. This is a good way to send prepared documents, or you can use a word processor or other program to produce and edit a lengthy file for the MAIL program.

The command is simple:

```
MAIL> SEND [File_Name]
```

The system will then prompt you for the name of the user to receive the file.

It is also possible to include all of the elements of the command in a single line from within MAIL:

```
MAIL> SEND Filename Username
```

In an even more convenient method, you can do the whole job from the DCL prompt without entering the MAIL program:

```
$ MAIL Filename Username
```

For example,

```
$ MAIL MEETING_DATES.TXT BLUEFISH::TESSA
```

will send the file called Meeting_Dates.Txt to the user named Tessa in the node Bluefish. The node name is optional, required only when the recipient is not in your default node. The system will assume that the file you are sending exists in your default directory; otherwise you will need to specify its location.

It is also possible to include a short message identifying the nature of the mail you are sending. Here is an example of such a command:

```
$ MAIL[/subject="August's meeting schedule"]
    MEETING_DATES.TXT TESSA
```

## SENDING AN ELECTRONIC CHAIN LETTER

You can send one message to multiple users by stringing their mailbox names together with commas, as in:

```
_To: TESSA,WILLIAM,JANICE
```

You can also create your own list of mailbox names to allow you to send a single message to a group of accounts. To do so, create a file with the extension of .Dis (for distribution). The file can be made by using the command CREATE from DCL or under the EDT text editor. Here is an example using CREATE:

```
$ CREATE STAFF.DIS
TESSA
WILLIAM
JANICE
ARLENE
HERBERT
SONYA
DAN
Ctrl-Z
```

If it would help you to remember the purpose of a particular distribution list, you can add comments to the file. A comment is a line of text that begins with an exclamation point. Here is a commented version of Staff.Dis:

```
$ CREATE STAFF.DIS
!Boston office staff:
TESSA
```

```
WILLIAM
JANICE
ARLENE
HERBERT
SONYA
DAN
Ctrl-Z
```

To send a memo to the members of the Staff.Dis listing, precede the name of the .Dis file with an @ sign in place of an ordinary mailbox name. Here's an example:

```
$ MAIL
MAIL> MAIL
_Text: "Enter text here . . ."
_To:    @STAFF
_Subj: "4Q 1987 Sales figures"
Ctrl-Z
```

The file name extension .Dis is assumed by the system and is not required to be entered.

Let's suppose you have a second distribution list, with office staff in your San Francisco branch on node Swordfish as well as a group of secretaries on your default node. Here's another list:

```
$ CREATE SUPPORT_STAFF.DIS
!San Francisco branch and Home office support
    !San Francisco:
    SWORDFISH::KEEFE
    SWORDFISH::SANDLER
    !Boston support staff:
    NEIL
    STEVEN
    Ctrl-Z
```

Distribution lists can also be mixed in with ordinary account names:

```
_To: KENNEDY,@STAFF
```

The distribution list must be at the end of the command.

It is not possible to include more than one distribution list in a single mailbox command. However, you can nest one distribution list within another, as in:

```
$ CREATE ALL_STAFF.DIS
@STAFF
@SUPPORT_STAFF
Ctrl-Z
```

If you mix ordinary mailbox account names with nested distribution lists, the distribution lists must be at the end of the main distribution list file.

## Extending the Powers of SEND

There are three useful command qualifiers to MAIL and SEND.

```
MAIL> MAIL/EDIT
```

allows you to use the text editor EDT to compose a message. It is also possible to change the default text editor; see your system manager for details.

```
MAIL> MAIL/SELF
```

sends a copy of the message to your own folder.

```
MAIL> MAIL/SUBJECT=text
```

specifies a heading to the message. If the text is more than one word, it must be enclosed in quote marks.

Here is an example:

```
MAIL> MAIL/SUBJECT="Your vacation schedule"
FILENAME.EXT
```

## USING THE KEYPAD FOR COMMANDS IN MAIL

The MAIL program includes a set of predefined commands assigned to the numeric keypad of the LK-201 keyboard used on the VT-220. These commands are imitated by most terminals designed to be compatible with the VT-220. Most of the keys have two functions, one given by pressing the key, and the second issued by pressing the Gold key (PF1) and then striking the keypad key.

Here are the default key assignments, with the primary assignment listed first, and the secondary assignment, which must be preceded by the Gold key, listed second:

**Table B-1.** The numeric keypad on the VT100/LK201

| PF1<br>GOLD | PF2<br>HELP<br>DIR/FOLD | PF3<br>EXT/MAIL<br>EXTRACT | PF4<br>ERASE<br>SEL MAIL |
|---|---|---|---|
| 7<br>SEND<br>SEND/EDIT | 8<br>REPLY<br>RP/ED/EX | 9<br>FORWARD<br>FRWD/EDIT | —<br>READ/NEW<br>SHOW NEW |
| 4<br>CURRENT<br>CURR/EDIT | 5<br>FIRST<br>FIRS/EDIT | 6<br>LAST<br>LAST/EDIT | ,<br>DIR/NEW<br>DIR MAIL |
| 1<br>BACK<br>BACK/EDIT | 2<br>PRINT<br>P/P/NOTI | 3<br>DIR<br>DIR/9999 | ENTER<br>ENTER<br>SELECT |
| 0<br>NEXT<br>NEXT/EDIT | | .<br>FILE<br>DELETE | |

None of this, however, is necessarily binding on you, the user. MAIL allows the user to redefine any of the keys on the keypad to personalize commands in as many groupings as you'd like, using the command and parameter DEFINE/KEY.

The format to define a key:

```
MAIL>DEFINE/KEY key-name string
```

The name of the key to be redefined is followed by the string, or command to be assigned to that key.

Note that you cannot redefine the arrow keys or function keys 1 through 14.

To program the function key PF3 with the command READ/NEW, enter the following line:

```
MAIL>DEFINE/KEY PF3 "READ/NEW"
```

**Table B-2.** Keys Available for Redefinition within MAIL

| **Key name** | **LK201 (VT200)** | **VT100** | **VT52** |
| --- | --- | --- | --- |
| PF1 | PF1 | PF1 | red key |
| PF2 | PF2 | PF2 | blue key |
| PF3 | PF3 | PF3 | black key |
| PF4 | PF4 | PF4 | n/a |
| KP0-KP9 | keypad 0-9 | keypad 0-9 | keypad 0-9 |
| Period | period key | period key | period key |
| Comma | comma key | comma key | comma key |
| Minus | minus key | minus key | minus key |
| Enter | enter key | enter key | enter key |
| E1 | Find key | n/a | n/a |
| E2 | Insert key | n/a | n/a |
| E3 | Remove key | n/a | n/a |
| E4 | Select key | n/a | n/a |
| E5 | Previous screen | n/a | n/a |
| E6 | Next screen | n/a | n/a |
| Help | Help (15) | n/a | n/a |
| DO | Do (16) | n/a | n/a |
| F17-F20 | Function keys | n/a | n/a |

A valuable command qualifier is /TERMINATE, which tells the computer to execute the command associated with a particular key. This is equivalent to pressing the special key and then hitting the return key. Here is an example:

```
MAIL> DEFINE/KEY PERIOD "DIRECTORY"/TERMINATE
```

You can use /NOECHO to turn off the display of a command when a special key is struck:

```
MAIL> DEFINE/KEY COMMA "FORWARD"/NOECHO
```

You can have an unlimited number of key redefinitions if you subdivide your new choices into "states" for various purposes. For example, you could have a keypad redefinition for use during an editing session while retaining a basic mail command set and an advanced mail set.

The command qualifiers necessary:

```
/IF_STATE=state_list
```

One of the states from the list must be set to enable use of a redefined key. If this qualifier is not used, the current state is assumed.

```
/LOCK_STATE
```

sets the default at the most recently specified state.

```
/SET_STATE=state
```

associates a state with the key being defined.

Here are some examples:

```
MAIL> DEFINE/KEY F17 "SET" /SET
STATE=ADVANCED_MAIL
```

This makes key F17 on the LK-201 keyboard issue a SET command and change the state to Advanced_Mail.

```
MAIL> DEFINE/KEY F18 "FORWARD" /TERMINATE
/IF_STATE=ADVANCED_MAIL
```

Under these two redefinitions, if F17 is pressed, followed by F18, MAIL will use the Advanced_Mail redefinition of F18.

Keypad reassignments made during a mail session will not be retained by the computer when you exit from the MAIL program. In order to retain these redefinitions, it is necessary to create a file in your top-level (root) directory with the definitions and then add a pointer to that file in your LOGIN.COM command file.

Here is an example of how to create such a file of keypad redefinitions, starting from the VMS prompt:

```
$ CREATE MAIL$KEYS.DEF
DEFINE/KEY PF1 "MAIL"
DEFINE/KEY PF3 "READ/NEW"
DEFINE/KEY PERIOD "DIRECTORY"
DEFINE/KEY COMMA "DIRECTORY/FOLDER"
Ctrl-Z
```

Next you must add to your LOGIN.COM file the following statement:

```
$ DEFINE MAIL$INIT SYS$LOGIN:MAIL$KEYS.DEF
```

The list of redefinitions will be read into the computer and made active as part of MAIL the next time the LOGIN.COM file is read at login.

## READING A MAP OF MAIL

Finally, it is valuable to know about one command, SHOW, that will display the current state of any keyboard definitions as well as other qualifiers, including terminate, echo and state:

```
MAIL> SHOW KEY [key-name]
```

will tell you the definition given to a particular key.

```
MAIL> SHOW KEY/ALL

MAIL> SHOW KEY/ALL/STATE=(state,state, .....)
```

will list the definitions of all keys in the default state, or if a state or states are specified, the definitions of those states. Note that if states are specified, they are listed within parentheses and are separated by commas.

```
MAIL>SHOW KEY/BRIEF
```

displays only definitions of keys, leaving out other qualifiers.

```
MAIL>SHOW KEY/DIRECTORY
```

identifies the names of all states for which keys have been identified.

## A SHORT NOTE ABOUT LONG MAIL MESSAGES

You may notice in your directory one or more file listings with a combination of alphanumeric characters and a .MAI extension, as in:

```
MAIL$nnnnnnnnnnnnnnnnn.MAI
```

This is a temporary file created by MAIL to hold a mail message of more than three blocks in size. This file will be automatically deleted when you delete the message from MAIL. If you delete the file yourself from the VMS prompt, you will still find the message listed in your mail directory, and you will receive an error message if you attempt to read the file.

## A SPECIAL MAIL DICTIONARY

Following are definitions and examples of use of some of the most important MAIL commands.

**ANSWER and REPLY**  Allow the user to send a message to the originator of the message being read or the one last read. ANSWER and REPLY are interchangeable. The command can include the name of a prepared file to be sent to the originator:

## A SPECIAL MAIL DICTIONARY  □  225

**MAIL> ANSWER Filename.Ext**

Or you can wait for the system to prompt you for the text of a message. To use REPLY, though, you must have read a recent message and have it as your current message.

The following command qualifiers are available for use with ANSWER and REPLY:

**MAIL> ANSWER/EDIT**

lets you use EDT to edit the reply you compose. When you exit from EDT, the message is automatically sent. (To cancel the message, use the EDT command QUIT.)

**MAIL> ANSWER/EXTRACT**

allows you to use EDT to edit the text of the message you are reading.

**MAIL> ANSWER/LAST**

tells the system that the last mail message that was sent, regardless of who the addressee was, is to be used as the text for the reply.

**MAIL> ANSWER/SELF**

tells MAIL to send a copy of the response to you so that you can retain a record.

## COPY

COPY places a duplicate of an existing file in another folder within the MAIL program. (If you want to copy a mail message to a program outside of MAIL, use EXTRACT File_Name copies the current mail message to a VMS text file in your current directory.

The form for the command:

**MAIL> COPY foldername [filename]**

Here are examples of use:

**MAIL> COPY PHONECALLS**

This instruction makes a copy of the current message and places it in the folder Phonecalls in MAIL.

Note: If the specified folder name does not exist, it will be created by the system, following a request for confirmation.

```
MAIL> COPY PHONECALLS/NOCONFIRM
```

eliminates the confirmation request by the system and automatically creates a new folder if an unknown folder is requested.

```
MAIL> COPY PHONECALLS/ALL
```

tells the system to copy all selected messages to the specified folder. If the /ALL switch is not used, only the current message is copied.

As with most commands, the system will prompt the user for information:

```
MAIL> COPY
Folder: foldername
File:
MAIL>
```

## CURRENT

CURRENT displays the beginning of the message being read, an easy way to reexamine the top of a lengthy message.

```
MAIL> CURRENT
```

To move to the top of the current message and invoke EDT, enter

```
MAIL> CURRENT/EDIT
```

## DELETE

This command deletes the message being read or most recently read. The form is

```
MAIL> DELETE
```

to remove the current or most recently read message.

> MAIL> DELETE [message number]

deletes a specific message as listed in the directory.

> MAIL> DELETE/ALL

will delete messages specified by the command SELECT.

Note: Messages are not immediately erased, but are placed in the WASTEBASKET folder that is a part of every mail account. The WASTEBASKET is automatically emptied when an EXIT or PURGE is used.

If you want to recover a message accidentally deleted but not yet purged, select the WASTEBASKET folder, call for a directory to see the message numbers in that folder, read the message you wish to retain, and then move it to another folder.

## EDIT

This command invokes EDT to allow editing of a message before it is sent. See the VAX EDT Reference Manual for details on EDT commands.

The command qualifier /EDIT is available for a number of MAIL commands, automatically calling forth EDT for such uses as FORWARD and ANSWER.

As a command of its own EDIT has the following form:

> MAIL> EDIT filename

The command also has a number of qualifiers, including

> MAIL> EDIT/COMMAND=ini-filename

This command invokes EDT and calls the EDT start-up command file EDTINI. See details in the VAX EDT Reference Manual. If the user does not call for a special start-up command file, the default file EDTINI.EDT is automatically called.

> MAIL> EDIT/CREATE

tells MAIL to invoke EDT and create a file. If a file name is not included in the command, the editor will prompt the user for a file name.

## ERASE

MAIL> ERASE

A simple command to clear the screen during a MAIL session, it uses no qualifiers.

## EXIT

MAIL> EXIT

To leave MAIL, enter the command EXIT or type Ctrl-Z. When you exit the program, all messages in the WASTEBASKET folder are deleted unless the command SET NOAUTO_PURGE has been issued. (See SET.)

## EXTRACT

One of the more useful attributes of MAIL is that you can take a file out of MAIL and work on it under another program, archive it, or place it in a database. The key is to extract it from MAIL and put in a separate file under VMS so that it can later be retrieved and worked on. The form of the command:

MAIL> EXTRACT filename-spec

The verb EXTRACT applies to the current message, and the file name is applied to the output file. The default file specification .TXT is used unless a different extension is given.

The following command qualifiers are among those available for use with EXTRACT:

MAIL> EXTRACT/ALL

This copies to a single file all files chosen with SELECT.

MAIL> EXTRACT/APPEND

Adds the current or selected message or messages to the end of an existing file. If the file name does not exist, a new file with that name is created.

MAIL> EXTRACT/NOHEADER

Extracts a message file, removing the header information (To:, From:, and Subject:) from the mail message.

## FILE and MOVE

FILE and MOVE, which are interchangeable commands, move the current message to the specified folder. If you enter FILE, supply a folder name, and then decide that you do not want to file the message, enter Ctrl-Z to abort the operation and stay within MAIL.

The format for the command:

MAIL> FILE folder-name [File_Name]

## FORWARD

This command sends a copy of the current message to a user or group of users. The system will prompt the user for the mailbox names of addressees. The form:

MAIL> FORWARD

To edit a file, issue:

MAIL> FORWARD/EDIT

This invokes the EDT file editor to allow changes to the current message before it is forwarded.

MAIL> FORWARD/NOHEADER

Strips off the header information before a message is forwarded.

## PRINT

To send a copy of the current message to a printer, use PRINT:

    **MAIL> PRINT**

The files are not ordinarily released to the printer until the user exits from MAIL, so all files are printed at the same time.
The default print queue for MAIL is SYS$PRINT.
The following command qualifiers are available:

    **MAIL> PRINT/ALL**

This prints all of the messages indicated by SELECT.

    **MAIL> PRINT/COPIES=n**

This orders the specified number of copies of a file to be printed.

    **MAIL> PRINT/NOTIFY**

This calls for a broadcast message to be sent to your account when your printing request has been completed.

    **MAIL> PRINT/PRINT**

This releases messages queued by previous PRINT commands without the need for an EXIT command. PRINT/PRINT will not order a print of the current message.

    **MAIL> PRINT/QUEUE=queue-name**

Orders printing of a file or files on a print queue other than the default SYS$PRINT. For example, if your system has a laser printer with a queue called SYS$LASER, the command is:

    **MAIL> PRINT/QUEUE=SYS$LASER**

## PURGE

As we've seen, files that are deleted from MAIL folders are not immediately erased from the system but are instead placed in the

Wastebasket folder. The files in that folder are automatically discarded when the user exits from MAIL. PURGE is used to remove files from that folder while remaining within MAIL.

The form of the command is

```
MAIL> PURGE
```

The following command qualifiers are available:

```
MAIL> PURGE/RECLAIM
```

This releases space from deleted messages to the VAX record management services for reuse. Note that while a PURGE/RECLAIM operation is under way, you will not be able to receive new mail, and users sending mail during that time will receive an error message.

```
MAIL> PURGE/STATISTICS
```

This gives a report on the amount of space reclaimed.

## QUIT

To leave MAIL without clearing the Wastebasket folder, use QUIT:

```
MAIL> QUIT
```

Ctrl-Y performs the same command.

## READ

The verb to display messages is READ:

```
MAIL> READ [foldername] [message-number]
```

Pressing the return key with MAIL in most instances is interpreted by the system as equivalent to a request to read the current message.

To display a list of available messages in the current directory, along with the message numbers, use DIRECTORY.

If READ is entered without parameters or a file name, MAIL will display the oldest message in NEWMAIL, the unread mail folder. If there are no messages in that folder, MAIL will display the oldest message in the Mail folder.

To specify a folder other than the current one, enter

```
MAIL> READ [foldername]
```

To read a specific file in the current folder, enter

```
MAIL> READ [message-number]
```

If you enter a number higher than that of the last message in a folder, the system will display the last message. This allows a quick way to get to the end of a folder without knowing the message numbers — simply specify a number that you know is larger than the number of messages in a folder.

The following command qualifiers are available:

```
MAIL> READ/BEFORE=date
```

displays messages received before the indicated date. If no date is included in the command, all messages before the current date are displayed. The form:

```
MAIL> READ/BEFORE=19-JUL
MAIL> READ/EDIT
```

invokes EDT with READ.

```
MAIL> READ/NEW
```

displays any new mail messages received while you are using MAIL.

```
MAIL> READ/SINCE=date
```

displays messages received after the indicated date. Use the form

```
MAIL> READ/SINCE=06-JUL
```

## REPLY

This command is interchangeable with ANSWER.

## SEARCH

If you accumulate a large folder of files, it may become difficult to find previous messages. SEARCH will look through the files in the current folder for the first occurrence of a string of characters. The form:

```
MAIL> SEARCH search-string
```

Here is an example:

```
MAIL> SEARCH Bluefish futures
```

## SELECT

```
MAIL> SELECT [foldername]
```

identifies a set of messages that can be acted upon as a group. The selected group is acted upon as if it were in a separate folder. The following commands can be applied to a set that has been selected:

```
COPY

DELETE

DIRECTORY

EXTRACT

FILE

MOVE

READ

SEARCH
```

If no folder name is indicated in the command, the current folder is used.

You can use the following command qualifiers:

```
MAIL> SELECT/BEFORE=date
```

to choose all messages earlier than the indicated date. The form:

```
MAIL> SELECT/BEFORE=06-JUL

MAIL> SELECT/NEW
```

to choose only unread messages.

```
MAIL> SELECT/SINCE=date
```

to choose all messages dated since the indicated date. The form:

```
MAIL> SELECT/SINCE=19-JUL
```

## SEND

See Sending a File by MAIL.

# NAVIGATIONAL COMMANDS WITHIN MAIL FILES

Another class of commands within MAIL can be considered to be navigational. They can be used in the selection or manipulation of files within the folders of MAIL.

## BACK

Entered at the **MAIL>** prompt, BACK displays the message preceding the current or most recently read message. If the most recent command was DIRECTORY, issuing a BACK command displays the preceding screen of the directory. The form:

```
MAIL> BACK
```

Another option with BACK:

**MAIL> BACK/EDIT**

which performs as above and invokes EDT to work on the displayed message.

## FIRST

FIRST selects as the current message, then displays, the first message in the current file. The form:

**MAIL> FIRST**

Another way to invoke the command:

**MAIL> FIRST/EDIT**

which displays the first message and invokes EDT.

## LAST

LAST selects as the current message, then displays, the last message in the current folder. The form:

**MAIL> LAST**

Another way to use this command:

**MAIL> LAST/EDIT**

which invokes EDT and then displays the last message in the current folder.

## NEXT

NEXT moves on to the next message in a directory of Mail messages. The form:

**MAIL> NEXT**

If the cursor is at the bottom of a message, hitting the return key will move you on to the next message automatically; NEXT is most useful, then, in moving through long messages.

MAIL> NEXT/EDIT

moves you to the next message and invokes EDT.

## SYSTEM COMMANDS WITHIN MAIL

### SPAWN and ATTACH

The command SPAWN allows you to create a subprocess from the current process. The context of the subprocess is copied from that of the current process. You can use SPAWN to leave MAIL temporarily, perform other functions such as displaying a directory listing or printing a file, and then return to MAIL. Going in the other direction, while editing a file, the user can spawn a subprocess to read a new mail message and then return back to the editing process.

ATTACH switches control between processes created using SPAWN. Attach is used to activate the desired process started with SPAWN. New processes can be named and you switch among processes with the command:

ATTACH processname

Be aware that your system configuration and the load of users and processes on your system may combine to make SPAWN an attractive concept but unworkable because of loss of speed. Consult your system manager for instructions about your system.

SPAWN uses the following form:

MAIL> SPAWN [command]

Here is an example of moving in and out of a MAIL session:

MAIL> SPAWN PHONE

to suspend MAIL and conduct a PHONE session.

The following qualifiers are available within MAIL:

**MAIL> SPAWN/INPUT=filename**

tells the program to use an input file containing one or more DCL command strings to be executed within the spawned subprocess. If a command string is specified along with the name of an input file, the program processes the string before moving on to the command file.

**MAIL> SPAWN/LOGICAL_NAMES**

instructs the system to copy the logical names (see glossary) of the parent process to the spawned subprocess. The default is /LOGICAL_NAMES. To block passage, use /NOLOGICAL_NAMES.

**MAIL> SPAWN/SYMBOLS**

instructs the system to pass DCL global and local symbols to the subprocess. The default is /SYMBOLS. To block passage, use /NOSYMBOLS.

**MAIL> SPAWN/PROCESS=subprocess-name**

allows the user to specify the name of the subprocess to be created. If this qualifier is not used, the default name is the user name and an incremented number, as in User_Name_n.

**MAIL> SPAWN/OUTPUT=filename**

tells MAIL to direct output of a SPAWN subprocess to the indicated file. This command should be used in conjunction with the qualifier /NOWAIT.

**MAIL> SPAWN/WAIT**

instructs the system to wait until a subprocess is completed before accepting further commands.

**MAIL> SPAWN/NOWAIT**

allows the user to specify new commands while the subprocess is running. This command qualifier should be used with /OUTPUT=file-spec to direct the output to a file instead of the screen.

It is also possible to spawn a MAIL session from the DCL command level. Here is an example:

```
$ SPAWN MAIL
%DCL-S-SPAWNED, process XXXXXXXNAME_1 spawned
%DCL-S-ATTACHED, terminal now attached to process
XXXXXNAME_1
MAIL>
```

To return from MAIL, use the following command:

```
MAIL> ATTACH XXXXXNAME_1

%DCL-S-RETURNED, control returned to process
XXXXXXNAME
```

## ATTACH

This command allows the user to move between processes created with SPAWN. For example, while editing a file, the user can spawn a subprocess (MAIL) to read a new mail message and later attach to the editing session again. The form is:

```
ATTACH [/PARENT] [process-name]
```

Process_name is optional. The name defaults to username_n, where n is the numeral of the subprocess you have spawned.

## COMPRESS

This command compresses ISAM (indexed sequential access method) mail files so that they take up less space in disk storage.

When a file is compressed, a temporary file named MAIL_nnnn_COMPRESS.TMP is created. (Nnnn is an unique four-digit number.) The contents of the file to be compressed are copied to the temporary file and compressed. The original uncompressed file is renamed with a file type OLD. Finally, the newly compressed file is renamed from MAIL_nnnn_COMPRESS.TMP to its original name.

The form:

```
COMPRESS [filename]
```

## SET and SHOW

SET allows the user to customize some of the features of MAIL. SHOW displays the current state of those commands.

Here are some commands:

```
MAIL> SET NOAUTO_PURGE
```

This command instructs the system not to purge the contents of the WASTEBASKET folder when an EXIT or SET FILE is commanded. With this instruction in place, the user must enter PURGE to clean out the WASTEBASKET folder.

To turn the automatic purge back on, issue the command

```
MAIL> SET AUTO_PURGE
```

To display the current state of the AUTO_PURGE default, issue the command

```
MAIL> SHOW AUTO_PURGE

MAIL> SET COPY_SELF
```

This command determines the default instruction for SEND or REPLY to deliver or withold a copy of a message to the sender.

To display the current state of the COPY_SELF default, issue the command

```
MAIL> SHOW COPY_SELF

MAIL> SET FILE [filename]
```

This command establishes or opens another file as the current mail file.

```
MAIL> SHOW FILE
```

This command displays the current file.

```
MAIL> SET FOLDER [foldername]
```

This command establishes or opens another folder as the current mail folder.

```
MAIL> SHOW FOLDER
```

This command displays the current folder.
SET FOLDER has the following command qualifiers:

```
MAIL> SET FOLDER/BEFORE=date
MAIL> SET FOLDER/SINCE=date
```

to set the folder and select messages within it that are either before or since the indicated date.
Use

```
MAIL> SET FOLDER/NEW
```

to select the Newmail folder with unread mail.

```
MAIL> SET FORWARD address
```

to establish a default forwarding address for mail. This default stays in effect until a SET NOFORWARD command is given.
To determine what the default forwarding address is, issue the command:

```
MAIL> SHOW FORWARD
```

You can personalize your mail's return address label with the following command:

```
MAIL> SET PERSONAL_NAME "text string"
```

This command adds a string of characters to the "From:" field of a message, allowing personalization of messages with information beyond that of the account name. The string can be no more than 127 characters in length.

Here is an example of use:

```
MAIL> SET PERSONAL_NAME "The man who signs your
paycheck"
```

This will yield the following on-screen message at a recipient's terminal when a message is sent:

```
New mail on node SWORDFISH from BLUEFISH::SANDLER
"The man who signs your paycheck"
```

On a less frivolous note, the message could also include a short note such as

```
MAIL> SET PERSONAL_NAME "Urgent update on
prices."
```

To display any personal names, use the command

```
MAIL> SHOW PERSONAL_NAME
```

To cancel personal names, issue the following:

```
MAIL> SET NOPERSONAL_NAME
```

Another command allows changing the name of the folder ordinarily named Wastebasket. The form:

```
MAIL> SET WASTEBASKET_NAME foldername
```

The contents of the Wastebasket, if any, are transferred to the new file.

```
MAIL> SHOW WASTEBASKET_NAME
```

will display the name of the Wastebasket folder.

## EVERYTHING YOU NEED TO KNOW ABOUT YOUR MAIL ACCOUNT

After you have completed—or before you have begun—to customize your Mail account, issue the following simple command:

```
MAIL> SHOW ALL
```

This instruction will yield the following:

- The name of the mail file directory
- The current mail file and folder
- The name of the Wastebasket folder (adjusted by SET WASTEBASKET_NAME)
- The amount of deleted message space
- The number of new (unread) messages
- The forwarding address for mail; use SET FORWARD
- The personal name; use SET PERSONAL_NAME
- Whether the user will receive copies of mail messages under SEND or ANSWER, as set by SET command, and COPY_SELF
- Whether MAIL will empty the Wastebasket when EXIT or SET FILE is used (unless disabled by SET AUTO_PURGE)

## THE HELP IS IN THE MAIL

MAIL has a full set of help messages and explanations of commands, available any time MAIL is being used.

The following is a list of help topics under MAIL in a typical system:

| | | | | |
|---|---|---|---|---|
| /EDIT | ANSWER | ATTACH | BACK | COMPRESS |
| Convert_files | | | | |
| COPY | CURRENT | DEFINE | DELETE | DIRECTORY | EDIT |
| ERASE | | | | |
| EXIT | EXTRACT | FILE | FIRST | Folders | FORWARD |
| GETTING_STARTED | | HELP | KEYPAD | LAST | MAIL |
| MOVE | | | | |
| NEXT | PRINT | PURGE | QUIT | READ | REPLY |
| SEARCH | | | | |
| SELECT | SEND | SET-SHOW | SPAWN | Syntax |
| V4_CHANGES | | | | |

The form to ask for help is

```
MAIL> HELP
```

for a prompted help session, or

```
MAIL> HELP
```

for information about all MAIL commands, or

```
MAIL> HELP [topic]
```

for instructions about a specific command or topic. The list of available subjects is displayed with a basic HELP command.

# Appendix C

# VMS PHONE Notebook

Forget about all of the fancy number-crunching, database management, and computerized graphics and design capabilities of your VAX system. Here's a really neat use of your million-dollar system: as a telephone.

Well, it's not quite as simple as all that. The VAX/VMS system includes a facility called PHONE that allows for direct, interactive written text communication between users.

Like any modern telephone system, VMS PHONE has a whole set of sophisticated features that Alexander Graham Bell never envisioned. They include conference calls, hold buttons, and facsimile transmission. Here is one way in which the system works:

You sign on to your VAX from a distant branch office and are reading your mail when you realize that you need some help from headquarters. You make a quick check of the names of the users signed on to the system and find that the account of the person you want is active. You "phone" him or her online and discuss the files you need. You learn that a coworker on another VAX system, tied in to the network from overseas, has the information you need. You put your first call on hold, dial up the European user, and reconnect the first party. The three of you watch the information stream into your account and then hold a three-way conversation.

When you enter VMS PHONE, your screen will split into three parts, a command input line at the top, a viewport with your node and user name for the display of messages you type into the system, and a viewport for the response from the called party. If you make a conference call, the screen will be subdivided further for additional users.

## PHONE COMMANDS

To enter a command from within the program PHONE, you must begin with the command character. The default character is the percent sign; PHONE will allow you to redefine the command character if necessary.

```
$ PHONE
```

Enters program and displays the PHONE command screen. At this point commands require a percent sign as the first character. To call another user, for example, enter:

```
%DIAL BLUEFISH
```

An alternate way to enter PHONE and place an immediate call is to enter the following from the VMS prompt:

```
$ PHONE BLUEFISH
```

This command enters the program and dials the user named Bluefish in one instruction.

The verb PHONE has several qualifiers that allow you to customize your account.

```
$ PHONE/NOSCROLL
```

determines how new lines of text are displayed on the screen as the viewing section of the screen becomes full. If the qualifier /NOSCROLL is used, text lines are wrapped and new text appears at the top line of the viewport. If /SCROLL, the default, is left in place, new text appears at the bottom of the viewport, and the text scrolls up and off the screen as new text is entered.

$ PHONE/SWITCH_HOOK="character"

allows you to select your own switch hook, or command character, to precede each command. The character can be any nonalphanumeric character. The default character is the percent mark. Here is an example of use of the command:

$ PHONE/SWITCH_HOOK="&"

to change the switch hook to an ampersand. The switch hook character is necessary if you are in a conversation on PHONE and you want to issue a program command. The default is the percent sign (%).

$ PHONE/VIEWPORT_SIZE=n

allows the user to choose the maximum number of lines in a viewport. The range is three to ten, with a default size of ten.

## DIALING A CALL

Placing a call to another VAX user is about as simple as can be. Just use the verb DIAL or the verb PHONE followed by the name of the called user account. If the user is on your default node, you do not need to add that information to the command.

PHONE KENNEDY

If you need to speak with a user in another node, add that information and a pair of colons before the user name:

DIAL BLUEFISH::TESSA

A third way to place a call is to enter the name of a user at the PHONE prompt; the system assumes the verb PHONE and places the call.

When you issue the command DIAL or PHONE, the computer will send a message to the party you are calling to indicate that you are phoning. The message will flash on the recipient's screen every ten seconds until:

1. The recipient answers the phone;
2. The recipient rejects the incoming call; or
3. The sender cancels the call by pressing any key on the keyboard.

## CONFERENCE CALLS

You can add as many as four other VAX users to your conversation in a conference call.

In setting up the conference, one participant who is already online serves as the operator, calling other users and adding them to the conversation. If you call someone who is already on the phone, only the direct recipient of your call can be added to your conference.

To add new parties to a conversation, just use the command DIAL or PHONE, preceded by the switch hook:

    %PHONE KENNEDY

## DIRECTORY ASSISTANCE

Since PHONE is an online interactive means of communication (as opposed to the send-and-hold design of VMS MAIL), the user you call must be signed on to the system and willing to accept a call. There are three ways to determine who is available for a phone conversation. First, you could just place the call and let the system inform you if the user is not online. Second, you could command SHOW USER from the VMS prompt and read the names of the accounts presently signed on. This will not tell you whether a particular user is willing to accept a broadcast message, and it could require you to exit PHONE, command SHOW USER, and then reenter PHONE. The most direct way to obtain a listing of available users is to use the PHONE command DIRECTORY:

    %DIRECTORY

lists users on the default node.

    %DIRECTORY BLUEFISH

lists users on another node.
The directory will list the following information for each user:

Process name
User name
Terminal device name
Phone status

The status indicator will tell you whether a particular user has issued the command SET BROADCAST=NONE from the VMS prompt. This command screens out all classes of messages, including VMS MAIL and VMS PHONE, from the issuer's terminal. SET also allows the user to screen out phone calls only; the command is SET NOPHONE.

## ANSWERING THE CALL

When you receive a broadcast message that you are being called, go to the VMS prompt and enter PHONE by typing

`$PHONE`

Once inside the program, type the command

`%ANSWER`

to complete the link to your caller.
If you are already in PHONE when a broadcast message comes in, simply type the switch hook plus ANSWER.

## HANGING UP

There are three ways to end a phone conversation.

`%EXIT`

ends a conversation with an automatic HANGUP command and then exits the program and returns the user to the VMS prompt.

    Ctrl-Z

when there is no ongoing conversation is equivalent to EXIT. Typing Ctrl-Z during a conversation merely ends the conversation, equivalent to HANGUP.

    %HANGUP

disconnects all links, including active conversations, calls on hold, and any caller who has placed you on hold. You will, however, stay within the program PHONE.

## SENDING A FILE FROM WITHIN VMS PHONE

The command FACSIMILE allows you to send the contents of a file to all participants in a conversation. The transmission of the file continues until the end of the file is reached or until the sender presses any key on the keyboard. The command:

    %FACSIMILE Filename

PHONE will continue to send the file until it reaches end of the file or until you type any key at your keyboard.

## HOW TO PHONE FOR HELP

VMS maintains a file of help messages within PHONE. To obtain assistance, issue the following command:

    %HELP

The system will display a list of help topics; a typical selection includes

| | | | | | |
|---|---|---|---|---|---|
| ANSWER | Characters | DIAL | DIRECTORY | EXIT | FACSIMILE |
| HANGUP | | | | | |
| HELP | HOLD | MAIL | REJECT | Switch_hook | |
| UNHOLD | | | | | |

A more direct route to help is to issue a specific command:

%HELP FACSIMILE

Here is an example of the system's response to the HELP FACSIMILE request:

VAX/VMS Phone Facility

Press any key to cancel the help information and continue.

FACSIMILE

The FACSIMILE command allows you to include the contents of a file into your conversation. It requires a file specification, and proceeds to send the contents of that file to everyone in the conversation. Thus the complete syntax is:

FACSIMILE file-spec

PHONE continues to send the file until it reaches end of file or until you type any key at your keyboard.

## PLACING A CALL ON HOLD

The user can temporarily suspend the link to participants in a one-on-one or conference call by issuing the command HOLD. A message is sent to each terminal announcing that the user has been put on hold.

The user can place other calls while a conversation is on hold.
To place a conversation on hold, issue the command

%HOLD

To resume a conversation, issue the command

%UNHOLD

## THE COMPUTER AS AN ANSWERING MACHINE

PHONE lets you leave a message with another user. This facility is useful if you call someone who is not online or if a user has rejected your call.

The command is as follows:

%MAIL [node::]user "message"

The node is necessary only if the recipient is not on your default node. The message itself can be no longer than one line. Here is an example:

%MAIL TESSA "Please phone me when you are available."

## REJECTING AN INCOMING PHONE CALL

While you are signed on to PHONE, you can reject an incoming request for a conversation. Adding the optional verb EXIT after the command will return you to the VMS prompt after you have rejected a call.

%REJECT

tells the calling party that his or her request for a phone conversation has been rejected. The sender of the REJECT will remain within PHONE.

%REJECT EXIT

rejects a call, exits PHONE, and returns the user to the VMS prompt.

Contrast this with SET BROADCAST=NONE, which signifies your account is offline for phone messages.

Here is an explanation of some of the keyboard characters you can use when it is your turn to "talk."

| | |
|---|---|
| Delete | Deletes the previous character from your screen as well as those of your "listeners." |
| Line feed | Deletes the previous word from your screen and from receiving viewports. |
| Return | Starts a new line. |
| Tab | Advances to the next tab stop. |
| Ctrl-G | Sounds the beeper at your terminal and at the terminal of any users linked to the conversation. |
| Ctrl-L | Clears all text in the viewport. |
| Ctrl-Q | Reopens your viewport to the receipt of text, negating a Ctrl-S. |
| Ctrl-S | Freezes your viewport to block further characters. |
| Ctrl-U | Clears the current line of the viewport. |
| Ctrl-W | Refreshes (redraws) the entire screen. |
| Ctrl-Z | HANGUP if used during a conversation; EXIT if used when no conversation is under way. |

# Appendix D

# The VT-Series Terminals

There are three major families of terminals in use with VAXs: the VT-100, VT-200, and VT-300 series. Each series was designed by Digital and is still supported by the company. When we talk about the VT series, we are talking about a specific line of Digital terminals as well as a whole marketplace of VT-compatible terminals from third-party manufacturers. The third parties typically compete with Digital on the basis of price or features.

Of the three families, the VT-200 series is the most widely used, supplanting the older VT-100s in almost every instance. According to the company, it had sold more than a million terminals by mid-1987, when Digital's VT-300 series was introduced. The initial release of the VT-300 family comprised three models—a monochrome alphanumeric text terminal, a monochrome graphics model, and a color graphics terminal.

The VT-200 family added its advanced features to those of the VT-100 series; similarly, the VT-300s include a superset of the features and commands of the VT-200s. Digital made several changes with its VT-300 family. The VT-320 text terminal broke a price barrier at its launch as well as enhancing the resolution of the screen. The VT-330 (Figure D-1) and VT-340 include better screens, while adding a new capability, that of maintaining connections to two separate hosts, or two separate sessions on a single host, over a single standard cable connection.

Here are some of the features of the models in the VT-200 and VT-300 lines. You can expect competitive models from third-party manufacturers to equal or surpass the specifications for each device.

**VT-220.** Twelve-inch curved nonglare monochrome screen. Resolution is 800 pixels across by 240 lines in depth. In 80-column mode, characters are displayed in a 7x9-dot matrix. In 132-column mode, characters are displayed in a 7x12-dot matrix. Includes ASCII, Digital Special Graphics, Digital Supplemental Graphics character sets. Communicates at speeds from 75 to 19.2 Kb/s. Includes twenty-five-pin EIA RS-232C, 20mA current loop host port connector, nine-pin printer port connector, and composite video output.

**VT-240.** Twelve-inch nonglare monochrome screen, available in white, green, or amber phosphor. Resolution is 800 pixels across by 240 lines in depth. In 80-column mode, characters are dis-

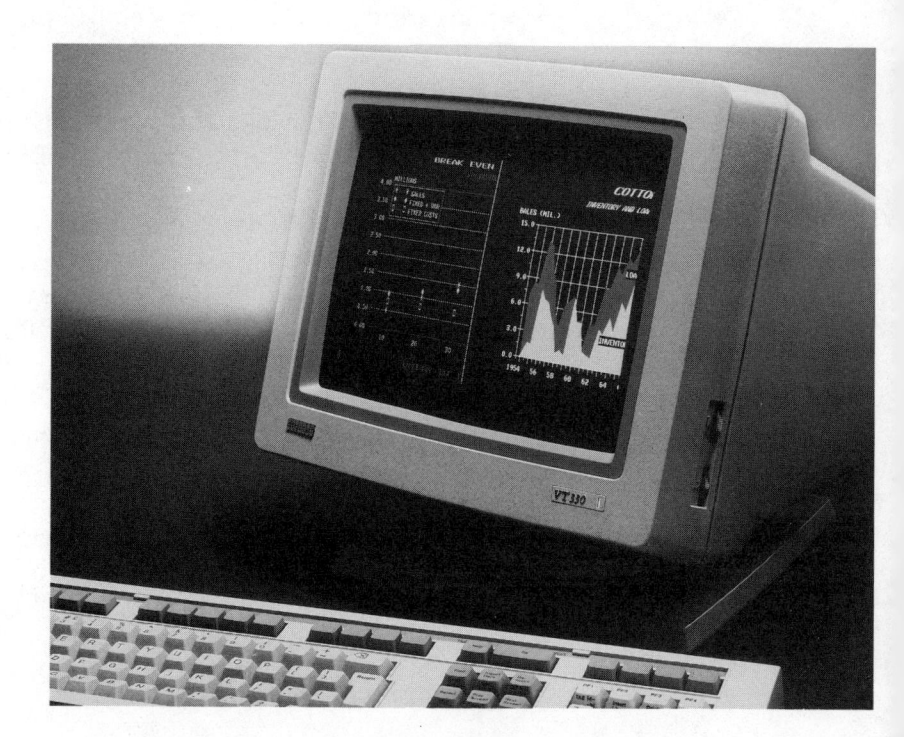

*Figure D-1*

played in an 8x10-dot matrix. In 132-column mode, characters are displayed in a 5x10-dot matrix. Supports ReGIS, Tektronix 4010, and Tektronix 4014 graphics protocols. Includes ASCII, UK National, Digital Special Graphics, Digital Supplemental Graphics character sets. Communicates at speeds from 75 b/s to 19.2 Kb/s. Includes EIA RS-232C, RS-423, and 20mA interfaces.

**VT-241.** Thirteen-inch nonglare color screen with four colors displayable from a palette of sixty-four. Resolution is 800 pixels across by 240 lines in depth. In 80-column mode, characters are displayed in an 8x10-dot matrix. In 132-column mode, characters are displayed in a 5x10-dot matrix. Supports ReGIS, Tektronix 4010, and Tektronix 4014 graphics protocols. Includes ASCII, UK National, Digital Special Graphics, Digital Supplemental Graphics character sets. Communicates at speeds from 75 to 19.2 Kb/s. Includes EIA RS-232C, RS-423, and 20mA interfaces.

**VT-320.** Fourteen-inch flat-surface antiglare monochrome screen, available in paper white, green, or amber phosphor. Resolution is 1,200 pixels across by 300 lines in depth. In 80-column mode, characters are displayed in a 7x12-dot matrix. In 132-column mode, characters are displayed in a 7x7-dot matrix. Includes ASCII (seven-bit National Replacement Character Set) and eight-bit ISO Latin 1 international character sets (on international models), and Digital Special Graphic (VT-100 line drawing) set. Communicates at speeds from 75 b/s to 19.2 Kb/s. Includes six-pin RS-423 host port and six-pin RS-423 printer port. International model adds twenty-five-pin EIA RS-232C host port. (See Figures D-2 and D-3 for a comparison of the I/O ports between the VT-220 and VT-330 series.)

**VT-330.** Fourteen-inch flat-surface antiglare monochrome screen, available in paper white, green or amber phosphor, with the ability to display graphics in four shades of gray. Resolution is 800 pixels across by 500 lines in depth. In 80-column mode, characters are displayed in an 8x11 or 9x11-dot matrix. In 132-column mode, characters are displayed in a 4x9 or 5x9-dot matrix. Includes up to six pages of local memory. Supports ReGIS, Sixel, Tektronix 4010, and Tektronix 4014 graphics protocols. Includes ASCII (seven-bit National Replacement Character Set) and eight-bit ISO Latin 1 international character sets, and Digital Technical character set. Communicates at speeds from 75 b/s to 19.2 K/bs. Includes EIA RS-232C, three RS-423, and MicroDIN connector for mouse, tablet, or other device.

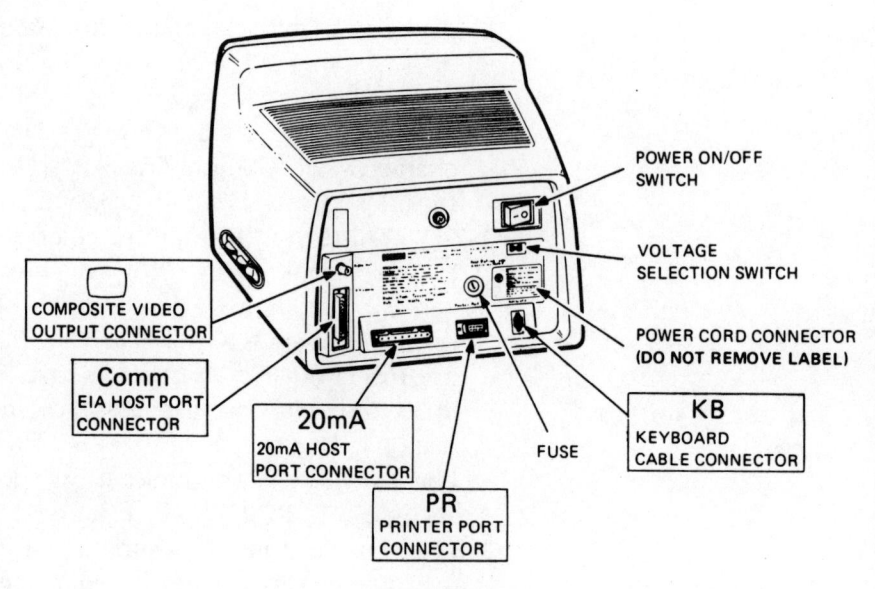

*Figure D-2*

**VT-340.** Thirteen-inch convex antiglare color screen with 16 colors displayable from a palette of 4,096 colors. Resolution is 800 pixels across by 500 lines in depth. In 80-column mode, characters are displayed in an 8x11 or 9x11-dot matrix. In 132-column mode, characters are displayed in a 4x9 or 5x9-dot matrix. Includes up to six pages of local memory. Supports ReGIS, Sixel, Tektronix 4010, and Tektronix 4014 graphics protocols. Includes ASCII (seven-bit National Replacement Character Set) and eight-bit ISO Latin 1, international character sets, and DEC Technical. Communicates at speeds from 75 b/s to 19.2 Kb/s. Includes EIA RS-232C, three RS-423, and MicroDIN connector for mouse, tablet, or other device.

## CHARACTER ATTRIBUTES

Table D-1 indicates the various character attributes of the three principal alphanumeric terminals. The pattern is generally followed by third-party clones, although some manufacturers have enhanced these capabilities.

*Figure D-3*

**Table D-1.** Compatibility Chart

|  | VT-320 | VT-220 | VT-102 |
|---|---|---|---|
| **Character Attributes** | | | |
| Blinking | Yes | Yes | Yes |
| Bold | Yes | Yes | Yes |
| Double height | Yes | Yes | Yes |
| Double width | Yes | Yes | Yes |
| Reverse video | Yes | Yes | Yes |
| Underline | Yes | Yes | Yes |
| **Character Sets** | | | |
| ASCII | Yes | Yes | No* |
| DEC Special Graphics | Yes | Yes | Yes |
| DEC Supplemental Graphics | Yes | Yes | No |
| Downline loadable | Yes | Yes | No |
| ISO Latin 1 | Yes | No | No |
| National replacement (NRC) | Yes | Yes | No** |

## Table D-1. (continued)

|  | VT-320 | VT-220 | VT-102 |
|---|---|---|---|
| **Communication** | | | |
| Baud rate to 19.2 K | Yes | Yes | Yes |
| Composite video output | No | Yes | Yes |
| Communication ports: | | | |
|   DEC-423 serial | Yes | No | No |
|   RS-232 serial | Yes | Yes | Yes |
|   20 milliamp | No | Yes | Yes |
| Optional internal modem | No | Yes | No |
| Printer port | | | |
|   Connector | 6-pin DEC-423 | 9-pin RS-232 | 25-pin RS-232 |
|   Bidirectional | Yes | Yes | Yes |
| **Compatibility** | | | |
| VT-52 | Yes | Yes | Yes |
| VT-100 | Yes | Yes | Yes |
| VT-102 | Yes | Yes | Yes |
| VT-220 | Yes | Yes | No |
| Conformance Level | 3 | 2 | 1 |
|  | (VT-300 mode) | (VT-200 mode) | (VT-100 mode) |
| **Display Features** | | | |
| Character cell | | | |
|   80 columns | 10x20 | 10x10 | 7x10 |
|   132 columns | 6x20 | 6x10 | 6x10 |
| Display size (diagonal) | 14 in. | 12 in. | 12 in. |
| Display type | Flat | Convex | Convex |
| Nonglare screen | Etched | Coated | Coated |
| Pixel aspect ratio | Square | Rectangular | Rectangular |
| **External Features** | | | |
| Rear panel cable cover | Yes | No | No |
| Tilt-swivel base | Optional | No | No |
| 25th status line | Yes | No | No |

*VT-102 terminal's United States character set differs slightly from the ASCII set.
**VT-102 terminal's United Kingdom character set differs slightly from the United Kingdom NRC set.

## OPERATING MODES

The VT-220's four operating modes for communications are selectable by the user:

**VT-200 mode, seven-bit controls.** This is the standard setting. It produces standard ANSI functions and the full range of the VT-220's capabilities, communicating with a host computer and application programs via control characters made up of seven bits of code.

**VT-200 mode, eight-bit controls.** Same as the previous setting, with the addition of an eighth bit in control characters. Use this setting only when an application program or a modification to your host computer's operating system requires it.

**VT-100 mode.** This setting selects a subset of the VT-220's capabilities to emulate the standard ANSI functions and the character set and control characters of the VT-100 line. Use this setting only when an application program or operating system requires use of the less capable VT-100 terminal or its equivalent.

**VT-52 mode.** This text-only mode emulates Digital's VT-52 terminal and its proprietary functions. Use this setting only when an application program or operating system requires use of the less capable VT-52 terminal or its equivalent.

## THE STANDARD DIGITAL KEYBOARD

The standard keyboard for VT-200 and VT-300 terminals is called the LK-201. There have been minor adjustments by Digital as well as some minor and not-so-minor changes by third-party manufacturers, but the general layout has remained the same.

Some application programs, such as word processors, may assign nonstandard functions to some keys. Some such software comes with replacement key caps to indicate the new definitions. Do not replace the VT-220 key caps unless you will be using that application quite heavily. If you make this change, save the original keycaps in case you change programs or move the terminal. Digital and some third-party companies also sell versions of their keyboards with special notations on the front face of the key caps for such command-driven programs as WPS-Plus, Digital's most common word processor.

The LK-201 keyboard (Figure D-4) has four areas: the main keyboard, an editing keypad, an auxiliary numeric keypad, and function keys, each discussed below.

**Main Keyboard**

Very much like a standard typewriter keyboard, this section includes the alphabet, numerals 0 through 9, punctuation marks, and the following:

| | |
|---|---|
| Tab | Moves the cursor to the next tab stop. |
| Shift | Holding down the shift key and typing another key yields an uppercase character. This can be a capital letter or a special character. Some control-key combinations act differently in the shifted and unshifted mode. |
| Ctrl | The control key is like a shift key. Just as a shift-A sends "A" instead of "a," Ctrl-A sends a different character, usually a command or part of one. The user invokes a control character by holding down the control key while typing a second character. |
| Lock | This locks the alphabetic keys into their shifted equivalents. Unaffected are the numeric keys, function keys, and other special keys. |
| Return | This key has different meanings depending upon the context or assignment given it. Pressing Return generates either a carriage return or a carriage return plus line feed, as determined by the setup. It can also signify 'Enter' in communication with the operating system or an application program. |
| Delete | This key sends a "delete" to the computer. In most applications this command erases one character to the left of the cursor. A shift-delete combination produces a "cancel" character. The effect of the "cancel" is determined by the application program. |
| Compose | This key allows the user to send special commands or characters not standard on the keyboard. |

THE STANDARD DIGITAL KEYBOARD □ 263

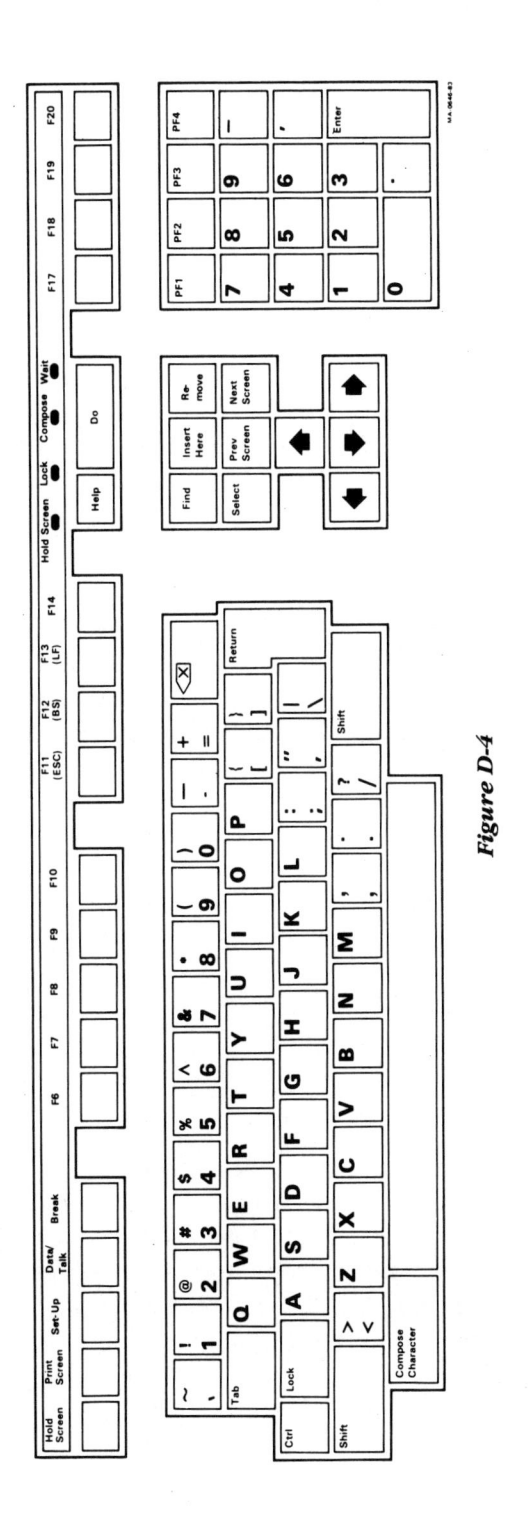

*Figure D-4*

**Editing Keypad**

This section of the keyboard is used to send commands to the computer to move the on-screen cursor and manipulate text or other data.

Cursor keys

These four keys move the cursor in the direction of the arrow shown on them. The right cursor key used at the end of a line moves the cursor to the beginning of the next line and vice-versa. This is called line wrap. Note that the behavior of cursor keys may vary slightly from application to application; line wrap may be disabled, for example.

Editing commands

These keys ask the application program or the operating system to perform certain tasks: Prev Screen displays the previous twenty-four or twenty-five lines of text; Next Screen displays the next twenty-four or twenty-five lines of text. These keys can be used as quick substitutes for the cursor keys in many, but not all, application programs. The keys Find, Remove, Select, and Insert Here can generate certain editing functions in certain application programs.

**Auxiliary Keypad**

The auxiliary, or numeric, keypad is intended for entering numeric data as if to a calculator. The four function keys, PF1, PF2, PF3, and PF4, can be assigned special functions by the application program. Further, some programs, word processors chief among them, will assign this area of the keyboard to special editing commands. The enter key on this keypad may be used to transmit commands or data, as a return key, or for special purposes, including setup of the screen.

## Function Keys

The keyboard includes a number of special keys that can issue predefined codes or commands and which application programs can use to perform various functions. Function keys are found across the top of the keyboard as well as in the auxiliary keypad.

### Top-Row Function Keys

Across the top of the VT-220 keyboard are twenty special-purpose keys that command the operating system or certain application programs. Although applications can assign custom functions to these keys, the VT-220 is supplied with preassigned functions:

Hold Screen
: This key freezes the on-screen display and is particularly useful when looking at information that is larger than the normal twenty-five lines of display and would otherwise scroll off the screen too fast to be read. The key acts as a toggle; strike it once to hold the screen, and again to release the screen.

Print Screen
: This key, if enabled by the operating system or an application program, will send the text on the screen to the printer. This is a quick means to obtain a copy of downloaded data or a portion of a data file. Typing Ctrl–Print Screen sets or resets the auto-print mode.

Setup
: This key temporarily disconnects the terminal from the host and displays the setup screen.

Data/Talk
: Infrequently used and eliminated in the VT-300 series, this key works in conjunction with a modem connected to the EIA modem port on the terminal.

Break
: A multiple-function key.
**Break**. Sends a break command if such authorization is given in the setup configuration.
**Shift-Break**. Initiates a disconnect.
**Ctrl-Break**. Sends to the host computer the message selected in the setup configuration.

### Other Function Keys

The following keys are given special assignments by many applications programs.

F11    In VT-100 and VT-52 modes, F11 sends an ESC (escape) character to the host computer.

F12    In VT-100 and VT-52 modes, F12 sends a backspace character to the host computer.

F13    In VT-100 and VT-52 modes, F13 sends a line feed character to the host computer.

Help    This key calls for context-sensitive help from within many application programs.

Do    This key has special functions in some application programs.

## Visual Indicators

The keyboard includes four status lights that indicate previously issued commands:

Hold screen    Glows when the screen is frozen.

Lock    Glows when the shift lock key has been struck, showing that uppercase letters will be generated.

Compose    Glows when the user is in the midst of issuing a multikey compose command.

Wait    A signal that the host computer is unable to accept new information from the terminal. If the keyboard remains unlocked, the user can command CLEAR COMMUNICATIONS from the setup menus.

## Audible Indicators

Audible feedback helps interpret the keyboard and software.

Keyclick    This option gives audible assurance that a typed key has been properly delivered from the keyboard. Essentially it is an audible aid for the very light typist. If you punch the keys so hard they bottom out and click by themselves, this feature is of no value; and some users would rather have near-silence as they type. The keyclick can be turned off from the setup menus. Note that the

|          | shift and control keys never generate a click, since they are intended to be used only in combination with other keys. |
|----------|---|
| Bell     | The bell sounds during the automatic self-test at power-up and when the computer receives the character BEL (bell) from the host. Depending upon the setup, the bell can also sound when a compose error is made or when the cursor approaches the right margin. The term "bell" is a holdover from the old mechanical teletype days. With modern terminals the same ASCII code is used to generate the signal, but the resulting sound is an electronic beep, not a bell. |

## Control Commands

The control key serves as another shift key on the LK-201 keyboard. In various application programs, the keyboard can issue any number of special commands by combining alphabetic characters with the control, control-shift, or control-Alt commands.

As delivered, the LK-201 keyboard will issue the following commands from the DCL prompt:

| Ctrl-A or F14* | Sets DCL into insert mode rather than overstrike. Useful in editing a DCL line already on your screen. The default for this mode is commanded with SET TERMINAL/LINE_EDIT and is reset at the beginning of each line. |
|---|---|
| Ctrl-B | Recalls and displays previous DCL commands, starting with the most recent entry and working backward through the last twenty commands in the recall arrow buffer. Displayed commands can be edited; the arrow keys move the cursor to the point to be edited. New typing will overwrite existing letters unless Ctrl-A is issued to set DCL into insert mode. Typing Enter sends the command to the computer for execution. |
| Ctrl-C or F6* | Interrupts a command or program. Use care with this command and Ctrl-Y while in a program with an open file. In certain circumstances the use of an interrupt command can |

| | |
|---|---|
| | lose a working file. Displays a statement of cancellation on screen. |
| Ctrl-D or Left Arrow | In line editing moves the cursor one character to the left. |
| Ctrl-E | In line editing moves the cursor to the end of the line. |
| Ctrl-F or Right Arrow | In line editing moves the cursor one character to the right. |
| Ctrl-H or F12* or Backspace | In line editing moves the cursor to the beginning of the line. |
| Ctrl-I | Tab. Preset at eight spaces, the tab can be reset in various editing programs. |
| Ctrl-J or Line Feed or F13* | Deletes the word to the left of the cursor. |
| Ctrl-K | Advances the current line to the next vertical tab position. |
| Ctrl-L | Calls up the beginning of the next page. This key is ignored when line editing is enabled. |
| Ctrl-O | Suppresses the display on a terminal. The command does not interrupt or stop execution but merely darkens the screen. Typing the command again resumes display. Displayed on the screen as "Output off" and "Output on" respectively. |
| Ctrl-Q | Restarts terminal output to the screen or an I/O port that has been suspended by Ctrl-S. |
| Ctrl-R | Retypes the current input line and leaves the cursor at the end of the line. |
| Ctrl-S | Suspends terminal output to the screen or I/O port. To restart use Ctrl-Q. |
| Ctrl-T | Temporarily suspends terminal output to display information about the process running in your account on the VAX. Information includes your user name, the time, the sort of process you are running, and the total amount of CPU time you have used since you logged in. |
| | Invoking the process display does not affect execution of your called command or program, and the system will resume terminal output after the line has been displayed. |

|  |  |
|---|---|
|  | Ctrl-T will work only if the systemwide login command file includes the specification SET CONTROL=T or if the user adds the line to his own LOGIN.COM file or enters it as an interactive command. |
| Ctrl-U | Clears the command line without executing it. In line editing mode, Ctrl-U deletes characters from the beginning of the line to the cursor position. |
| Ctrl-V | In line editing mode, allows the user to enter one of the line editing function keys but suppresses the line editing function. Can be used to enter control sequence in text rather than initiating the edit function. |
| Ctrl-W | Redraws, or refreshes, the screen. This can be used to eliminate error messages, system notices, or mail notices that may have appeared on the screen. |
| Ctrl-X | Discards the current line by clearing out the type-ahead buffer, also causing the computer to disregard commands not yet executed. |
| Ctrl-Y | Interrupts a command or program and returns the user to the DCL prompt.** |

---

*Keys available on the LK-201 keyboard, used with VT-200 and VT-300 terminals.

**The user can choose whether to enable or disable Ctrl-Y and Ctrl-T. Some applications automatically shut off this capability as part of their protection schemes. To disable Ctrl-T or Ctrl-Y, enter the following from the DCL prompt:

```
$ SET NO_CONTROL=T
```

or

```
$ SET NO_CONTROL=Y
```

To restore to the default condition, enter:

```
$ SET CONTROL = T
```

or

```
$ SET CONTROL = Y
```

| | |
|---|---|
| Ctrl-Z or F10 | Notifies the computer that the end of data has been reached. Used to end a file under CREATE, MAIL, PHONE, and other modes. Displayed on screen with the message "Exit." |
| Delete | Removes the last character entered. Labeled "rubout" on some keyboards. |
| Tab | Moves the cursor or printhead to the next tab stop. |
| Down Arrow | Displays the next line in the command recall buffer. See Ctrl-B or Up Arrow. |

## Composing Characters

VT-200 and VT-300 terminals are not limited to the characters that appear on the LK-201 keyboard. Compose sequences consist of the Compose character followed by two other characters. To compose a special character you press the Compose key, then press one or two additional keys to produce the desired symbol from the Compose symbol table in your terminal manual.

Characters can be selected from the character set selected from the setup menu. The default character set is the DEC multinational set. Make sure that Compose is enabled (the ordinary setting) within the keyboard setup screen.

Compose characters are generated using either a three-stroke or a two-stroke sequence.

Three-stroke sequences can be generated on all keyboards by first pressing Compose Character and then striking two other keys that are among the recognized sequences. Two-stroke sequences can be generated on all keyboards except for North American keyboards and are initiated with what Digital calls a "nonspacing diacritical mark"—essentially a grave accent, acute accent, circumflex accent, tilde, dieresis mark [umlaut] or ring mark. These diacritical marks are not present on most North American keyboards.

To compose a character, find the one you want in the first column of the table that follows. Press Compose Character on the keyboard. The Compose light will illuminate, indicating that the terminal is in the middle of a compose operation. Then type the two characters in the second column for the character you are composing. A portion of the Compose Table for the multinational character set is reproduced in Table D-2.

When the sequence is completed, the composed character appears on the screen and the Compose indicator light turns off.

If you attempt to use an invalid sequence, the terminal will end the compose sequence and sound a warning bell. If you make a mistake and wish to end the sequence or start over, use any of the following characters:

Tab
Return
Enter
Any function key in the top row
The period key on the numeric keypad
Any combination of Ctrl and another key

If you strike Compose Character while composing a character, a new compose sequence begins at that point and the original sequence is canceled.

## Type-Ahead Buffer

One of the features of the VAX is a special section of memory, referred to as a type-ahead buffer, that stores commands issued from the keyboard but not yet executed by the computer — typically commands issued while the VAX was processing another command.

This is in effect an extension of the abilities of the terminal.

Commands enter into the type-ahead buffer after they have been sent to the computer when the return key is struck. The commands are executed in FIFO order.

The Digital VT-200 and VT-300 terminals have a buffer with a capacity of 256 and 254 characters respectively. When the buffer fills to the 64- or 128-character level (as selected in the setup menus) the terminal sends an XOFF to the host computer. This signals the host to stop sending more characters. A second XOFF is sent at 220 characters if the host computer continues to transmit, and a third warning is sent if the buffer becomes completely full.

When the buffer falls below 32 characters, an XON signal is sent to the host computer to tell it to resume transmitting.

If you have made an error in typing in a command and it has not yet been executed, or if you change your mind about a command in the buffer, you can clear the type-ahead buffer by striking Ctrl-X.

**Table D-2.** Compose Sequence for Multinational Characters

| (1) | | (2) | (3)[b] | (1) | | (2) | (3)[b] |
|---|---|---|---|---|---|---|---|
| " | quotation mark | "(sp)[a] | "(sp) | ± | plus or minus sign | +− | |
| # | number sign | ++ | | ² | superscript 2 | 2^ | |
| ' | apostrophe | '(sp) | '(sp) | ³ | superscript 3 | 3^ | |
| @ | commercial at | A A | | µ | micro sign | /U* | |
| [ | opening bracket | (( | | ¶ | paragraph sign | P! | |
| \ | backslash | // or /< | | · | middle dot | .^ | |
| ] | closing bracket | )) | | ¹ | superscript 1 | 1^ | |
| ^ | circumflex accent | ^(sp) | ^(sp) | º | masculine ordinal | O_ | |
| ` | grave accent | `(sp) | `(sp) | ›› | closed angle brackets | >> | |
| { | opening brace | (- | | ¼ | fraction one-quarter | 1 4* | |
| \| | vertical line | /^ | | ½ | fraction one-half | 1 2* | |
| } | closing brace | )- | | ¿ | inverted ? | ?? | |
| ~ | tilde | ~(sp) | ~(sp) | À | A grave | A` | `A |
| ¡ | inverted ! | !! | | Á | A acute | A' | 'A |
| ¢ | cent sign | C/ or C\| | | Â | A circumflex | A^ | ^A |
| £ | pound sign | L- or L= | | Ã | A tilde | A~ | ~A |
| ¥ | yen sign | Y- or Y= | | Ä | A umlaut | A" or "A | "A |
| § | section sign | SO or S! or S0 | | Å | A ring | A* or A° (degree sign) | °A |
| ¤ | currency sign | XO or X0 | | Æ | A E diphthong | AE* | |
| © | copyright sign | CO or C0 | | Ç | C cedilla | C, | |
| ª | feminine ordinal | A_ | | È | E grave | E` | `E |
| « | open angle brackets | << | | É | E acute | E' | 'E |
| Ë | E umlaut | E" or "E | "E | Ê | E circumflex | E^ | ^E |
| Ì | I grave | I` | `I | å | a ring | a* or a° (degree sign) | °a |
| Í | I acute | I' | 'I | | | | |
| Î | I circumflex | I^ | ^I | æ | a e diphthong | a e* | |
| Ï | I umlaut | I" or "I | "I | ç | c cedilla | c, (comma) | |
| Ñ | N tilde | N~ | ~N | è | e grave | e` | `e |

**Table D-2.** (continued)

| (1) |  | (2) | (3)[b] | (1) |  | (2) | (3)[b] |
|---|---|---|---|---|---|---|---|
| Ò | O grave | O ` | `O | é | e acute | e' | 'e |
| Ó | O acute | O ' | 'O | ê | e circumflex | e^ | ^e |
| Ô | O circumflex | O^ | ^O | ë | e umlaut | e" or "e | "e |
| Õ | O tilde | O~ | ~O | ì | i grave | i` | `i |
| Ö | O umlaut | O" or "O | "O | í | i acute | i' | 'i |
| Œ | O E diphthong[c] | O E* |  | î | i circumflex | i^ | ^i |
| Ø | O slash | o/ |  | ï | i umlaut | i" or "i | "i |
| Ù | U grave | U` | `U | ñ | n tilde | n~ | ~n |
| Ú | U acute | U' | 'U | ò | o grave | o` | `o |
| Û | U circumflex | U^ | ^U | ó | o acute | o' | 'o |
| Ü | U umlaut | U" or "U | "U | ô | o circumflex | a^ | ^o |
| Ÿ | Y umlaut[c] | Y" or "Y | "Y | õ | o tilde | o~ | ~o |
| ß | German small sharp s | ss |  | ö | o umlaut | o" or "o | "o |
| ° | degree sign | 0^ |  | œ | o e diphthong[c] | o e* |  |
| à | a grave | a` | `a | ù | u grave | u` | `u |
| á | a acute | a' | 'a | ú | u acute | u' | 'u |
| â | a circumflex | a^ | ^a | û | u circumflex | u^ | ^u |
| ã | a tilde | a~ | ~a | ü | u umlaut | u" or "u | "u |
| ä | a umlaut | a" or "a | "a | ÿ | y umlaut[c] | y" or "y | "y |
| NBSP | no break space | sp sp |  | ´ | acute accent | ' |  |
| ¦ | broken vertical bar | \| \| or ! |  | ¸ | cedilla | , , |  |
| ¬ | logical not | -,* |  | ¨ | diaresis | " " | "(sp) |
| | soft (syllable) hyphen | - - |  | Ý | Y acute | Y' | 'Y |
| ® | registered trademark | R O |  | ý | y acute | y' | 'y |
| — | macron | -^ |  | Þ | capital Icelandic thorn | T H |  |
| ¾ | three quarters | 3 4* |  | þ | small Icelandic thorn | t h |  |
| ÷ | division sign | -: |  | Ð | capital Icelandic Eth | -D |  |
| × | multiplication sign | x x |  | ð | small Icelandic Eth | -d |  |
| ø | o slash | o/ |  |  |  |  |  |

[a] (sp) = space bar.

[b] You must type the characters for these sequences in the order shown (includes all two-stroke and some three-stroke sequences).

[c] This character is available only when you use the DEC Multinational character set.

[d] These characters are available only when you use the ISO Latin-1 multinational character set.

# Appendix E

# Serial Communications Notebook

In any host computer environment, the issue of serial communications is an important one. The majority of terminals connect to VAXs over serial lines; many printers use serial connections to a host or terminal server; and all modem and dial-up links involve serial communications.

This section discusses the popular RS-232C serial communications standard, showing the physical connections required and presenting some of the problems you are likely to encounter because of the loose interpretation of the standards among some hardware and software vendors.

## A MATTER OF STANDARDS

We all take it for granted that when we buy a package of hundred-watt light bulbs, they will screw into the sockets in the lamps in our home. We also assume that the lamp will have a plug that fits properly into the electrical outlet and that the outlet will provide voltage in the proper range. Finally, we feel confident that the bulb that carries a rating of sixteen hundred lumens will glow at an expected, repeatable intensity equal to other bulbs with the same rating.

We take all of this for granted because there is an established set of standards: hardware specifications for the bulb, socket, and plug, and outlet; a "software" standard for voltage, and an agreed-upon measure of brightness for the bulb's rating.

So it must be with computer telecommunications. Consider the following process:

You sit down at a computer keyboard to send a message across the country. The keyboard is familiar because the pressures of the marketplace have worked to make all such devices quite similar. Further, virtually all typewriter keyboards in this country have the same arrangement of keys—the so-called QWERTY layout.

You start by typing "hello," which you assume the recipient will understand, since you share language. If you were French speakers, you would start by typing "bonjour." If you were multilingual, you might start by typing "hello," and the called person might be able to translate the message into "bonjour"; communication would continue.

We are able to use written characters for this spoken word because we have a standard alphabet. The computer understands the typed characters after it looks them up and converts them to 0s and 1s in another standard—ASCII code.

Next, the computer sends those 0s and 1s to a modem. Converted to a standard modulated signal, the signal can travel over a nationally standardized telephone system across the country. At the other end, another modem demodulates the signal and reconverts it to 0s and 1s for the computer to look up in its table and translate to characters.

The final step calls for the human mind to convert the lines on a video screen to the outlines of characters, pick out the words, and finally, read the message.

Here's an illustration of the process, with the telecommunications standards indicated alongside:

# A MATTER OF STANDARDS  277

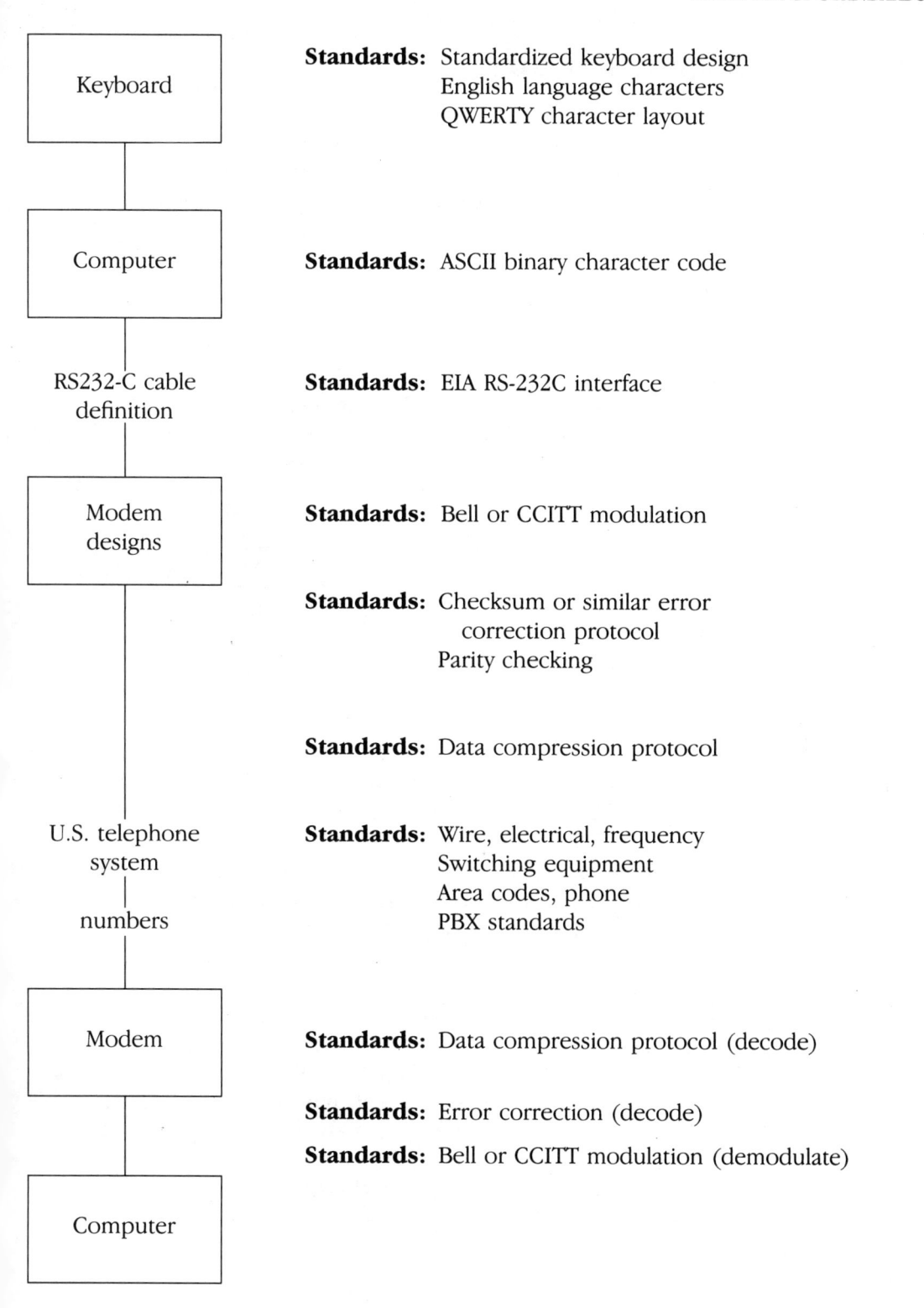

**Keyboard**

**Standards:** Standardized keyboard design
English language characters
QWERTY character layout

**Computer**

**Standards:** ASCII binary character code

RS232-C cable definition

**Standards:** EIA RS-232C interface

**Modem designs**

**Standards:** Bell or CCITT modulation

**Standards:** Checksum or similar error correction protocol
Parity checking

**Standards:** Data compression protocol

U.S. telephone system

numbers

**Standards:** Wire, electrical, frequency
Switching equipment
Area codes, phone
PBX standards

**Modem**

**Standards:** Data compression protocol (decode)

**Standards:** Error correction (decode)

**Standards:** Bell or CCITT modulation (demodulate)

**Computer**

## THE RS-232C NONSTANDARD STANDARD

The spinal cord for most microcomputer telecommunication is an RS-232C cable. The "recommended standard" used is a creation of the Electronic Industries Association (EIA), a United States trade association.[17] The standard was created in 1969 to establish once and for all the official way to make an interface between data terminal equipment (DTE) and data communications equipment (DCE) using serial digital data transmission. In most cases today, an item of DTE is more commonly referred to as a computer; an item of DCE is a modem or a printer.

The importance of the RS-232C standard is that it assigns certain types of signals to certain wires, or pins, in a standard twenty-five-pin cable. The standard defined the EIA position on characteristics of electrical signals, the mechanical elements of the connection, and a functional assignment for interchange circuits. The RS-232C specification guarantees the integrity of signals transmitted up to fifty feet. In practice data integrity will probably be all right at lengths of as much as two hundred feet. Use of special cable and signal repeaters can increase that distance.

With this in mind, you might think any computer or modem whose manufacturer claimed to adhere to the RS-232C standard would work with any other computer or modem following the same rules.

Unfortunately, not everything is so neat and simple. It seems that the EIA drafters decided not to require that DCE and DTE interfaces be identical at both ends nor that all wires be connected straight through from one end to another. Finally, though they ordered use of a DB-25 connector plug, they made no official pronouncement as to which end needed to be male and which end female.

To make things even more complicated, Apple's implementation of the RS-232C standard does not include the DB-25 plug for the Macintosh. Apple is not alone. The IBM PC serial port adapter terminates in a male connector; most other machines terminate their serial interfaces with a female outlet. Furthermore, the IBM PC AT terminates with a nonstandard nine-pin C-shell, sort of like the miniplug used by Apple but not the same. Users must purchase an adapter cable to attach the nine-pin PC-AT to a standard twenty-five-pin RS-232C cable.

Finally, taking a page from *Alice in Wonderland*, the EIA says that there are actually thirteen standard but different implementations of the signal connections for an RS-232C interface. They've designated them A to M, but just to make absolutely certain that even that attempt at standardization is of no value, they added Interface Type Z. What is Z? Why, it's "anything else."

Do you have any doubt as to why one of the growth areas of microcomputers in the past several years has been specialty cables? If you find an outfit that is able to understand your system and work with you, consider yourself well-armed.

## An Expedition Across an RS-232C Cable

Actually, the twenty-five pins of the RS-232C cable are far more than are needed for most ordinary serial communication. (See Table E-1.) For full duplex telecommunications between an IBM PC and a modem, for example, only ten pins are used. Here is a representation of communication using an IBM or IBM-like standard for microcomputers, indicating first the pin assignment, then the official RS-232C name for the signal, and finally a translation of the purpose of the wire.

**Table E-1.** Common RS-232 PIN Assignments

| DTE (Computer) | | DCE (Modem) | The Message |
|---|---|---|---|
| 1 | Frame ground | 1 | |
| 2 | Transmit data | 2 | "Sending data." |
| 3 | Receive data | 3 | "Receiving data." |
| 4 | Request to send | 4 | "May I send?" |
| 5 | Clear to send | 5 | "Yes, you may." |
| 6 | Data set ready | 6 | "The modem is ready." |
| 7 | Signal ground | 7 | Common signal wire |
| 8 | Data carrier detect | 8 | "The link is okay." |
| 20 | Data ready terminal | 20 | "The terminal is ready." |
| 22 | Ring indicator | 22 | "The phone is ringing." |

Here's another way to look at the link: a guided tour from computer to modem to modem to computer using an RS-232C interface and cable.

1. The computer (DTE) raises the voltage on pin 20, signaling to the modem (DCE) that the computer is ready to communicate. The signal is called data terminal ready.

2. The telephone number is dialed, either manually by the user or by the modem under direction of software.
3. The remote, or answering, modem at the other end of the phone line detects the incoming ring signal and sends back an answer in the form of a carrier signal.
4. The dialing, or originating, modem detects the carrier tone and raises the voltage on two wires going back to the computer: data set ready on pin 6 and the data carrier detect on pin 8. (The official Bell term for modem is "data set".)
5. The computer asks permission to send information by raising the voltage on pin 4, request to send (RTS).
6. The modem responds to the RTS query with a clear to send (CTS) signal on pin 5.
7. Data begins to flow from the computer to the modem, which converts it from digital 0s and 1s to an analog warble. Data is sent out on line 2 and enters the receiving computer on pin 3. Both computers continually monitor lines 4, 6, 8, and 20 to determine that communication is possible. This is the hardware handshaking.

See Table E-2 for a complete list of Pin assignments.

## NONSTANDARD STANDARD CABLES

In the simplest scheme of all, a computer could be connected to a modem with just three wires: the signal ground on pin 7, the transmitted data on pin 2, and the received data incoming on pin 3. In such an arrangement, of course, there is no handshaking between systems to arrange for timing and error checking, and it would probably be best not to use such a cable with a "smart" modem—with timing, error checking, and other functions built in—since it could become confused by the unorthodox wiring scheme.

In many short-distance applications, the easiest way to connect two computers is through a direct link between their serial ports, using an RS-232C cable. There is no need to use a pair of modems in such a link if the distance is less than fifty feet, but there is one important consideration: the transmission line of one computer must not be connected to the transmission line of another, which would be the case if the two serial ports were connected with an unaltered RS-232C cable.

What's required here is a cable that connects the transmission wire (pin 2) of computer A to the reception wire (pin 3) of computer B, and vice versa. Such a cable is called a null modem, a crossover, or a modem eliminator.

Here's another type of cable, one that can be used to connect two computers of unequal "intelligence." This wiring scheme fools a transmitting computer into thinking it has CTS when it asks RTS. It also assures the more demanding computer that the data set is ready (DSR) and that a carrier signal has been detected (CD).

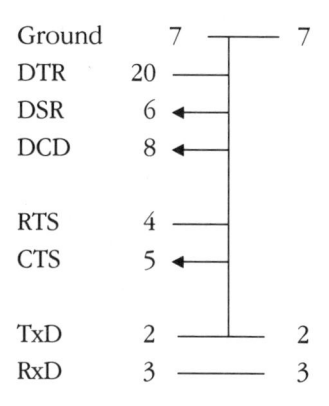

```
Ground    7 ───┬─── 7
DTR      20 ───┤
DSR       6 ◄──┤
DCD       8 ◄──┤
                │
RTS       4 ───┤
CTS       5 ◄──┤
                │
TxD       2 ───┴─── 2
RxD       3 ──────── 3
```

## LEFTOVERS

Current loop is a method of data transmission left over from old Teletype circuits. It is highly unlikely you will run into a current loop connection in a state-of-the-art computer shop, but in case you are that lucky, here is an explanation and some hints.

The current loop interface consists of two separate circuits with one data line traveling in each direction between two devices. Each circuit has an outgoing line and an incoming line; the two lines form a complete electrical circuit, or loop. Data is represented by the presence or absence of current in the loop. Current indicates 1; no current indicates 0.

The four connectors marked "current loop" are not used in the official RS-232C description for microcomputers, but they appear in one of the secondary standards set by the EIA.

## SHOPPING FOR CABLES

Market pressures, coupled with the increasing emergence of the microcomputer for nontechnical users, are reducing some of the problems brought about by the RS-232 non-standard standard. You are quite likely to find prepackaged cables in computer stores marked "Apple Macintosh to Hayes Smartmodem." However, your best bet still is to deal with a well-informed dealer and a cooperative hardware manufacturer. If you are running a large department using many different types of computers, modems, and peripherals, you might want to look into purchase of a breakout box, a smart cable, or specialized reference sources.

## GOOD-BYE, RS-232C?

Committees of the EIA have been hard at work on a new standard for telecommunications, prodded along by the federal government, which as perhaps the single largest purchaser and user of computers has the clout to complain about the RS-232C non-standard.

The new standard suggested by the EIA is the RS-449. The connectors on this standard are RS-422, a thirty-seven-pin primary connector, and RS-423, a fifteen-pin secondary connector. Already RS-449 has been attacked as being expensive and complex, which may or may not block its implementation.

RS-449 can handle higher speeds, can deal with transmission distances of more than fifty feet, provides a better specification for connectors, and includes standards that balance the electrical characteristics of the signal.

The other major standard for communications is parallel transmission, in which the seven or eight bits of the signal march down seven or eight parallel wires, with each computer word arriving at the same moment.

The principal standard here is the Centronics standard, named after the printer company that popularized it. IEEE-488 is another parallel standard, used in some Commodore computers and other brands. IEEE-488 signals require conversion before they can be used with Centronics devices.

## STANDARDS FOR MODEMS

In theory, any type of modulation that is compatible with and does not damage the public telephone or common carrier network can transmit information from point to point. In the early days of telecommunications, there were in fact several standards in use.

In the early 1970s, Racal-Vadic became the first American firm to sell a 1200-baud modem, using what the company called the 3,400 protocol. A few years later, Bell Labs entered the marketplace with a 1,200-baud device based on what Bell called the 212A standard. Bell's system won out because of the company's overwhelming size. There are still Racal-Vadic modems in use, but they either now include the 212A standard or they can only be used to communicate with other 3,400-protocol devices.

The Bell standards are divided into 100 and 200 series. The Bell 100 Series operates at speeds up to 300 baud and can transmit and receive simultaneously (full duplex). Standards 113A and 113B also run at 300 baud, but only in half-duplex mode.

The Bell 200 series encompasses 1,200-baud communication. Bell standard 202 is 1,200 baud, but only half duplex. Bell standard 212A is 1,200 baud, full duplex, and capable of downshifting to slower rates.

## THE INTERNATIONAL ARENA

The international community for the most part relies upon recommendations from the Comité Consultatif International Télégraphique et Téléphonique (CCITT), a committee of the United Nations International Telecommunications Union (ITU). That agency comprises representatives from more than 80 countries as well as delegations from several major private telecommunications agencies, including AT&T, Western Union, RCA Global Communications Corp., and Nippon Telephone and Telegraphic Public Co.

All CCITT recommendations for small computers are assigned a V or X prefix. The V series of standards are for data communication over the existing switched telephone network, while the X code denotes standards for data communication networks and other communications that do not use switched phone lines. Revisions or alternate recommendations for the same standard are indicated by "bis" (second) or "ter" (third), as in the *X.25 bis* standard for networking.

In addition to standards for modems, the CCITT has recommendations V.24 and V.28, which generally parallel the RS-232C interface standard from the EIA.

The Bell 212A standard is likely to be around a long time because of the huge installed base. The CCITT has come up with a corresponding—but incompatible—standard called V.22.

CCITT has a 300-baud standard, V.21, that is not compatible with Bell 103. V.22 is nearly equivalent to Bell 212A but not fully compatible. There is also a V.23 standard which is used in European videotext; it has an unusual bidirectional speed limit: 1,200 baud for incoming graphics and information and 75 baud for outgoing commands from terminals.

Before you despair of ever finding a way to link your American and European offices, let's differentiate direct dial-up from public telecommunications networks. In order to communicate directly at 1,200 baud, you will have to have either Bell 212A devices at both ends (illegally at the European side) or V.22 devices at both ends.

One solution is to use one of the international networks such as Tymenet, Telenet, or Euronet, which provide their own protocol converters. All the user needs is a modem that is compatible from the micro to the node and from the node to the micro.

## The 2,400-Baud Battle

At 2,400 baud there is not yet a clear winner, although the Bell 201 standard is being used heavily. At least one American modem manufacturer has made a device that can be switched from 201 to the CCITT V.26 standard for 2,400-baud communication. AT&T is working on its own standard.

It may be reasonable to expect that the former Bell operating companies, no longer linked to AT&T, may be more amenable to CCITT standards or joint and compatible standards rather than being locked in to Bell codes. For example, industry experts are hoping that

V.32 recommendations, now under study by CCITT, will be compatible with AT&T plans for 4,800- and 9,600-baud communication.

**Table E-2.** The RS-232C Standard

| Pin | Name of Signal | Direction |
|-----|----------------|-----------|
| 1 | Earth ground | |
| 2 | Transmitted data | To DCE |
| 3 | Received data | To DTE |
| 4 | Request to send | To DCE |
| 5 | Clear to send | To DTE |
| 6 | Data set ready | To DTE |
| 7 | Logic ground | |
| 8 | Carrier detect | To DTE |
| 9 | Reserved* (+Transmit current loop return 20 ma) | |
| 10 | Reserved | |
| 11 | Reserved* (−Transmit current loop data 20 ma) | |
| 12 | Secondary carrier detect | To DTE |
| 13 | Secondary clear to send | To DTE |
| 14 | Secondary transmitted data | To DCE |
| 15 | Transmit clock | To DTE |
| 16 | Secondary received data | To DTE |
| 17 | Receiver clock | To DTE |
| 18 | Reserved* (+Receive current loop data 20 ma) | |
| 19 | Secondary request to send | To DCE |
| 20 | Data terminal ready | To DCE |
| 21 | Signal quality detect | To DTE |
| 22 | Ring detect | To DTE |
| 23 | Data rate select | To DCE |
| 24 | Transmit clock | To DCE |
| 25 | Reserved* (−Receive current loop return 20 ma) | |

*Pins 9, 11, 18, and 25 are IBM implementation of current loop.

# CENTRONICS STANDARD

The thirty-six-pin Centronics standard (Figure E-1) is set up to carry the eight bits of a computer word along eight parallel lines so that each byte arrives at its destination in a single instant.

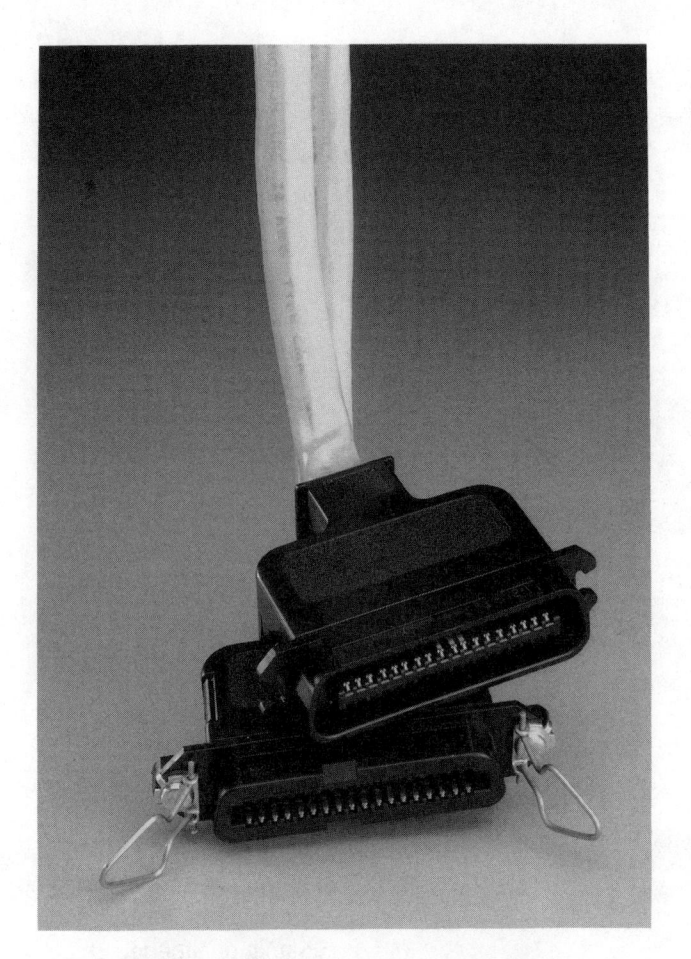

**Figure E-1** The thirty-six pin Centronics connector attaches to the printer rear panel or to switch and buffer boxes. Some terminals and workstations have a matching connector on the rear panel; others use a DB-25 connector for one end of the Centronics attachment. (Source: Black Box Corporation)

The plug facing you with the wider face to the right, the pins are numbered from 1 at left bottom up the left side to 18; and from 19 at the right bottom up the right side to 36 (Table E-3).

Note that since the Centronics signal was designed for use as a printer standard, it includes specialized printer signals such as "paper end" and "select."

**Table E-3.** Official Assignments of the Centronics Standard

| Signal Designation | Pin Number | Pin Number | Signal Designation |
|---|---|---|---|
| +5V | 18 | 36 | Undefined |
| Chassis gnd | 17 | 35 | Undefined |
| Logic ground | 16 | 34 | Undefined |
| OSCXT | 15 | 33 | Undefined |
| Supply ground | 14 | 32 | Fault |
| Select | 13 | 31 | (R) Input prime |
| Paper end | 12 | 30 | (R) Input prime |
| Busy | 11 | 29 | (R) Busy |
| Acknowledge | 10 | 28 | (R) Acknowledge |
| Data bit 8 | 9 | 27 | (R) Data bit 8 |
| Data bit 7 | 8 | 26 | (R) Data bit 7 |
| Data bit 6 | 7 | 25 | (R) Data bit 6 |
| Data bit 5 | 6 | 24 | (R) Data bit 5 |
| Data bit 4 | 5 | 23 | (R) Data bit 4 |
| Data bit 3 | 4 | 22 | (R) Data bit 3 |
| Data bit 2 | 3 | 21 | (R) Data bit 2 |
| Data bit 1 | 2 | 20 | (R) Data bit 1 |
| Data strobe | 1 | 19 | (R) Data strobe |

(R) Indicates signal ground return.

# Appendix F

# Modem Notebook

The modem is an integral part of any communications discussion. You will find additional information on modems in chapters 4, 5, 6, and 13. The term is mentioned as part of other discussions in several other sections.

This appendix will help you understand some of the finer points of the operation and selection of modems. Once you have determined that telecommunications will be part of your environment, a modem must be selected and installed. The following section discusses the purchase decision for a modem.

## BUYING A MODEM

Congratulations! You've made the decision to connect your workstation with the VAX via a modem. That was simple, wasn't it?

Not exactly. There are modems and there are modems. Here are some of the decisions you still must make:

- 300, 1,200, 2,400 or 9,600 baud?
- Error correcting? Using which protocol?
- Direct-connect or acoustically coupled?
- Internal or external?
- Smart or dumb?
- Hayes-compatible?

## Specifications for Modems

In many ways the modem has become a commodity. There is not a great deal of difference in performance between models with similar features from different manufacturers. Decide first on the capabilities you need, and then look at the specification sheets for modems that offer those features. You'll also find regular roundups of modem reviews in computer magazines — one such recent gathering had more than fifty manufacturers listed.

How much speed do you need in a modem? Well, part of the answer lies in defining how fast is fast. Let's start by striking the 300-baud modem off your list: the price differential between a 300-baud and a 1,200-baud modem — once several hundred dollars — is now so slight as to be inconsequential. Besides, any user would find 300-baud communication to be the electronic equivalent of watching cement dry. The only real reason to use a 300-baud modem these days is if the quality of your dial-up telephone service is so poor that nothing faster will work.

Remember, too, that almost all 1,200-baud modems can be instructed to operate at 300 baud; 2,400-baud models can be downshifted to 1,200 or 300 baud in most cases. This will allow you some flexibility for communicating with other users. Because 300-baud devices are less demanding of a perfect phone connection, you may be able to use the slower speed as a backup. A few years back in a certain distant suburb of New York it was necessary regularly to grit one's teeth and work all day at 300 baud when the telephone line from Manhattan was particularly noisy.

One measure of the quality of design of a modem is the carrier-detect threshold, or strength of signal required by the modem, indicated in decibels. The greater the negative decibel (dB) value, the better the modem is at finding a weak carrier signal on a noisy telephone line. A threshold of $-45$ dB or lower is a good indication.

These days, to transmit occasional short dispatches from point to point or to and from an electronic mail utility, 1,200 baud is likely to be quite sufficient. Similarly, at speeds beyond 1,200 baud, the contents of an electronic database may zip on—and off—your screen faster than you can read them.

## A Measure of Speed

You can approximate the transmission time of a document with a simple mathematical progression. Assume your modem is rated 1,200 baud, or 120 characters per second. First determine the size of the file in bytes.

Let's say the file you've selected is 30,720 bytes long. Each byte represents a character. Simply divide the number of bytes by the speed of your modem in characters per second. Add about one-third more time to account for framing bits and other control characters. The result will be the approximate transmission time in seconds for the file. In this instance we divide 30,720 by 120 cps to yield 256 seconds. Multiply that figure by 1.3 for framing bits to yield an approximate transmission time of 333 seconds, or 5 minutes, 33 seconds. To send this file with a 300-baud modem would take about 22 minutes, 12 seconds.

You can also look at the number of bytes in a file and come up with an approximation of the number of words in it. In English text the average length of a word is 5.5 characters. Adding another character to represent the space produces a word length of 6.5. Divide the number of bytes in a simple ASCII text file by 6.5, and you will obtain a rough word count for the file.

It is not quite so simple to apply this method to a file created in a special format for a word processor; the file may contain a very high percentage of extra characters for overhead, including formatting and indexing codes.

It is possible to purchase a word counter. Most of these programs work by counting the number of spaces between sets of characters and presenting that result as the number of words in the file. In our experience such utilities generally come within about 10 percent of the actual number of words.

Let's say you know the number of words in a file. Table F-1 shows transmission times.

**Table F-1.** Transmission Times for Typical Documents

| Words in Document | At 300 Baud | At 1,200 Baud | At 2,400 Baud |
|---|---|---|---|
| 1,000 | 3:20 | 0:50 | 0:25 |
| 3,000 | 10:00 | 2:30 | 1:15 |
| 5,000 | 16:40 | 4:10 | 2:05 |
| 10,000 | 33:20 | 8:20 | 4:10 |

The chart in Table F-1 assumes nearly perfect line conditions. Remember that a 1,200-baud modem that is forced by a poor telephone connection to send every block of data four times is no faster than a 300-baud modem with an acceptable connection.

# TYPES OF MODEMS

There are two types of modems in common usage for microcomputers: the acoustic coupler and the direct-connect device. Buy and use a direct-connect device unless you have no choice in the matter.

## Direct-Connect Modems

A direct-connect modem plugs directly in to the phone lines through a wall jack or RJ-11 modular jack or in to the phone itself. The phone line goes into the modem, and a serial communications cable goes from the computer to the modem.

If your home or office has the older four-prong phone plug, it is an easy matter to rewire the plugs or purchase converter plugs from Radio Shack, AT&T, or other sources.

The advantage of the direct-connect modem is that it offers a continuous electrical link between the phone line and modem. The analog signal carried on the phone line is received by the modem and converted into pulses of electricity by a microchip; going the other direction, the 0s and 1s from the computer are converted by the chip into the analog signal carried by the phone line.

## Acoustically Coupled Modems

By contrast, acoustic couplers use two additional mechanical devices, essentially giving your computer a voice and an ear. It provides a pair of foam or rubber cups that attach to the earpiece and mouthpiece of a standard telephone handset. The incoming phone signal is routed to the speaker of the telephone, where it converts the FSK analog signal into an audible warble; a microphone in the coupler picks up the sound and converts it to an electrical signal which is then converted again to digital pulses for a computer.

The extra work involved in the acoustic connection allows the possibility of corruption of the signal because of extraneous noise or the poor acoustics of some phones.

The only good reason to use an acoustic connection in a PC-to-VAX link may be for use with laptop or portable computers. Most portable computers and portable internal or external modems will still be intended for use with direct connections; however, many hotel rooms have their telephones hard-wired into the wall, blocking access to the phone plugs. In such a case, an acoustic modem may be the only choice.

A few hints: be wary of unusually shaped phones—an acoustic coupler may not work properly with modern flat phones and almost certainly will not attach properly to designer phones, Mickey Mouse units, or Elliot Ness specials. Older telephones with carbon microphones may lose some of their frequency range over time as the carbon granules compact. You may be able to improve the transmission ability of an older phone used with an acoustic coupler by rapping the handpiece sharply to jar loose some of the carbon. You could buy a replacement mouthpiece and carry it with you. Experienced telecommunicating travelers usually come equipped with gaffer's tape, rubber bands, Velcro straps and other devices in anticipation of a need to adapt a strange telephone.

## Going for a Short Haul

A third type of modem is a short-haul device, also called a line driver. Priced in the midrange, line drivers are high-speed units designed for use over short distances using standard computer cable, special twisted-pair wire circuits, or dedicated telephone circuits; they are not designed for use with dial-up phone circuits. A typical model might work at 19,200 baud for up to a mile, 9,600 baud for a six-mile range, and 2,400 baud for ten-mile transmissions. Units are available to carry asynchronous as well as synchronous communication, and some devices include multiplexing circuitry, allowing transmission of several piggy-backed signals on the same line.

**Intelligent Modems**

A "smart" modem has its own microprocessor and a small amount of memory, capable of receiving instructions directly from the user or indirectly from a communications program.

Some standard features of intelligent modems:

- **Auto dialing.** Uses software or keyboard to dial phone numbers automatically, usually presenting a choice between pulse (a simulation of a rotary dialing phone) or tone (electronic equivalence to the Bell touch-tone system).

  Auto dialing can save time, allowing the user to initiate an automatic dialing, logon, and selection of a phone number from a database. Conversely, the modem can work as part of an automatic system, calling and downloading information or transmitting without the operator's involvement.
- **Auto answer.** Allows the modem to detect incoming calls and to function without an operator for bulletin board and other systems. Some modems can also operate in the background without affecting other tasks performed by the computer.
- **Programmable parameters.** Parameters such as baud rate, protocols, and other features can be selected through direct command by the user or instruction passed along by communications software.
- **Autobaud.** Provides capability to determine the baud rate of an incoming signal and automatically adjust to match it. This is a particularly important feature for remote systems.
- **Originate/Answer Selection.** Frees the operator from having to switch modes between sending and receiving.

Other useful features available in modems:

- **Voice and data transmission.** The ability to switch back and forth between data and voice transmission with the aid of hardware or software switches. This is very valuable for giving

quick instructions to the party at the other end. You will, of course, require a telephone handset plugged in to the system at some point.
- **Positive tone detection**. A feature that allows a smart modem to listen in on the line for secondary dial tones such as those required by PBX systems in offices or by some long distance services. For example, if you must dial 9 and wait for a second dial tone to get an outside line, a smart modem can be instructed to wait for a specified time or for a second carrier tone.
- **Error and indicator lights**. A visual indication of the status of the modem. Some internal modems display messages on the screen.
- **Volume control and speaker shutoff**. Most autodialing modems include a small speaker to allow the user to listen for the dial tone, pulses or touch tones, rings, and carrier signal as an aural check on the progress of the call. Valuable features to accompany the speaker are a volume control and an automatic shutoff of the speaker once a connection is made.
- **Test mode**. Some devices include a self-diagnosis program that checks out the system when it is turned on. Others report on the quality of the phone line when activated.

## THE HAYES STANDARD

Hayes Microcomputer Products was an early success in the modem business and remains an important force in the industry. Its initial products were among the first modems with a built-in microprocessor capable of responding to instructions from the host computer—to change parameters or protocols and to dial numbers, among other tasks. Though many other companies have since come out with modems with equal or enhanced features, the Hayes became the unofficial standard. Many software packages were written to take advantage of the Hayes instruction set, and you will find many unrelated modem manufacturers advertising their devices as Hayes-compatible.

Why might it be advantageous to use a modem with a particular command set? The answer is mostly related to the software. The use of a standard should allow the software to automate such procedures as dialing, connecting, responding with passwords and requests for specific services, and the like. Almost all communications software expects to find a Hayes or Hayes-compatible modem; check for support of your particular piece of hardware before making a purchase.

There are two parts to the unofficial Hayes standard: the panel of indicator lights on the external model and the set of attention codes and instructions for the microprocessor. (On a modem mounted internally, it is not possible to read the indicator lights directly, although some units echo status messages to the screen.)

## The Hayes Indicator Lights

From right to left on a Hayes Smartmodem 1,200, the indicator lights are

MR     Modem ready. Remains lit while power to the modem is on.

TR     Terminal ready. Shows that a signal has been sent to the Smartmodem and that the terminal or computer attached to the modem is ready to receive or send data or to accept commands from the terminal. Depending upon a configuration switch setting, TR will be illuminated whenever power to the modem is on or only when power is on to the computer or terminal as well as the modem. The second setting can be used only if the computer or terminal supports the RS-232C signal data terminal ready (pin 20).

SD     Send data. Lights up when data or commands are sent from the serial port to the modem. SD indicates signals coming to the modem from the local computer or terminal.

RD     Receive data. An indication that data is being sent from the modem to its controlling computer. In full duplex mode, RD will also light as the modem echoes back data sent by the controlling computer. RD will also illuminate when the modem sends result codes to the local computer, indicating the presence of a carrier or the discontinuance of a link.

OH     Off hook. Lights up when the modem is using the telephone line.

CD      Carrier detect. Indicates when the modem has detected a carrier signal from a remote modem.

AA      Auto-answer. Lights up if the modem has been placed in the automatic answering mode, either by a hardware switch or a software code. When the phone rings, the AA light goes off during each ring, and the line is answered after a specified number of rings.

HS      High speed. Lights up to indicate that the modem is set at its highest speed. In the case of the Smartmodem 1200 this is 1,200 baud.

## AT Commands

The Hayes software command structure is based on the instruction "AT" (attention) and the "S" registers. Most commands must begin with AT; this is used by the modem both as an indicator of an upcoming instruction and as a benchmark for automatic settings. The modem looks at the incoming capital A to determine the speed of transmission of the computer or terminal; the capital T gives enough information for word length and parity to be determined.

Depending upon how you use your modem and the type of communications software you will employ, you may never issue an AT command directly, or you may constantly be giving the modem direct instructions. Either way it's worthwhile to have some understanding of the nature of the communication between the computer and modem.

Here are a few of the AT dialing commands as implemented on the Smartmodem 1200:

D      Dial. Puts the modem in origination mode to dial a number.

,      Pause. Makes the modem wait for a second dial tone. Used with PBX systems to get an outside line and with secondary long-distance services like MCI, Sprint, and SBS.

T      Touch-tone dialing. Uses Bell standard DTMF tones.

P      Pulse dialing. Mimics a rotary-dial phone.

R      Reverse mode. Allows the modem to dial an *originate-only* modem.

A/      Repeats the last command. Often used to redial a phone number.

;      Puts the modem back in the command state after dialing.

For example, the command

```
ATDT 5551212
```

sets the modem on touch-tone dialing and calls the phone number. You hear the dial tone and then the electronic tones as the call is placed.

The command

```
ATDP 12125551212
```

adds an access code, an area code, and the instruction to dial using pulses instead of touch-tone signals. You can place spaces or dashes in the phone number to help visualize the number, as in

```
ATDP 1-212 555-1212
```

Dialing out with a PBX system, one or more commas tell the modem to pause and wait for secondary dial tones. You can also change from pulse to touch-tone if, for example, the PBX is an old-style pulse or rotary dial system, while the phone exchange can accept tones. Here is an example:

```
ATDP 9,T1518 555-1212
```

## Hayes Modem Registers

The S registers of the Hayes and compatible modems allow settings for a number of parameters. Timing for several modem events are as follows:

- S0  Sets the number of rings before the Smartmodem will answer a call. A value of 0 instructs the modem not to answer the phone. A value of 1 through 255 indicates the number of times the phone is to be allowed to ring before auto-answering takes over.
- S6  Sets length of time the Smartmodem will wait for a dial tone before dialing the first digit of a phone number. Default value is two seconds.
- S7  Sets length of time the modem will wait for a carrier signal after conclusion of dialing. Default value is thirty seconds.
- S8  Sets length of pause for each comma in command. Default value is two seconds.

**S9** Sets duration of time the modem will listen to a carrier signal before recognition. Default value is six hundred milliseconds.

**S10** Sets time between loss of carrier signal and disconnection of line. Default value is seven hundred milliseconds.

**S11** Sets duration and spacing of touch-tone dialing tones. Default value is seventy milliseconds.

Commands sent to the S register follow the format AT SX = n. For example, if your PBX system is particularly slow and the modem must wait longer for a dial tone for an outside line, the command could be

    AT S6=5

The modem will echo the response "OK" to the monitor if the command has been successfully acted upon.

## ALTERNATIVES TO MODEMS

We've already seen how the worldwide telephone system offers the possibility of almost-instant connection between any two points. To send a file from one office in New York to another in San Francisco, a telephone-based modem is still the most obvious and simplest way to go. But to communicate across the room or down a floor or from a laptop portable to a desktop PC, there are other ways that are generally faster, cheaper, and simpler.

The connection from the computer to a modem is made by taking the output of a serial or asynchronous port and piping it into a standard RS-232C cable that leads to a modem. Over short distances it is possible to eliminate the trouble and expense of having a modem for each end of the telecommunications link by directly connecting the two computers with a slightly modified RS-232C cable.

### The Null Modem

The secret device here is a null modem, also known as a crossover cable or modem eliminator. Stop for a moment and look at a typical implementation of an RS-232C cable. Six pins must be connected: #1 for frame grounding; #2 for data transmission; #3 for data reception; and #7 for signal ground. Add two wires for handshaking, #4 for request to send, and #5 for clear to send, and you are nearly able to communicate from computer to computer. If we were connecting a computer to a smart modem, we might need to attach #6 for data set ready, #8 for data carrier detect, #20 for data ready terminal, and #22 for ring indicator.

This cable would work just fine using a modem. But if we were to plug one end of it in to a transmitting computer and the other end directly in to a receiving computer, we would have a problem: the data transmission and the data reception pins are misconnected. The first bit of communication would produce both data collisions and data vacuums.

The entire trick involved for a null modem is that the wires connecting pins 2 and 3 are swapped somewhere along the line: outgoing pin 2 from computer A connects to incoming pin 3 of computer B, and pin 3 from computer B will go to pin 2 of computer A. In addition, some of the handshaking lines need to be shifted for null modem operation.

You'll find null modems for sale in most comprehensive computer stores and listed in the catalogues of most mail order supply houses. Versions with ten feet of cable typically sell for about $30; plug adapters that make the conversion at the end of any RS-232C cable cost about $25.

Plug the null modem into serial ports of each computer and use any standard telecommunications software to communicate just as if you were using a modem, at speeds up to 9,600 baud.

The official RS-232C standard is supposed to guarantee the integrity of signals for as much as fifty feet. If you need to go further, another type of low-cost device can serve as a signal amplifier. One such unit, the Cable-Stretcher from Inmac, sells for about $110, draws power from an AC line and plugs in to the middle of the stretch of cable, allowing transmission (synchronous or asynchronous) at speeds up to 19,200 baud.

## Line Drivers

Another device worth considering for direct connections is the line driver, which changes the way RS-232C signals are driven down a wire. Using inexpensive twisted-pair cable or dedicated phone lines, a line driver can zip data along using synchronous or asynchronous protocols at speeds up to 19,200 baud over short distances and 2,400 to 9,600 baud at distances to about fifteen miles.

The problem with line drivers is that they are like the old current loops: they require a continuous, unswitched pathway from transmitter to receiver—think of it as an unbroken wire from one point to another. That makes them perfectly acceptable in a dedicated line but less than wonderful if you have to go through a PBX or phone company switchers.

Another step up the ladder, but still faster and cheaper than an ordinary modem, are devices called short-range or short-haul modems. These modems are capable of baud rates up to 19,200 over simple four-wire cables or over dedicated telephone lines. Signals produced by short-range modems can go through PBXs and other switches.

Should you consider a line driver or a short-range modem instead of a modem? My suggestion is that you ignore price for a moment and answer these questions:

Do you need to exchange information regularly over a short distance at a high speed? Can you arrange to string a cable or obtain a dedicated telephone line? If so, a line driver or short-range modem may fit the bill even if you have to buy an ordinary modem for database services or more distant computers. At fifty feet or so, you might find it best to connect the two computers with a null modem cable.

## Multiplexers

Multiplexers accept two or more lines of data from computers and then transmit them at high speed to a central computer. They are typically used with terminals or remote computers in synchronous or asynchronous communication over dedicated phone lines. In a typical setup, RS-232C output cables from terminals or computers are plugged into a line multiplexer, and the output of that device is plugged into a standard modem. The output of the modem enters the phone line. At the other end, the phone line goes into the modem and the output of the modem goes into another multiplexer, which splits the signal up into outputs for the central computer.

Many multiplex units include automatic adjustments to match exchange rates with modems as well as error correction circuitry. The principal advantages of using multiplex units come in simplicity of-connection and cost savings over expensive dedicated lines and individual modems. Table F-2 compares the expense of four 2,400-baud modems plus four dedicated phone lines with that of a pair of modems and a pair of multiplexers with a single dedicated line. Note that the cost savings is significant not only in the first year, when capital costs are included, but also in later years, when the expense of dedicated phone lines is the only factor.

**Table F-2.** Telecommunication Expenses

| 2,400-Baud Modems | Dedicated Phone Lines (Annual Rent) | Multiplexer | Total (1st year) | Total (2nd year and later) |
|---|---|---|---|---|
| Direct Connection $8,000 (8 units) | $24,000 (4 lines) | — | $32,000 | $24,000 |
| Multiplexed System $2,000 (2 units) | $6,000 (1 line) | $2,000 (2 units) | $10,000 | $6,000 |

**Concentrators**

A variant of the multiplexer is the concentrator. Concentrators combine data from many slow terminals and transmit the recombined data stream to the host at a very high speed, reducing the need for leased lines. Typically it has more than two lines.

# Endnotes

1. Though the IBM PC and its clones claim to be sixteen-bit devices, in fact they are hybrid systems that move data in eight-bit words on ther internal bus and sixteen-bit words within the microprocessor chip. Similarly, the PC AT, its clones, and the Apple Macintosh are thirty-two/sixteen-bit hybrids.
2. KEA Systems Ltd., 412-2150 West Broadway, Vancouver, B.C., Canada, V6K 4L9, 604-732-7411.
3. Diversified Computer Systems, Inc., 3775 Iris Avenue, Suite 1B, Boulder, CO 80301, 303-447-9251.
4. The Headlands Press, PO Box 862, Tiburon, CA 94920, 415-435-9775.
5. Datastorm Technologies, Inc., PO Box 1471, Columbia, MO 65205.
6. Ptel, PO Box 130, West Hill, Ontario, Canada M1E 4R4.
7. The Forbin Project, Inc., and John Friel III, 715 Walnut Street, Cedar Falls, IA 50613.
8. Bit Software, Inc., 830 Hillview Court, Suite 160, Milpitas, CA 95035.
9. Everex Systems, Inc., 48431 Milmont Drive, Fremont, CA 94538.

10. Datamedia Corporation, 11 Trafalgar Square, Nashua, NH 03063, 800-362-4636.
11. Novell, Inc., 122 East 1700 South, Provo, UT 84601, 801-379-5900, 800-453-1267.
12. Datability Software Systems, Inc., 322 Eighth Avenue, New York, NY 10001, 212-807-7800, 800-342-5377.
13. Technology Concepts, Inc., 40 Tall Pine Drive, Sudbury, MA 01776, 800-777-2323.
14. Persoft, 465 Science Drive, Madison, WI 53711, 608-273-6000.
15. Polygon, 1024 Executive Parkway, Sain Louis, MO 63141, 314-576-7709.
16. Walker, Richer & Quinn, 2825 Eastlake Avenue East, Seattle, WA 98102, 206-324-0330.
17. Electronic Industries Association, 2001 Eye Street, N.W., Washington, DC 20006.

# Glossary

20MA HOST PORT CONNECTOR   A port used to connect a VT terminal to a nearby host computer using a 20-milliamp connection.

68020   A high-speed, sixteen-bit microprocessor that is common in workstations and network processors. The 68020 is being superseded in new applications by the 68030 processor.

80188   A true sixteen-bit version of the Intel 8088 chip. Used in some IBM PC–compatible machines.

80286   A true sixteen-bit high-speed member of the Intel 8088 family. Used as the brain of the PC AT.

80287   The sixteen-bit equivalent of the 8087 math coprocessor. Available for use with the 80286 chip in the PC AT.

8088   The Intel microprocessor that is the brain of the IBM PC and most IBM PC–compatible machines. Processes sixteen-bit words internally but deals with the computer through an eight-bit bus.

A   Ampere. A measurement of the strength of a current of electricity.

AC   Alternating current. An electrical flow that reverses its direction at regular intervals.

ACCESS CONTROL   The process of validating a connection, login, or file access request to see if the action is permitted under the instructions set by the system manager. Access control is usually implemented through passwords.

ACCESS LINE   The direct connection from the telephone equipment at your premises to the nearest telephone office. Also called a local loop.

ACCESS PROTOCOL  The scheme employed by a network to avoid data collisions, such as carrier sense multiple access. Also called media access control.

ACCESS TIME  The amount of time required to store or retrieve information. Memory chip speeds are typically measured in nanoseconds; disk speeds are measured in microseconds.

ACCOUNT  The heart of the system's library functions. Every user of the system, and many of the parts of the system itself, have an account assigned by the system manager. The computer keeps track of the privileges assigned to each account as well as the physical location of the files created by or sent to each account.

ACCUMULATOR  A register in a microprocessor in which the result of an operation is gathered and stored.

ACOUSTIC COUPLER  A form of modem in which the digital signals of the computer are converted into audio tones and transmitted by a speaker to a telephone handset. At the receiving end, a microphone picks up incoming audio tones and converts them to digital signals. Compare DIRECT-CONNECTION MODEM.

ACTIVE POSITION  The location on the screen, indicated by the cursor, where the next typed character will appear.

ACTIVE WINDOW  The frontmost window displayed on a screen.

ADDRESS  A number used by the operating system to locate information in storage. Can be regarded as VIRTUAL ADDRESS (qv) or PHYSICAL ADDRESS (qv). In many computers, address locations are identified in terms of a starting address for a block of memory and an offset address identifying how far into that block a particular bit of data is located.

ADDRESS BUS  One or more conductors used to carry the binary-encoded address from the microprocessor through the rest of the system.

ALGORITHM  A formula or logical method used to solve a problem or accomplish a task. Conversion of binary data to ASCII characters requires an algorithm, for example. The efficiency of an algorithm is an unseen contributor to the speed of a modem, computer, or process of communications.

ALIAS  A different name for the same entity, allowing use of shorter or more familiar names for complex commands, files, and specifications.

ALLOCATE A DEVICE  Reserve a device for exclusive use. Such an action can be made only when the device is not allocated by another process.

ALPHANUMERIC CHARACTER  Any alphabetic letter in upper or lower case, any decimal digit, the dollar sign, and the underscore.

ANALOG  The representation of numerical quantities by the measurement of continuous physical variables. For example, the rise and fall of a wavelike signal is an analog signal, an analogy of the effect being measured—the stronger the signal the higher the wave. In telephone communication the signal carries information by continuously varying the electrical frequency wave to match the sound frequencies and volume of the input signal. In an automobile the standard speedometer registers on an analog scale, with greater speed indicated by greater deflection of the needle. The other form of data manipulated by a computer is digital and based on purely numerical codes.

ANSI   American National Standards Institute. The principal American standards development organization; represents the United States at the International Standards Organization (ISO).

ANSI CHARACTERS   A standard set of characters established by the American National Standards Institute. Two types: GRAPHIC CHARACTERS (qv) and CONTROL CHARACTERS (qv).

APPC   Advanced program-to-program communications. An IBM protocol similar to the OSI session layer. It allows multiple application programs to send data across a network.

APPLICATION LAYER   The topmost layer of the OSI model, responsible for defining how application programs work with the operating system.

APPLICATION PROGRAM   A set of computer instructions intended to perform a specific task, such as a spreadsheet, word processor, or database program.

ARBITRATION   In a computer, the management by a piece of hardware or software of multiple requests for the same channel at the same time. For example, on a network there must be a form of arbitration to handle the possibility that two stations will seek to transmit at the same time. The arbitration can be random or it can be based on a logical assessment of priorities.

ARCHITECTURE   The hardware design of a computer or peripheral that determines its compatibility with other such devices.

ARCHIVING   The act of backing up a file to a different disk for the purpose of safeguarding the data against loss.

ARCNET   Attached Resources Computing Network. A token-passing bus network.

ASCII   Abbreviation for American Standard Code for Information Interchange, a standard that defines the coding for letters, numbers, and symbols manipulated by computers, printers, or plotters. Pronounced "as key."

ASCII CHARACTERS   A set of eight-bit binary numbers used to represent the alphabet and other symbols used by the computer in many communication, display, and printing applications.

ASSEMBLY LANGUAGE   A programming language that speaks directly to the computer. The VAX assembly language is VAX MACRO.

ASSIGN A CHANNEL   Create a software link between an application and a device to allow communication with a device.

ASYNCHRONOUS COMMUNICATION   The transmission of information over a single wire one bit at a time. Each character is framed by a start bit and one or more stop bits. Thus the transmission of information is not dependent upon precise timing between receiver and transmitter. Compare SYNCHRONOUS COMMUNICATION.

ATTACHED PROCESSOR   A secondary processor in certain types of VAX systems.

ATTENUATION   The reduction or loss of signal strength, measured in decibels (dB) or in decibels per unit of length. Virtually all electrical conductors suffer from attenuation. At some point a signal cannot be sent any farther without amplification or retransmission. The opposite of attenuation is gain.

AUDITING   A notation by the system that a particular event has taken place.

AUTHENTICATION   The establishment of the identity and privileges of users signing on to a computer.

AUTO-ANSWER   The capability of a modem automatically to establish a connection with an incoming call. Usually coupled with AUTO-DIAL.

AUTO-DIAL   The ability of a modem or associated software to place a telephone call for voice or data communication.

AUTO PRINT MODE   A printing mode that sends the currently displayed line to a printer each time the on-screen cursor moves down a line because of a line feed, form feed, vertical tab code or auto wrap. Auto print is selectable from the print menu. All printing functions, including Print Screen, can be initiated from the keyboard while in this mode. See PRINTING MODES for other conditions.

AUXILIARY KEYPAD   See NUMERIC KEYPAD.

BACKGROUND   A procedure run during idle moments by a processor or server, allowing another procedure to take precedence in the foreground. For example, a printing job could be undertaken while the computer is mostly occupied with another text editing procedure.

BACKUP COPY   A copy of a program made for storage and used only in case of loss or damage of the original or working copy.

BACKUP FILE   A copy of the most recently edited version of a file, kept in case the current version is somehow destroyed or altered inappropriately. Some word processors automatically create a backup file anytime an existing file is edited. A truly cautious user will make backup files of irreplaceable documents on separate disks that will be stored in a different place from data files in daily use. As a verb, to backup means to create a protective file. The act of recovering a backed-up file is to restore.

BANDWIDTH   The frequency range of a channel—the difference between the highest and lowest frequencies of a transmission signal. Usually measured in kilohertz or megahertz. The wider the bandwidth, the greater the theoretical capacity of the channel.

BASIC   Acronym for Beginner's All-purpose Symbolic Instruction Code. The most popular microcomputer programming language for nontechnical users.

BASIC-GROUP SIGNAL   In an analog telephone network, a signal that combines twelve voiceband channels within a bandwidth of 60 to 108 KHzz.

BASIC RATE INTERFACE   See BRI.

BATCH PROCESSING   A system under which a computer accepts and stores for execution all of the commands of a particular process or program and then executes them as a group. Compare REAL-TIME PROCESSING.

BAUD RATE   The speed at which a terminal or modem communicates with the host system, printer, or other device. The measurement is the number of discrete signal changes per second. At slower speeds each signal change may represent a single bit; if so, the baud rate is the same as the number of bits per second. At higher speeds one change in signal can represent two or more bits. For successful serial communication, the baud rate of computer and peripheral must be the same. The name is derived from J.M.E. Baudot (1845-1903), a French pioneer in telegraphy.

BAUDOT CODE   The five-bit code used in Telex systems.

BELL 103   The AT&T standard for asynchronous telecommunication at speeds up to 300 baud.

BELL 201   The AT&T standard for asynchronous telecommunication at speeds up to 2,400 bits per second.

BELL 202   The AT&T standard for asynchronous telecommunication at speeds up to 1,800 bits per second. Requires a four-wire line for full duplex transmission.

BELL 208   The AT&T standard for synchronous telecommunication at speeds up to 4,800 bits per second.

BELL 209   The AT&T standard for synchronous telecommunication at up to 9,600 bits per second.

BELL 212   The AT&T standard for full-duplex asynchronous or synchronous transmission at speeds up to 1,200 bits per second on dial-up phone lines.

BINARY MACHINE CODE   The internal language of the computer, which has only the characters zero and one. Programmers use higher-level languages, compiler, and the macro assembler to generate binary code.

BINARY SYNCHRONOUS COMMUNICATION (BSC)   An IBM protocol using a standard set of control characters and protocols for the synchronous exchange of information. The transmitter and receiver are synchronized with control characters as they communicate. See SYNCHRONOUS COMMUNICATION.

BIT   The basic unit of information recognized by a computer. Derived from "binary digit." A bit is either off or on, either 0 or 1.

BIT MAP   A video screen expressed in a grid of pixels (picture elements). Each pixel is controlled by bits that set intensity and color. Bit map graphics can also be used to produce an image using a dot matrix printer.

BLOCK GRAPHICS   Pictures produced by a monitor or printer using ASCII characters such as lines, boxes, slashes, and parts of curves.

BOOT   To start a machine or program. Derived from "by one's bootstraps" because the computer or program generates its own environment.

BOOT NAME   The name of the device used to boot software.

BPS   Bits per second. The rate at which data moves. See also BAUD RATE.

**BREAK KEY** A key that is recognized by some programs and operating states as meaning a halt to a particular process or program or a disconnect. The break key sends different commands in its ordinary, shifted, and control combinations.

**BREAKOUT BOX** A device for troubleshooting or temporary fixes for telecommunications wiring; allows enabling or disabling, jumping, or merging of signals.

**BRI** Basic rate interface. Within ISDN, a format consisting of two bearer (B) channels operating at 64 Kb/s and one signaling (D) channel operating at 16 Kb/s.

**BRIDGES** Devices that connect networks, allowing nodes on either network to work with nodes on the other. A standard bridge does not amplify signals or control their flow. See GATEWAYS.

**BROADCAST ADDRESSING** A means of sending a message to all nodes of a system.

**BROADCAST CIRCUIT** A circuit to which multiple nodes are connected and across which a message can be sent to multiple receivers.

**BUFFER** A storage place for data that compensates for differences in speed of data flow between two devices. A printer or plotter typically operates much more slowly than a computer, and a buffer can be used to accept and store instructions. Also, some word processors allow placement of a block of copy in a buffer within the computer's RAM. This copy can later be recalled and inserted elsewhere in the file. Programs that have an Undelete function will place the most recent character manipulation into a buffer to allow resetting.

**BUFFERED REPEATERS** Amplifier not electrically continuous to the cable. Controls the flow of signals by issuing "start" and "stop" commands to avoid collisions. See REPEATERS.

**BULLETIN BOARD** A community service for posting or reading of messages, files, and programs.

**BUS** A network design in which a signal passes through all nodes en route to the designated recipient. A bus has a certain topology that determines the pathways in which data moves to all of the stations, or nodes, on the network. Each point on the network must be able to recognize those messages addressed to it, and there must be a means of arbitration by the system so that different points on the network do not attempt to send data at the same instant. On a microcomputer, the system bus carries the electrical connections between the microprocessor and its memory, controllers, and peripherals. The bus generally is part of the backplane or motherboard and actually consists of an address bus, a data bus, power supply lines, and other control lines.

**BYTE** Eight bits (qv). Used by the computer to store numbers or characters. Bits are numbered from 0 to 7, going from right to left. Bit 7 is the sign bit, which indicates a positive or negative integer. Bits are binary; thus a seven-bit byte can be in the range from $-128$ to $+128$. Without the sign bit, the number can range from 0 to 255 in decimal counting.

C   A programming language used on a wide range of microcomputers and highly regarded because of the relative ease with which programs can be translated from one system to another.

CACHE   A means to speed access to data by setting aside a block of RAM to hold data the system expects to access repeatedly. Access to RAM is quicker than access to fixed storage.

CALL   To transfer control to a specified routine.

CAPTIVE ACCOUNT   A VAX/VMS account with limited privileges.

CARRIER SIGNAL   The base signal onto which information is modulated for transmission.

CCITT   Comité Consultatif International de Télégraphique et Téléphonique (International Telegraph and Telephone Consultative Committee), a European communications standards committee.

CENTRAL OFFICE   A local telephone exchange, or switching system, that connects various local loops (communication links to customers) to other local central offices or to toll offices for long-distance communication.

CENTREX   Service leased by telephone companies to larger users, performing at a central office the functions ordinarily undertaken by a private branch exchange (PBX).

CENTRONICS PARALLEL   A standard for parallel communication. See PARALLEL COMMUNICATION.

CHANNEL   In networks, a logical path connecting an application to a physical device, as assigned by the operating system. In telecommunications, a transmission path or circuit between two points.

CHARACTER   A symbol represented by an ASCII code.

CHARACTER BUFFER   The temporary storage area used by EDT and some other programs to hold the last deleted character.

CHARACTER CELL   The pixel area on the screen used to display a single graphic character.

CHARACTER CODE   An integer value representing a character. It can be generated by a single key on the keyboard or a combination of keys, including control keys.

CHARACTER ENCODING   The method used by a terminal or a computer to encode information. Most systems use eight-bit codes; other systems are based on a smaller seven-bit set.

CHARACTER SET   A complete group of characters. A hard character set is built into the internal memory of a terminal. Typical hard character sets include ASCII and DEC Supplemental Graphic . A soft character set is a group of characters downloaded to the terminal from a computer or other source.

CHARACTER STRING   A contiguous set of bytes. The computer identifies a character string by giving it an address and a length. The address is the location of the byte holding the first character of the string. The length is the number of characters in the string, stored in subsequent bytes of increasing address.

CHIP   An integrated circuit used as a microprocessor or a memory storage unit in microcomputers. The chip is constructed on a tiny silicon flake with gates and paths formed out of films of metal. Also called a microchip.

CLUSTER   1) A set of pages brought into memory in a single paging operation. 2) A configuration of VAX processors.

COAXIAL CABLE   A solid or stranded copper conductor surrounded by foam or plastic insulation, a woven copper or foil shield, and a rubber or plastic outer covering. Used in some computer networks as well as in cable television and in other applications. The copper braid or foil shield on the coaxial cable allows it to resist interference better than some other types of wiring, such as twisted-pair.

COBOL   An abbreviation of Common Business-Oriented-Language. A high-level programming language often used for business applications.

CODEC   A microchip for coding and decoding, used to produce digital output from analog signals and vice versa.

COLUMN   A vertical row of character positions on a screen. Most terminals can display 80 or 132 columns.

COMMAND   An instruction requesting the computer to perform a defined action.

COMMAND FILE   See COMMAND PROCEDURE.

COMMAND INTERPRETER   The element of the operating system that receives, checks for errors, and parses command files.

COMMAND PROCEDURE   A file containing commands and any necessary data upon which the command interpreter can act as if the instructions had been typed in by the user.

COMPATIBLE   In hardware, the ability to work with or act like another piece of equipment. In software, the ability to interchange files or data without reentering them from the keyboard.

COMPATIBILITY MODE   A mode that permits the VAX's central processor to execute nonprivileged PDP-11 instructions, assuring compatibility with software intended for an earlier series of DEC machines. See NATIVE MODE.

COMPILER   Computer software that translates a program written in a high-level language, such as BASIC, Pascal, COBOL, or C, into binary machine code. The program being translated is the source code, and the translated (compiled) result is the object code. Compiled programs generally run much faster than interpreted programs.

COMPOSE CHARACTER KEY   A key used to initiate display and transmission of certain special characters not part of the ordinary computer keyboard. Characters are sent by typing the Compose Character key and then one or two keyboard characters. On the LK-201 keyboard used with VT-220 and VT-300 series terminals, a Compose indicator illuminates while a compose character function is underway.

COMPOSE SEQUENCE:   See COMPOSE CHARACTER KEY.

COMPOSITE VIDEO OUTPUT CONNECTOR   A connector on a VT terminal or other display device that provides a video output signal to drive an external display. Also called NTSC video (for National Television Standards Committee), this system sends information on brightness, color, and timing on a single wire. The resulting image is not as sharp as with an RGB system.

CONCEALED DEVICE   An input/output device that has been given a logical name. The logical name rather than the device name is used in most system commands and responses.

CONDITION   An error state that exists when an exception occurs. See EXCEPTION and CONDITION HANDLER.

CONDITION HANDLER   A procedure executed by the system when a process exception such as an error occurs. When the exception occurs, the computer will look for an appropriate condition handler and within the context of the situation, follow the instructions given there.

CONFIGURATION   The combination of various parts, options, and cards that makes up a computer system.

CONFIGURATION DATABASE   A database of files containing information about the system and network components.

CONSOLE   The control unit used by the system operator to start and stop the system, monitor system operation, and perform diagnostics.

CONSOLE TERMINAL   The hard-copy terminal connected to the central processor console.

CONTEXT SWITCHING   The act of interrupting the activity in progress and switching to another. The switching can be done by the system as it concludes one process and moves on to the next, or can be performed by the user in certain circumstances.

CONTROL CHARACTERS   A set of characters not usually displayed on the screen that make the terminal perform a specific function. Examples include carriage return and line feed. Control characters can be generated by a program or by holding down the control key while typing another key. Special signals can also be sent by using the Alt key in the same manner. In some applications manuals and on-screen displays, control is signified with the symbol: ^A.

CONTROL KEY   A key that works like the shift key, sending control characters to the computer for action. The command is issued by holding down the control key while typing a second character. In this book and in most application programs, a command calling for use of a control character is printed as Ctrl-A.

CORE   The center of a fiber-optic cable, used to conduct light pulses generated by a laser or light-emitting diode (LED). Also a type of main memory in older computer systems.

CPU   Central processing unit. The "brain" of the computer, as opposed to ancillary units such as memory and storage.

CRC  Cyclical redundancy check. A form of error checking used during the transfer of data in I/O operations such as with disk drives and communications links.

CROSSOVER CABLE  See NULL MODEM.

CTRL  See CONTROL KEY.

CURSOR  A dash or block displayed on the screen to indicate where the next character will appear. The cursor can be customized as part of the setup choices on most VT terminals.

CURSOR KEYS  The arrow keys on a terminal's keyboard, used to move the cursor from point to point on the screen.

DATA FLOW CONTROL  A method of synchronizing communication between a terminal and its host system or printer.

DATA LINK LAYER  The second layer of the OSI model, responsible for managing the flow of data from a network device to a receiving device and ensuring that the information arrives safely.

DC  Direct current. An electrical current that flows in one direction only.

DCL  Digital Command Language. A component of the VMS operating system through which the user can issue commands.

DEBUG  To repair operating problems in a piece of hardware or software.

DECIBEL  A unit of measurement of the change in strength of a transmission signal. Calculated as a ratio between two amounts of electrical or acoustic signals. Abbreviated dB.

DEC MULTINATIONAL CHARACTER SET  The standard character set of the VT-220 and VT-300 series of terminals.

DECRYPTION  The process of restoring encoded information to its original, unencoded form.

DEC SPECIAL GRAPHIC CHARACTER SET  A group of characters with special symbols and line segments as well as equivalents to many ASCII graphics characters. Also called the VT-100 line drawing character set.

DEC SUPPLEMENTAL GRAPHIC CHARACTER SET  A set of 94 graphic characters including special characters such as letters with accents and diacritical marks used by European languages.

DEDICATED  Assigned to a single purpose or user.

DEFAULT  The ordinary or expected form of a command. In most cases, the operating system will substitute the default value in a command unless some other information is provided.

DETACHED PROCESS  A process that has no owner. Such processes are created by the job controller when a user logs in, when a batch job is begun, or when a logical link is requested. Detached jobs can continue to operate even if the originating user is conducting other operations.

DEVICE  Any peripheral unit connected to the processor for sending, receiving, or transmitting data. Devices include printers, terminals, magnetic disks, communication controllers, and modems. A pseudodevice is software that fools the computer into thinking hardware is present.

DEVICE DRIVER   Software associated with each device in the system; works as an interface between the operating system and the hardware controller.

DIACRITICAL MARKS   Symbols used in some languages to call for a change in the standard pronunciation of a letter, such as acute (´) and grave (`) accents and the tilde (~).

DIAGNOSTIC   A program to test hardware, logic, or memory and report any faults it finds.

DIALOGUE BOX   In a window application, a displayed box that requests information to complete a command or informs the user that the application is waiting for the completion of a process.

DIGITAL   In the form of digits; numerical. Analog, the other form of data manipulated by a computer, is based on a wave or other form of analogy to the actual event.

DIGITAL COMMAND LANGUAGE   The command interpreter in a VAX/VMS system.

DIGITAL SWITCH   An electronic switch that can alter the channel routing of digital signals without converting them to analog signals.

DIMMED   On a window display, an element drawn in gray tones rather than black.

DIP SWITCH   Abbreviation for dual inline package; a type of multiple switch found on many computers and peripherals and used to select options and protocols.

DIRECT-CONNECT MODEM   A type of modem that plugs directly into the phone jack. Compare ACOUSTIC COUPLER.

DIRECT MEMORY ACCESS   A means of transferring data between the main RAM storage and input/output devices that does not involve the microprocessor and therefore operates faster.

DIRECTORY   A file that catalogues the files stored in a particular physical location. Included in most directories are the file name, type, and version number as well as a number that identifies the file's actual location and points to a list of its attributes.

DISABLE   To stop operation of a circuit or device; opposite of enable.

DISPERSION   A gradual loss of integrity, or blurring, of light pulse during transmission along a fiber-optic cable.

DISPLAY ATTRIBUTE   On a video display, a property that can be assigned to all or part of a display. For example, a bit can be low-intensity, high-intensity, blinking, or a particular color.

DMA   See DIRECT MEMORY ACCESS.

DOT MATRIX PRINTER   A printer that produces letters, numbers, and graphics with dots drawn on a grid. Dot matrix printers can be impact or nonimpact.

DOT PITCH   The closeness of one phosphor dot to another on a monitor screen. The smaller or finer the dot pitch, the sharper the image. An ordinary television set typically has a dot pitch of about 0.62 millimeters, a high-resolution monitor is usually rated at 0.40 millimeters or less; and a medium-resolution device falls in between.

DOUBLE PRECISION   A system of storage of numbers that extends the value to two computer words. See SINGLE PRECISION.

DOWNLOAD   To move data or instructions from the host to the terminal. Also called downline load. Compare UPLOAD.

DOWNLOADABLE CHARACTER SET   A set of characters downloaded to a terminal from the host system to supplement or replace the built-in, or hard, character set of the terminal. Also called downline loadable character set, or soft character set.

DRCS   Dynamically redefinable character set. See DOWNLOADABLE CHARACTER SET.

DRIVE   The mechanical element of a mass storage unit. A magnetic tape or disk, for example, is mounted on a drive.

DRIVER   The code and data that oversee the physical input and output of data to a device. (See DEVICE DRIVER.) A set of instructions in a software package that operates a particular piece of hardware such as a printer or plotter.

DUPLEX   Simultaneous, independent transmission of data in both directions on a communication channel. A single-direction system is called half-duplex.

DVORAK KEYBOARD   A keyboard said to allow speedier typing than the familiar QWERTY keyboard. Some manufacturers offer replacement keyboards for the PC family, and there are software fixes to convert the standard keyboard to a different layout.

DYNAMIC RAM   Memory using transistors and capacitors as storage elements and therefore requiring a recharge (refresh) every few milliseconds. Memory that does not require a refresh is called static memory.

EBCDIC   Extended Binary Coded Decimal Interchange Code. A set of six-bit characters used to represent data in some IBM systems. Includes all fifty-one COBOL characters. Compare ASCII.

ECHO   A characteristic of a communication setup that calls for typed characters to be displayed on the screen or printer.

ECHOPLEX   A protocol that has the receiving station echo each character to the transmitting station as a check on proper communication.

EDITING KEYPAD   The supplemental keypad on some terminals designed to allow easy entry of editing commands, including cursor and page movement and insertion or deletion of characters.

EIA HOST PORT CONNECTOR   A port that connects a VT terminal to a host computer either directly or through a modem.

EMULATION   The ability of one piece of hardware or software to act like another. For example, the VT-320 terminal can emulate the earlier VT-220 and VT-100 terminals if required by a particular software application. Or a PC can run software allowing it to emulate the dissimilar VT-220 terminal in a direct connection or a telecommunications session.

EMULATORS   Device or software that allows one computer or piece of telecommunications equipment to mimic another. This allows the mixing of machines from different companies or of different internal architectures, and also allows one machine to have more than one use.

ENABLE   To allow a device or circuit to operate. Compare DISABLE.

ENCRYPTION   The process of encoding information so that it is not easily understood without a copy of the decryption code.

EPROM ERASABLE PROGRAMMABLE READ-ONLY MEMORY   See ROM.

ERROR MESSAGES   Notice from the program or operating system to the user of a problem in the program or machine.

ESC   The character Escape used to initiate an ESCAPE SEQUENCE.

ESCAPE SEQUENCE   A special command to the system. The sequence begins with ESC and is transmitted without interpretation to the software or operating system for action.

ETHERNET   A network protocol and cabling scheme used by Digital Equipment Corp., 3Com, and other manufacturers. Originally developed by Xerox.

EXCEPTION   An event detected by the hardware or software that changes the normal execution of instructions. Examples include attempts to perform a privileged or reserved instruction and arithmetic traps such as overflow, underflow, and division by 0. An event that is completely outside of the current instruction is called an INTERRUPT.

EXECUTIVE   The collection of procedures in the operating system to provide the basic control and monitoring functions.

EXECUTIVE MODE   A highly privileged processor access mode, used for many of the operating system's service procedures.

EXIT   Termination of an image execution, either normal or abnormal. The system deassigns I/O channels and other assignments made for the image.

EXIT HANDLER   A procedure executed when an image exits.

FAULT   A hardware exception that occurs in the middle of an instruction, leaving the computer's internal registers and memory in such a state that eliminating the fault and restarting the instruction will give correct results.

FIBER OPTICS CABLE   A cable made of fiberglass strands; transmits data in the form of pulses of light instead of pulses of electricity.

FIELD   A set of contiguous bytes in a logical record.

FIFO   First in, first out. The order in which processing is ordinarily performed; the computer acts upon the oldest command in its queue first. Compare LIFO.

FILE  Any named, stored program or set of data.

FILE CONTROL BLOCK  An element of the operating system; stores information about the access path for files.

FILE HEADER  A block in an index file describing a file.

FILE LOCKING  A means of protecting shared data from corruption by preventing simultaneous access by two users or two programs.

FILE NAME EXTENSION  See FILE TYPE.

FILES-11  The disk structure used by the VAX/VMS operating system as well as some other Digital systems. VMS uses Files-11 structure level 2, and supports level 1 for compatibility with earlier systems.

FILE SERVER  A computer on a network dedicated in full or part to storage of files in private or shared directories or subdirectories.

FILE SHARING  The capability of a relative or indexed file to allow access to more than one process.

FILE SPECIFICATION  The unique name of a file. On a VAX/VMS system, the file specification identifies the node, device, directory name, file type, and version number.

FILE TYPE  On a VAX/VMS system, the field of a file specification that identifies a particular class of files, such as compiler, assembly, data, and listings. Can be as many as thirty-nine alphanumeric characters in length.

FILTER  A procedure that allows some operating systems to read input (usually from a file) and then process it into a different form.

FLIP-FLOP  A circuit or device in which active elements are capable of assuming either of two stable states with the application of electrical current.

FONT  A style or design of characters.

FORMATTING  The preparation of a disk for writing and reading data by marking it off into wedges called sectors and concentric circles called tracks. There are several different formatting schemes, generally not compatible with each other.

FORM FEED  On a printer, the movement of the paper to the top of the next sheet of continuous-form paper. In the EDT word processor of a VAX/VMS system, the movement of the cursor position to the start of a new page.

FORTRAN  A programming language often used for scientific applications. Abbreviation for formula translation.

FRAME  A packet of information on a token-ring network; also, in serial communication, the elapsed time from the start bit to the last stop bit.

FREQUENCY  In an electrical signal, the number of waves of signal per second. Measured in Hertz. The range of frequencies allowed for a signal determines its bandwidth.

FREQUENCY-SHIFT KEYING (FSK)  A means of modulation used in 300-baud modems; uses one frequency to represent 0 and another for 1.

FSK  See FREQUENCY-SHIFT KEYING.

FULL DUPLEX   A mode of data communication between two devices in which signals can travel in both directions at the same time. For example, voice communication over a telephone is full duplex. Compare HALF-DUPLEX.

FUNCTION KEY   A keyboard character that can be temporarily or permanently assigned to perform a certain task when when struck.

GATEWAY   An intelligent device that reconciles networks running incompatible protocols; a link from one network to another. An internal local area network, for example, could have a gateway to a public network for transmission of electronic mail to outside addresses. One public network may have a gateway that allows its subscribers to tie in to the offerings of a different system without having to sign off the original network.

GIGABYTE   One billion eight-bit computer words.

GLOBAL   Affecting the entire file, system, or image. In a text file, a global replacement changes all instances of a particular string of characters to another string.

GLOBAL SECTION   A shareable section of an image that can be made available to all processes in a system. Access is set by privilege.

GLOBAL SYMBOL   A symbol that can be made to extend across a number of files or strings. The linker matches references with definitions.

GOLD KEY   A special key on a VAX terminal keyboard enabling alternate key functions. Used within WPS, EDT, and many other programs.

GRAPHIC CHARACTERS   A set of alphanumeric characters that can be displayed on the screen of a terminal.

GROUP   A set of users with access to each other's directories and files, unless the files have been specifically protected. VMS organizes users under the following hierarchy: system/owner/group/world.

HALF-DUPLEX   Data communication that allows signals to travel in only one direction at a time. For example, a walkie-talkie radio or a desktop intercom may be half-duplex. See FULL DUPLEX.

HANDSHAKING   A protocol of predefined signals to control the interchange of data and maintenance of a link.

HANGING   Slow response of the system because of a heavy load of users or computer-intensive jobs.

HARD CHARACTER SET   One of the sets of characters built into a terminal as a default design. Contrast DOWNLOADABLE CHARACTER SETS, also called SOFT CHARACTER SETS.

HARD-COPY TERMINAL   A terminal that prints on paper rather than on a video screen.

HELP SCREENS   Assistance to the user from within an applications program. Some packages allow you to adjust the help level so that once you know a system, you no longer have to go through unnecessary prompting.

**HEXADECIMAL** A numbering system based on 16 as opposed to the base 10 decimal system and the base 2 binary system. The letters A through F are used to indicate the numbers 10 through 15.

**H_FLOATING DATA** In a VAX/VMS system, an extended-range-floating point number, sixteen bytes in length, having a range of $\pm 0.8410^{-4932}$ to $\pm 0.5910^{4932}$ and a precision of approximately thirty-three decimal places. See also G_FLOATING DATA and FLOATING POINT DATA.

**HIBERNATION** Inactivation of a process still known to the system. The system keeps track of the process's status and can recall the process on the basis of a predefined wake request or a command from another process or the user. See SUSPENSION.

**HIERARCHICAL NETWORK** A communications systems designed to include various stages of signal routing and multiplexing for better efficiency in transmission.

**HIGH BIT** A slightly altered character set used by some word processors including WordStar and some other programs. Certain characters in storage are given a value higher than their ordinary ASCII value. High-bit characters are used in WordStar to indicate the end of each word so that microjustification can be accomplished. A high-bit stripper utility is often used to translate files from a high-bit program to a standard ASCII program or to DOS.

**HIGH-LEVEL LANGUAGE** A humanlike language that can give commands or create a program. High-level languages do not include machine-specific commands that directly address a computer, such as those in assembly and machine languages. High-level languages are translated into machine code by an interpreter or compiler before running or at the time of execution.

**HIGHLIGHTING** The brighter-than-ordinary display of characters, blocks, and other screen markers. Some systems use color, underlining, or dimming as a means of identifying blocks or characters.

**HOLDER** A user with a particular identifier.

**HOLD SCREEN** This key freezes the screen display and stops any other characters coming in from the host computer from being displayed. This function is useful when viewing a lengthy directory or file that would otherwise scroll off the screen too fast. The key is a toggle—pressing it once turns the mode on; pressing it a second time turns the mode off. On the LK-201 and similar keyboards, a Hold-Screen Indicator illuminates during a freeze.

**HOME** Usually defined as the top left corner of the screen or the active window of a screen.

**HORIZONTAL SCROLL** The shifting of the screen to the right to display text that is beyond the ordinary 80-column borders of a monitor.

**HOST** The computer or terminal server with which a terminal communicates

**HOST NODE** Under DECnet, the node that provides services to another node

**ICON** In a window environment, a graphic symbol that stands for a system resource or procedure. A drawing of a file folder may represent a data file to be opened or processed, for example; some systems use a garbage can to represent a delete or throwaway operation.

IDENTIFIER   The label of a user or group of users. VMS has three types of identifiers: UIC identifiers, system-defined identifiers and general identifiers.

IMAGE   The procedures and data bound together by the linker. VMS has three types of images, executable, shareable, and system.

IMAGE NAME   The name of the file in which an image is stored.

IMAGE PRIVILEGES   The privileges held by an image once installed.

INITIALIZE   To set counters, switches, or addresses to 0 or to a particular value, usually at the start of a session or a new program module. In some operating systems, to initialize means to format a disk.

INPUT STREAM   From the computer's point of view, the source of commands and data — the user's terminal, a batch stream, or a command procedure.

INSTRUCTION   An expression in a programming language that specifies a single operation.

INTEGER   Any whole number, including zero, either negative or positive.

INTEGRATED CIRCUIT   A complete electronic circuit on a microchip.

INTEGRATED OPTICAL CIRCUIT   Optical equivalent of a microelectronic circuit. Generates, detects, switches, and transmits light.

INTEGRATED SERVICES DIGITAL NETWORK   See ISDN.

INTERACTIVE SYSTEM   A system in which the user and the operating system communicate directly, with the operating system immediately acting upon commands and requests.

INTERFACE   The connection between two pieces of equipment.

INTERRUPT   The suspension of an operation caused by an event external to that process and performed in such a way that the process can later be resumed. For example, striking a key on the keyboard can interrupt particular programs. See EXCEPTIONS.

ISDN   Integrated services digital network. A plan for a hierarchy of digital transmission and switching systems, synchronized so that all digital elements work together for transmission of voice, data, and video signals. A true ISDN will do away with the need for modems, since the circuit will be able to carry and switch digital signals directly from computers without the need for an intermediate analog signal.

ISO   International Standards Organization, promulgator of the Open System Interconnection (OSI) model.

JOB   A record maintained by the computer to track a process and any subprocesses. A job can be either batch or interactive.

JOURNAL FILE   In an EDT editing session in a VAX/VMS system, a file that records all of the data and commands sent to the computer during one session. Can be used to reconstruct a file lost in an interrupted session.

**K** Short for kilo, or thousand. Used to measure memory and storage. A K is $2^{10}$, or 1,024, although it is commonly used to express a value of 1,000.

**KILOBIT** Informally, a thousand binary bits. A kilobit is actually 1,024 bits. Abbreviated Kb.

**KILOBYTE** Informally, a thousand bytes. A kilobyte is actually 1,024 bytes. Abbreviated KB.

**KILOHERTZ** One thousand cycles per second of electrical frequency. Abbreviated kHz.

**LABEL** A record that identifies the volume number or file section of a mass storage unit.

**LAN** See LOCAL AREA NETWORK.

**LASER** An electronic device that can produce light as rapid pulses within a very narrow frequency spectrum. Semiconductor-controlled lasers can operate at billions of pulses per second. Compare LED.

**LEAST SIGNIFICANT DIGIT** The rightmost or low-order digit of a number.

**LED** Light-emitting diode. A solid-state electronic device that can produce light within a broad frequency spectrum as rapid pulses for short-distance transmission on fiber-optic cable. Compare LASER.

**LIFO** Last in, first out. The order in which the most recently entered command is acted on first. Compare FIFO.

**LIGHT-EMITTING DIODE** See LED.

**LIGHT PEN** A device used to communicate position to a computer by shining the light at a CRT screen or touching the screen.

**LIMIT** The maximum size or number of resources allowed a particular job, as assigned by the system operator. See QUOTA.

**LINE PRINTER** A hard-copy output device that prints a single line at a time at very high speed.

**LINKER** A program that creates an executable program, referred to as an image, from one or more object modules produced by a language compiler or assembler. Programs must be linked before they can be executed.

**LK-201** The standard keyboard used by Digital with its VT-220 and VT-300 terminals.

**LOCAL AREA NETWORK (LAN)** Computers interconnected for the exchange of data and programs and the shared use of peripherals including printers and storage devices.

**LOCAL CONTROLLER MODE** Used to direct the keystrokes of a terminal in local mode to a directly connected printer. The mode is initiated from within the setup menus by selecting local mode from the main menu and then printer controller mode from the printer setup menu. See PRINTING MODES.

**LOCAL LOOP** Transmission lines that connect subscribers to the central switching office of a telephone company.

LOCAL MODE   The condition that exists when a terminal is set up as an offline device in direct communication with a printer or other device. Compare ONLINE MODE.

LOCK   A command that blocks unauthorized users from reading or writing to a file. Can protect the integrity of a file in use by several persons at the same time; can also prevent unauthorized access to sensitive material.

LOGICAL NAME   A name assigned by the user as a substitute for part or all of a file specification.

LOG IN   The process of identifying a user to the system. The user types in an Account Name and a Password in response to Prompts from the system. If the account name and password are registered in the system, the user will be given access to that account and all of its privileges.

LOGIN FILE   A command file containing instructions automatically executed at login.

LOGO   A programming language valued as an educational tool.

LOG OUT   To sign off a VMS account.

LOOPBACK   A diagnostic procedure in which a test message is sent from a transmitter and then back from the receiver to be compared with the original message.

LU   Logical unit, or the port through which users communicate in an SNA (qv) network.

MAC   1) Media access control. See ACCESS PROTOCOL. 2) Shortened form of Macintosh, as in Apple Computer Company's Macintosh line.

MACHINE LANGUAGE   Instructions for which the computer requires no interpreter. Usually each brand and sometimes each model within a company's line uses its own machine language.

MACRO   A statement that commands a language processor to generate a predefined set of instructions for action by the system.

MACROPROCESSOR   A program or utility that overlies a portion of an operating system to interpret and expand upon keystrokes or other input. For example, a keyboard macroprocessor can redefine single characters to stand for lengthy strings.

MAILBOX   A software equivalent of a physical mailbox. Used for communication between VMS users. Users can address mail to a particular mailbox, and recipients open their mailbox to retrieve messages.

MAP   Manufacturing automation protocol. A factory-floor network protocol, based on a token-passing design, promoted by General Motors.

MASS STORAGE DEVICE   An input/output device for the storage of data and other files while not in active use by the system. Such devices include magnetic disks, magnetic tapes, optical disks, and floppy disks.

MB   See MEGABYTE, MEGABIT.

MEDIUM   Cabling or wiring used to carry signals on a network, including coaxial, twisted-pair and fiber-optic cabling.

MEGABIT   Technically a thousand kilobits, or 1,048,576 bits. In common usage often taken as a million bits. Abbreviated Mb.

MEGABYTE   Technically a thousand kilobytes, or 1,048,576 bytes. In common usage often taken as a million bytes. Abbreviated MB.

MEMORY   Physical storage for data and instructions. Each memory location has an address to allow the system to find its contents.

MEMORY LIMITED PROGRAM   A program that will allow files only as large as the available space in the computer's memory, not allowing writing portions of the file to disk. Compare VIRTUAL MEMORY.

MENU   A list of choices that can be selected by use of a cursor or mouse-controlled pointer.

MODEM   Short for modulator-demodulator. Translates (modulates) digital impulses from a computer into analog waves for transmission. At the receiving end, the analog signal is demodulated to a digital signal.

MODULATION   The alteration of a carrier signal so that it can be transmitted. Most common forms of modulation are by means of altering amplitude, frequency, or phase angle of a signal.

MODULE   In software, a portion of a program or a program's library. In hardware, a physical element of a computer, as in logic module.

MOST SIGNIFICANT DIGIT   The leftmost nonzero digit of a number. Also called the high-order position. Its opposite is the least significant digit.

MOTHERBOARD   The main circuit board of a computer, including the microprocessor and some memory. Also called a system board. Secondary boards are sometimes called daughter boards.

MOUSE   A small device that can be held in the hand or moved on a desktop to position a cursor on the screen. Used in graphics and as a substitute for cursor keys. Buttons on the top of the mouse can also be used to transmit commands when the cursor is in the desired location.

MULTICAST ADDRESSING   A mode of addressing in which a message is sent to a group of predefined nodes.

MULTICAST GROUP ADDRESS   An address given to a group of nodes on an Ethernet and used to send a message to that group.

MULTIMODE FIBER   In lightwave systems, an optical fiber designed with a relatively large core that allows connection to light sources, such as LEDs, that are larger in frequency than lasers. Compare SINGLE-MODE FIBER.

MULTINATIONAL CHARACTER SET   A set of characters that goes beyond the ASCII eight-bit character set to include international alphanumeric characters, including characters with diacritical marks and special symbols.

MULTIPLEXER   A device that combines a number of communications channels to allow them to share a common circuit. In an analog system, frequency-division multiplexing is usually employed. In a digital system, time-division multiplexing is usually employed.

MVS   Multiple virtual storage. An IBM operating system that allows several users to use the mainframe as if it were dedicated to each user alone.

MVS/TSO   Multiple virtual storage/time-sharing option. A time-sharing version of MVS.

NATIVE IMAGE   An image whose instructions are executed in Native Mode (qv).

NATIVE MODE   The ordinary and primary mode of execution for a VAX processor. Under this definition, programmed instructions are interpreted as byte-aligned, variable-length instructions that operate on four data types: byte, word, longword and quadword integers; floating and double floating character strings; packed decimals, and variable-length bit fields. See COMPATIBILITY MODE.

NCP   Network control program. A resident program on some IBM devices to control routing, transmission, and packaging of data.

NETBIOS   Software that links a network to specific hardware. The original NetBIOS was developed by IBM, although other vendors have created equivalents.

NETWORK   A set of interconnected computer systems.

NETWORK FILE SYSTEM   A protocol, originally developed by Sun Microsystems, that allows computers and workstations on a network to use the files and attached peripherals of another member of the network as if they were local.

NETWORK LAYER   The third layer of the OSI model, including the rules for determination of pathways for data on a network.

NODE   An individual computer system in a network.

NODE ADDRESS   The unique numeric identification required for each node in a network. Also called "node ID."

NODE NAME   An optional alphanumeric identification for a node.

NONVOLATILE RAM   Computer memory that is able to retain data even after power to the system is shut off. Such RAM is used in many terminals to store configuration settings selected from the setup menus.

NORMAL MODE   The standard printing mode, which allows all keyboard printing functions including Print Screen to be initiated from the keyboard. See PRINTING MODE.

NULL   The ASCII character with a binary value of 000. In programming, a null is the absence of information. The character is used to fill a storage space or to consume a specific amount of time. A null character can be inserted into a sequence of characters without affecting the meaning of the sequence.

NULL MODEM   A special cable to link two identical input/output ports on computers. The key element is the crossing of the transmit and receive wires so that the output of one machine goes to the input of the other. Also called crossover cable, modem eliminator.

NUMERIC KEYPAD   A supplemental keypad on some terminals intended for rapid entry of numbers and punctuation marks. Can also be redefined to the special needs of a particular application program to allow quick entry of special commands. Often contains cursor keys.

NVR   See NON-VOLATILE RAM.

OBJECT   A process that is the recipient of a logical link request, called upon to perform a specific network function or a user-defined image for a special purpose. In hardware, an object is a system resource such as a file or device.

OBJECT CODE   See COMPILER.

OBJECT MODULE   The output of a language processor such as an assembler or compiler, in binary code, used as input to a linker.

OCTAL NUMBER   A number in the base 8 numbering system, which uses the numerals 0 to 7 only. Octal numbering is used in certain applications because it is easy to convert to binary numbers.

OFFSET ADDRESS   See ADDRESS.

ONLINE MODE   The condition that exists when a terminal is set up to communicate with a host computer. Offline modes include local and setup. See OPERATIONAL STATES.

OPEN ACCOUNT   An account that does not require a password for access.

OPEN SYSTEM INTERCONNECTION   See OSI.

OPERATING SYSTEM   A set of programs that controls the execution of computer programs, oversees system functions, and handles the communication with the user.

OPERATIONAL STATES   Type of operation invoked on a terminal. Includes online, for communications with a host computer; local, for operations not intended to be transmitted to a host computer; and setup for use of the terminal's built-in customization program.

OPERATOR   The person responsible for maintenance of a computer system and the accounts of users.

OPTICAL WAVEGUIDE   A solid glass fiber for transmission of communications signals generated by lasers or LEDs. Also called a lightguide.

OSI   Open System Interconnection. A network model promulgated by the International Standards Organization and intended to allow interconnection of heterogeneous computers and networks.

OUTPUT FILE   A file that contains the results of an operation.

PABX   See PBX.

PACKED DECIMAL   Allows two digits to be stored in a single byte.

PACKET   Assembled data to be routed from a source node to a destination node. Typically includes the identification of the sending and intended receiving nodes and error detection information.

PACKET SWITCHING   A scheme for more efficient use of a transmission channel by switching addressed packets in and out of the channel only as needed.

PAGE   In programming terms, a set of 512 contiguous byte locations, used as the unit of memory mapping and protection.

PAGING   Bringing pages of an executing process into physical memory when referenced; a process at the heart of the VAX architecture. When a process executes, all of its pages are placed in virtual memory. Only the pages in active use need to reside in physical memory; the remaining pages reside on disk until they are needed in physical memory. Under VAX/VMS, a process is paged when it references more pages than it is allowed in its working set or when it first activates an image in memory. If the process refers to a page not in its working set, a page fault occurs, which causes the operating system to read in the referenced pages from wherever they are located.

PARALLEL COMMUNICATION   Transmission of information over a pathway consisting of several wires, allowing the sending of more than one bit at a time.

PARITY   A setting in serial communications that requires that the number of bits in each word of transmitted data be even or odd. Used as part of the error-checking process.

PARITY BIT   In data communications, a bit that carries parity information to help verify accurate transmission of data.

PARITY CHECKING   A system of checking the integrity of data stored in memory by adding up the value of each of the eight bits that make up a computer word and then determining whether the total is odd or even. The answer is stored in a separate chip on the computer and regularly compared with the memory. If a mechanical or electrical error changes a bit in memory, the parity readings will differ and a parity error will result.

PARITY ERROR   A condition that results when the parity bit received by a device does not match the data.

PARSE   To break a command string into its various elements to interpret it for action.

PASCAL   A structured programming language named for the French mathematician Blaise Pascal.

PASSWORD   A character string entered by the user and examined by the operating system to validate access to the system.

PATCH   A change made in the assembly language code of a program.

PBX   Private branch exchange. Automated switching for an office telephone system. Available in both analog and digital systems. Digital models can switch both data and voice signals.

**PEER-TO-PEER**  A network design that allows any connected computer to make available to the network its resources while it runs local applications.

**PERIPHERAL DEVICES**  Any hardware, excluding the CPU and physical memory, that provides input or accepts output from the system. Peripherals include printers, terminals, and disk drives.

**PHOTODETECTOR**  A device used to turn pulses of light into bursts of electricity. Used at the receiving end of a lightwave system to convert light pulses into a signal that can be used by the computer.

**PHOTON**  The fundamental unit of light. Photons are to optical fibers what electrons are to copper wires.

**PHYSICAL ADDRESS**  To the computer, the address used by hardware to identify a specific location in physical memory or online secondary storage such as a disk drive. In network terms, the physical address is the unique address of a specific system on an Ethernet circuit.

**PHYSICAL LAYER**  The first layer of the OSI model, defining network wiring and electrical standards.

**PHYSICAL MEMORY**  The main internal memory of the computer.

**PID**  Process identification.

**PIXEL**  Picture element, the smallest unit of display on a video screen, used to create graphic characters and graphic displays.

**PORT**  A connector on a terminal to allow communication with a host or another device. Computers typically have parallel or serial ports for devices such as modems, keyboards, monitors, printers, and plotters as well as networks.

**PRESENTATION LAYER**  The sixth layer of the OSI model, where data is formatted for screen display. Terminal emulators, which make the PC act like a terminal, typically do their work here.

**PRIMARY PASSWORD**  The first password requested from the user. Some systems may ask for a second password.

**PRIMARY PROCESSOR**  The main processor in certain types of VAX computers. This processor handles input and output, scheduling, paging, and other system management functions. Such a system may have a secondary, or attached, processor for other assignments.

**PRIMARY RATE INTERFACE (PRI)**  A format within ISDN consisting of twenty-three B channels, each operating at 64 Kb/s, and one D channel, operating at 64 Kb/s. PRI is the next stage above BRI, the basic rate interface.

**PRINT QUEUE**  A feature of an operating system that stores files to be printed in a queue similar to a print spooler.

**PRINT SERVER**  A computer on the network dedicated in full or part to managing incoming and outgoing printing tasks. The server may maintain a print spooler and queue.

**PRINTER BUFFER**  See BUFFER.

**PRINTER CONTROLLER MODE** Condition selectable from the print setup menu; gives the host computer direct control of a locally connected printer. Characters sent by the host computer go directly to the printer and are not displayed on the screen. Ordinary printer control functions cannot be initiated from the keyboard while the terminal is in this mode. See PRINTING MODES for other conditions.

**PRINTER PORT CONNECTOR** A port on a VT terminal used to connect a printer directly to the terminal.

**PRINTING MODE** See NORMAL MODE; AUTO PRINTER MODE; PRINTER CONTROLLER MODE; LOCAL CONTROLLER MODE.

**PRIVATE BRANCH EXCHANGE** See PBX.

**PRIVATE SECTION** An image section of a process that is not open for sharing among processes. Compare GLOBAL SECTION.

**PRIVILEGED** Elements of the operating system that are restricted to the use of the system itself or to specific groups of users.

**PROCESS** The context within which an image executes.

**PROCESS IDENTIFICATION** A unique numeric value assigned by the computer to allow location and tracking of a process. Processes are assigned both process identification and a process name.

**PROCESS NAME** An alphanumeric string used to identify processes executing under the same group number. See PROCESS IDENTIFICATION.

**PROCESS PRIVILEGES** A combination of user privileges and image privileges granted to a process by the system.

**PROGRAM** A group of instructions intended to produce a particular result. See IMAGE.

**PROM** Programmable read-only memory. Compare ROM.

**PROMPT** The system's indication to the user that it expects input.

**PROTECTION** The attributes assigned to a resource that limit the type of access for users.

**PROTOCOL** A set of rules defining a communications link.

**PUBLIC SWITCHED NETWORK** A communications system, open to any subscriber, linking telephones and other devices.

**QUADWORD** On a VAX/VMS system, four contiguous words, sixty-four bits in total, with bits numbered from 0 to 63, right to left. The address of the quadword is the address of the byte containing bit 0. When interpreted as a number, a quadword is a two's complement integer (bit 63 is the sign bit in a signed integer). As a signed bit, a quadword ranges from $2^{-63}$ to $2^{63}$.

**QUALIFIER** The element of a command that modifies the command through selection of an option. For example, in the command DIR/FULL, the /FULL asks for a detailed listing of information about files rather than the short form that is yielded by the unmodified command.

QUEUE   An ordered list of jobs to be processed. Jobs are generally performed in FIFO order but can also be placed in different order on the basis of priority assigned them.

QUOTA   The amount of a system resource that a job is permitted to use during a particular period.

QWERTY   The keyboard layout used in the United States and most of the western world. Named after the first six letters at the top left side of the keyboard. See DVORAK KEYBOARD.

RAM   Random access memory, accessible in any order by the computer. RAM is usually volatile, meaning that when the electrical power to the circuit is shut off, RAM is erased.

RAM DISK   A segment of RAM set aside and formatted so as to imitate a physical disk in a disk drive. The memory can be used as an additional disk drive for storage while the computer is in use, adding utility and speed. The information must be copied to a real disk before the power is shut off. Other names for RAM disk include electronic disk, virtual disk, pseudodisk, and super drive.

RANDOM ACCESS   A memory or storage device on which all information is equally accessible at one time. Contrast with a serial storage device such as a reel of tape, in which the retrieval time for any one bit depends upon the location of the bit last retrieved.

RASTER   The pattern of horizontal lines on a video monitor.

READ-ONLY MEMORY   See ROM.

READ/WRITE HEADS   The recording heads inside a disk drive.

REAL-TIME PROCESS   A process that responds to particular events as they occur rather than when the computer is ready to respond to them. Examples include laboratory and manufacturing process control. Compare BATCH PROCESSING.

RECORD   A set of related data, usually organized into fields.

RECORD LENGTH   The size of a record in bytes.

REDIRECTION   Under some operating systems, taking input from a source other than the keyboard. For example, redirection can call up a file or another piece of hardware. Similarly, output can be redirected away from the standard goal of the display and instead be sent to a file or other device.

REDIRECTOR   Software resident at most stations on a network. It captures local requests for files and peripherals and routes them onto the network.

REFRESH MEMORY   The area of computer memory that holds values indicating whether a particular dot of a graphics raster is off or on. The memory may also contain information on color and brightness.

REGENERATORS   Device used along a digital transmission path to reshape and retime a digital signal. In a lightwave system optoelectronic modules refresh light pulses blurred by dispersion during transmission.

REGISTER   A storage device with a specified capacity such as a bit, a byte, a word, and so forth.

REMOTE DEVICE   A device not directly connected to the local node but available through a VAXcluster.

REMOTE FILE SERVICE   A distributed file protocol allowing sharing of network facilities as if they were local. Developed by AT&T and part of most implementations of UNIX.

REPEATER   Amplifier with electrical continuity to the cable to which it is connected. Signals enter one side of the amplifier and come out the other side stronger but with no switching or alteration. See BUFFERED REPEATER.

RESOLUTION   Clarity of the image on a screen. The number of pixels per unit of area determines resolution on a monitor; the greater the number of pixels per unit of area, the greater the resolution.

RESOURCE   A physical element of a computer system such as a device or memory.

RESUME   To reactivate a suspended process. Compare WAKE.

REVERSE VIDEO   The ability of some terminals to change from, for example, white letters on a black background to black letters on a white background.

RFS   See REMOTE FILE SERVICE.

RGB VIDEO   An acronym for a red/green/blue signal. Each of the color signals has its own transmitter and receiver and its own wire. Can transmit more information, and the resolution of an RGB monitor can be considerably greater than that of a composite monitor.

RING   Network topology in which each station is connected to another unit to the "left" and "right" as if it were in a circle. Messages pass through every station in turn but are retrieved only by the designated node.

ROM   Read-only memory. Blocks of memory with instructions for the computer or operating system that cannot be changed by the user or the system. Usually contains instructions and decoding information. ROMs are produced by designers in a single form. PROM is programmable ROM, which can be changed or updated. PROM includes the EPROM, which is erasable with ultraviolet light. An EEPROM is an Electrically Eraseable PROM that can be changed by sending an electrical signal.

ROUND ROBIN   A type of time sharing that gives equal access to the CPU for images of equal priority. Each process at a given priority level executes in turn before any other process at the level.

ROUTER   A dedicated machine in certain networks that reads the destination of a message and then determines the best route to that destination. See NETWORK LAYER.

RS-232C   A set of standards for mechanical and electrical design of an interface typically used for serial (asynchronous) communications in microcomputers. The interface includes a connector with twenty-five pins, each of which is lettered and provides a specific function. Although the standard is claimed by many manufacturers, it is still necessary to ensure that any two claimed RS-232C devices use standard pin assignments and cable construction in order to communicate properly.

RUN-TIME PROCEDURE LIBRARY   The collection of procedures available to native-mode images at run time.

SAA   See SYSTEMS APPLICATION ARCHITECTURE.

SCROLL   To move the window of text up or down, left or right, to see more of the copy.

SDLC   See SYNCHRONOUS DATA LINK CONTROL.

SECONDARY PASSWORD   A password that may be asked of the user at login time, after the primary password has been accepted.

SECTORS   The pie-wedge segments of a formatted disk. See FORMATTING.

SEGMENT   A part of an application; not all segments need to be loaded into memory at the same time.

SERIAL COMMUNICATIONS   A method of arranging data bits of a byte so that they follow one another down a cable. Compare PARALLEL COMMUNICATIONS, in which the bits of a byte travel alongside each other. See also ASYNCHRONOUS COMMUNICATION.

SERIAL COMMUNICATIONS CONTROLLER   A single chip or group of chips and associated circuitry that handle serial input and output.

SERVED DEVICE   A device available to remote nodes on a VAXcluster.

SESSION LAYER   The fifth layer of the OSI model, responsible for setting the conditions under which individual nodes can communicate with each other.

SETUP MENUS   The menus that let the user customize a terminal. See OPERATIONAL STATE.

SETUP MODE   The condition that exists when a terminal is set up to use its built-in customization program. See OPERATIONAL STATES, SETUP MENUS.

SHAREABLE IMAGE   An image that must be linked with one or more object modules in order to produce an executable image.

SIGNAL-TO-NOISE RATIO   The power relationship between a communications signal and "noise" — unwanted disturbances or interference — within the transmission bandwidth.

SIGNIFICANT DIGITS   The digits in a number from the leftmost digit that is not a zero to the rightmost digit declared to be relevant. The numbers 3789; 0.003789; and 3.789 all have four significant digits.

SINGLE-MODE FIBER   An optical fiber designed with a slender core capable of transmitting a narrow band of light frequencies, as generated by a laser. Compare MULTIMODE FIBER.

SINGLE PRECISION   A limit to the precision of a number based on a predetermined computer word length. See DOUBLE PRECISION.

SIXEL   A column of six pixels.

SNA   System network architecture. IBM's model for intercomputer communication.

SOCKET   A logical entity within the node of a network.

SOFT CHARACTER SETS   See DOWNLOADABLE CHARACTER SETS.

SORTING   The ordering of records in a particular sequence.

SOURCE CODE   See COMPILER.

SOURCE FILE   A text file with material ready for translation into an object module by an assembler or compiler.

SPOOLER   A piece of software that takes over a section of the computer's main memory (RAM) and uses it as storage for tasks under way such as printing or plotting. The hardware equivalent is the buffer.

STAR   A network topology in which all communication goes from the individual nodes to a central station for control.

START BIT   A serial communication bit that informs the system that the following bits are data.

STARTING ADDRESS   See ADDRESS.

STATIC MEMORY   RAM flip-flops as the memory elements. Data is thus retained for as long as power is applied to the flip-flops. Does not require regular refreshment. Compare DYNAMIC RAM.

STATUS LINE   A line of information that appears on many terminals in many applications to advise about the operating modes of the terminal.

STOP BIT   A serial communication bit that indicates the end of a block of data.

STRING   A connected series of characters.

SUBDIRECTORY   A subsidiary directory linked to a higher-level directory. For example, a system may have a directory containing a word processing program, a subdirectory of it containing memos, and another subdirectory with letters.

SUBPROCESS   A subsidiary process created by a process.

SUBRATE DATA   In a digital telephone network, data transmission at speeds less than 56 Kb/s, including standard modem rates of 300, 1,200, 2,400, 4,800 and 9,600 baud.

SUBROUTINE   A routine that executes when called by another routine.

SUBSCRIPT   A character or set of characters positioned a fraction of an inch beneath the rest of the copy on a line. Often used in scientific and mathematical notation.

SUPERSCRIPT   A character or characters positioned a fraction above the rest of the copy on a line.

SUSPENSION   A state in which a process is inactive but remains known to the system. It will become active if another process requests the operating system to resume it. Compare HIBERNATION.

SYMBOL   A character that represents a function or entity such as a command string or file name.

SYNCHRONOUS COMMUNICATION   A method of data transmission in which the transmitter and receiver are synchronized so that both ends can define start and stop of data bytes. Compare ASYNCHRONOUS COMMUNICATION.

SYNCHRONOUS DATA LINK CONTROL (SDLC)   An IBM protocol for data transfer.

SYNTAX   The grammatical form of a command.

SYSTEM BOARD   See MOTHERBOARD.

SYSTEM IMAGE   The image read into memory when a system is first started up.

SYSTEM NETWORK ARCHITECTURE   See SNA.

SYSTEM PASSWORD   The password asked of the user before login can begin.

SYSTEMS APPLICATION ARCHITECTURE   An IBM specification for the "look and feel" applications across a network.

TARGET NODE   The node that is to receive a memory image from another node.

TASK   In network terms, an image running in the context of a process.

TCP/IP   Transmission control protocol/internet protocol. A communication protocol, developed by the Department of Defense, for connection of heterogeneous computers and networks. Used in many UNIX-based networks as well as other systems.

TELEMETRY   Remote measurement or recording of data using communications channels between sensing devices and the computer or data recorder.

TELETEXT   One-way broadcast of video images in page format, based on images and data stored in a central computer database. Compare VIDEOTEX.

THROUGHPUT   The actual amount of work that can be accomplished by a particular device in a particular period. The fact that a printer, for example, claims a speed of 100 cps does not mean that it will print 10,000 characters in 100 seconds because it will be slowed down by other factors such as the speed of the incoming data, the amount of time the printer loses because of the need to change directions or return its print head, and paper handling time losses. Also used as a measure of the effective speed of a network.

TIME-OUT   The expiration of the time limit given a device or a user to provide a particular input.

TIME-SHARING   A means of allocating computer time by dividing up access to the processor into equal-sized slices and then sharing it among contending processes.

T INTERFACE   The four-wire physical link between ISDN terminal gear, limited to a distance of about a mile and a half.

TOGGLE   A key with an on/off function. Pressing the key once turns a particular feature or mode on; pressing the key a second time turns the feature or mode off. Examples include Hold Screen and Shift Lock.

**TOKEN-PASSING** A protocol design in which an electronic token circulates around a network; nodes find an available token and attach to it. The process is used for network communication to regulate access. A station seeking to transmit waits until a token message arrives, indicating availability of the network. The data is attached to the token and sent out on the network. Other stations cannot transmit until the token is freed.

**TOPOLOGY** The layout of a network in physical, electrical, or logical terms.

**TRACKS** The concentric circles of data on a formatted disk. See FORMATTING.

**TRANSMISSION CONTROL PROGRAM/INTERNET PROGRAM** See TCP/IP.

**TRANSPORT LAYER** The fourth layer of the OSI model, responsible for determining the integrity of data and the formatting of data.

**TRUNK** A multichannel communications link used to connect two switching offices in a network, or to link a central office to a PBX.

**TURNKEY ACCOUNT** See CAPTIVE ACCOUNT.

**TWISTED-PAIR WIRING** A type of electrical cabling made from a pair of wires twisted together in a particular design to provide electrical self-shielding. Many local telephone cables are twisted-pair.

**TWO'S COMPLEMENT** A means of representing an integer in binary code in which a negative number is one greater than the bit complement of the positive number.

**TYPE-AHEAD** The ability of a terminal to accept typed-in commands and data while the computer is processing a previously entered command. Input is held in a type-ahead buffer.

**UNIVERSAL SYMBOL** A global symbol in a shareable image that can be used by any module linked to the image.

**UNIX** An operating system with multiuser and multitasking abilities in use on large computers and on the new generation of sixteen-bit microcomputers. A variant of UNIX, called XENIX, is available for the PC AT.

**USER AUTHORIZATION FILE** A file created by the system manager to identify and grant access to the system for users. Included is user name, password, default account, quotas, limits, and privileges for each user.

**USER IDENTIFICATION FILE** A thirty-two-bit value given to users or files and other activities.

**USER NAME** The name of the user entered into the system at login.

**UTILITY** A program with functions related to the management of a system, account, or program.

**VARIABLE** Items or events that can take on differing numeric values dependent upon other events or items.

**VAX/VMS** Virtual Address Extension/Virtual Memory System.

**VERSION NUMBER** In a file specification, it represents the various revisions of a file since creation. The lowest version number is the oldest iteration of the file. In software terms it represents the revision level of the product. In general software version numbers are given a decimal number such as 4.25, in which the numbers to the left of the decimal represent major changes, while differences in the number to the right of the decimal stand for bug fixes or minor alterations and improvements.

VIDEOTEX   A two-way transmission system using a telephone network to transmit and receive data and graphics to and from a central computer. Compare TELETEXT.

VIRTUAL ADDRESS   A thirty-two-bit integer that identifies the location of a byte in virtual address space.

VIRTUAL ADDRESS SPACE   All possible virtual addresses where an image executing in the context of a process can seek or store information or instructions.

VIRTUAL CIRCUIT   A temporary link between two computers that creates the effect of a dedicated link.

VIRTUAL MEMORY   The storage locations in physical memory and on disk referred to by virtual addresses. As far as the program is concerned, all storage locations appear to be locations in physical memory.

VOICEBAND DATA TRANSMISSION   In telephone networks, a digital signal of 64 Kb/s or less, carried on the standard 4 kHz bandwidth of a voice channel.

VOLTAGE CONNECT SWITCH   A slide switch on many VT terminal models that allows selection of 110 volt (United States domestic power source) or 220 volts (many foreign countries). In addition to the voltage connect switch setting, most terminals require the proper fuse and power cord to be installed.

VOLUME   A mass storage medium such as a disk pack or magnetic tape. On a PC system, a piece of storage medium formatted for files that may be a disk or a part of a disk.

VT COMPATIBILITY   A claim by a third-party manufacturer to provide a functional equivalent to one of the VT terminals manufactured by Digital Equipment Corp. Compatibles typically are less expensive than Digital products, or provide enhanced features, or both. Compatibility does not always mean exact duplication—terminals may look different; the on-screen character display may be nonstandard; and even some of the key caps and locations of keys may be different. Buyers are advised to examine and test "compatibles" to be sure they meet particular needs.

VT-52 MODE   A terminal setting that conforms with the official definition, by Digital Equipment Corp., of the VT-52 terminals only. This mode employs Digital's proprietary text functions.

VT-100 MODE   A terminal setting that conforms with the official definition by Digital Equipment Corp. of the VT-100 terminals. This mode employs standard ANSI functions as well as the full range of VT-100 capabilities. The

VT-100 superseded the earlier VT-52 terminals and includes most of the earlier series's abilities as well.

VT-200 MODE   A terminal setting that conforms with the official definition, by Digital Equipment Corp., of the VT-200 terminals. This mode employs standard ANSI functions as well as the full range of VT-200 capabilities. The VT-200 superseded the earlier VT-100 and VT-52 series and includes most of the earlier series' abilities as well.

VTAM   Virtual telecommunications access method. Telecommunications software for MVS (multiple virtual storage) machines.

WAIT   A process enters a wait state and becomes inactive when it suspends itself, hibernates, or declares to the system that it needs to wait for an event or resource.

WAKE   To reactivate a hibernating process.

WAN   Wide area network. A data communications network that connects computers and terminals dispersed over a wide area, often through the linkage of several LANs.

WIDE AREA NETWORK   See WAN.

WILD CARD   A nonalphanumeric character used in a file name or directory in a file specification to indicate "all."

WINDOW   A marked-off area of the screen that presents information or messages; a screen within the screen.

WORD   Two contiguous bytes, sixteen bits in total, with bits numbered from 0 to 15, right to left. The address of the word is the address of the byte containing bit 0. When interpreted as a number, a word is a two's complement integer (bit 15 is the sign bit in a signed integer). As a signed bit, a word ranges from $-32,768$ to $32,767$. When interpreted as an unsigned integer, the value is in the range from 0 to 65,535.

WORKING SET   The set of pages in process space that an executing process can refer to without generating a page fault. Remaining pages of the process, if any, are in memory or in secondary storage.

WORLD   All users, including system operators, system managers, and users, in any group.

X.25   A protocol that specifies the interface for packet-mode communication on data networks. Examples include Telenet and Tymnet.

# Index

212A standard, 283
3Com, 79
80286, 85
80386, 29, 18, 86
80486, 90
ACK, 178
ADCCP—Advanced data communications control procedures, 22
Advanced Technology PC, 91
Alisa Systems, 47
American National Standards Institute, 20
ANSI, 20
Answering the call
  in VMS PHONE, 249
APPEND
  in DCL, 199
Apple Computer, Inc., 8
AppleTalk, 8
  AppleShare, 46
  AppleTalk filing protocol (AFP), 46
  AppleTalk-to-VAX vendors, 47
Application layer, 24
ASCII code table, 53
ATTACH
  in VMS MAIL, 238
Attenuation, 58

AUX, 119

BACK
  in VMS MAIL, 234
Backslash
  in MS-DOS, 128
  in Xenix, 128
Base numbering system, 52
Baseband, 10
Baud rate, 63
Begun, Michael, 189
Bell standard, 202, 283
Binary arithmetic, 52
Bridge, 26
Broadband, 10
Buffered repeater, 26

Cable television, 10
Cables
  ThickWire, 12
  ThinWire, 12
  Unshielded twisted pair, 12
Carrier sense multiple access/collision detection, 23
CASE, 25
CATV, 10
CCITT, 22, 25, 283

339

Centronics
  connector (Fig. E-1), 286
  pin assignments (Table E-3), 287
  standard, 285
Clear to send, 173
Clones
  Turbo, 85
  VAXmate, 100
CMIP, 44
Coaxial cable, 10
COM 1, 69, 119
COM 2-4, 119
Common application service elements, 25
Communications
  Ctrl-Q, 155
  Ctrl-S, 155
  DC1, 155
  DC3, 155
  Echoplex, defined, 172
  FIFO buffer, 155
  Full duplex, defined, 172
  Half duplex, defined, 172
  Serial, 275
  Simplex, defined, 172
  Terminal to host, 153
  XOFF, 155
  XON, 155
Community-DOS
  Technology Concepts, Inc., 188
Community-Mac, 47, 189
Compaq Computer Corporation, 8
COMPRESS
  in VMS MAIL, 238
Concentrators, 302
Conference calls
  in VMS PHONE, 248
Connectivity
  direct links, 65
  serial, 65
  serial attachments (Fig. 5-1), 67
Connectors, serial port, 69
Control codes, 155
Conventions in this book, 3
COPY
  in DCL, 200

  in VMS MAIL, 214, 225
CRC—Cyclical redundancy checking, 178
CSMA/CD, 23
Ctrl-C, 131
Ctrl-Q, 155
Ctrl-S, 155
Ctrl-Y, 131
CTS-Clear to send, 173
CURRENT
  in VMS MAIL, 226

Data communications, 60
Data compression, 175
Data link layer, 22
Data traffic, 31
Datability Software Systems, Inc., 185
Datastorm Technologies, Inc.
  Procomm, 162
DCL
  APPEND, 199
  Commands, 197
  COPY, 200
  DELETE, 201
  DIRECTORY, 202
  PRINT, 203
  Prompt, 132
  PURGE, 203
  RENAME, 205
  Self-prompting commands, 198
  TYPE, 205
DECmate III, 102
DECnet, 2, 43
  DECnet vs. OSI layers (Fig. 3-3), 38
  DECnet/OSI phase V, 40
  Definition, 36
  Enhancements, 44
  History, 35
  Network management, 41, 43
  OSI, 37
  OSI model, 36
  Overview, 35
  PCSA, 101, 182
DECnet enhancements, 95
  Message Router x.400 Gateway, 44
  Novell's Netware, 45

## INDEX □ 341

DECnet enhancements:, *continued*
  SNA, 45
  VAX DEC/MAP, 44
  VAX OSI, 44
  VAX packet-switching interface, 44
DECnet/OSI, 20
DECnet/OSI phase V
  data-link layer, 40
  DNA session control, 41
  network layer, 40
  physical layer, 40
  transport layer, 40
DECstation 3100
  DECstation 3100 (Fig. 7-5), 106
DECwindows, 33
Default specifications, 142
DELETE
  in DCL, 201
  in VMS MAIL, 226
Dell Computer Corporation
  enhanced PC keyboard (Fig. 10-3), 158
DIAL
  in VMS PHONE, 246
Dialing a call
  in VMS PHONE, 247
Digital
  intracompany network, 43
Digital networking architecture, 8
Digital-to-Digital communications, 21
DIR, 136
Direct serial link, 9
Direct-connect terminal, 130
Directories and subdirectories, 206
DIRECTORY
  consulting mail directory, 210
  in DCL, 202
Directory assistance
  in VMS PHONE, 248
Distributed processing, 16, 32
  architecture, 33
  PC network, 31
Diversified Computer Systems, 192
DNA, 8, 37
  design goals, 36
  security, 37
  standards, 37
  technologies and applications, 37
  transparent operation, 36
DOS
  commands, 117
  machine language, 117
Drive assignments
  MS-DOS, 122

EDIT, in VMS MAIL, 227
EOT—End of transmission, 179
ERASE, in VMS MAIL, 228
Error checking, 175, 178, 179
Ethernet
  adapters for PC, 72
  baseband, 10
  broadband, 10
  distance limits, 10
  hardware, 72
  software, 73
  ThickWire, 12
  ThinWire, 12
  transfer rate, 10
  twist-on connector (Fig. 2-1), 11
Everex, 163
Excelan (EXOS 205E, 205T), 189
EXIT, in VMS MAIL, 228
EXTRACT, in VMS MAIL, 228

FDDI, 16
  speed, 15
Fiber distributed data interface, 15
Fiber-optic cable, 10, 13
  disadvantages, 14
FILE and MOVE, in VMS MAIL, 229
File damage, avoiding, 133
File manipulation, 145
File transfer, 165
  software protocols, 167
File transfer access and
  management, 25
FIRST, in VMS MAIL, 235
Folders, in VMS MAIL, 212

Forrester research, 126
FORWARD, in VMS MAIL, 229
Freeware
　defined, 161
　user supported software, 163
Frequency, 58
Frequency modulation
　frequency shift keying, 61
　phase shift keying, 61
FTAM, 25
Function keys, VT series, 265

Gateway, 26
Global characters, 142
　DCL, 144

Handshaking, 172
　character delays, 173
　CTS—Clear to send, 173
　null characters, 173
　RTS—Request to send, 173
　Time delay loops, 173
Hanging up, in VMS PHONE, 250
Hayes Microcomputer Products
　AT commands, 297
　indicator lights, 296
　modem, 295
　modem registers, 298
　Smartmodem, 296
HDLC, 22
HELP, 137
　in VMS MAIL, 242
　in VMS PHONE, 250
　word list, 138
High level data link control, 22
HOLD, in VMS PHONE, 251
Host machines, 30

IBM, 83, 84
　original PC, described, 90
　PC AT, 85, 91
　PC XT, 85, 90
　PS/2 Model 30, 92
　PS/2 Model 50, 93

PS/2 Model 60, 93
PS/2 Model 80, 92, 93
SNA/SDLC, 175
IDC, 125
IEEE, 10
　802.3 standard, 10, 22
　802.4 standard, 25
　802.5 standard, 24
Institute of Electrical and Electronics
　　Engineers, 10, 24
Intel 8088, 84
Interface cards, network (Fig. 5-4), 73
International Data Corporation, 88, 125
International Standards Organization,
　　20
International Telephone and Telegraph
　　Consultative Committee, 22
ISO, 20
　8802.3 standard, 22
　8802.4 standard, 25
　8802.5 standard, 24

KEA Systems, 159, 192
Kermit, 165, 179
　data compression, 179
　sliding-window data exchange, 179
Keyboard
　auxiliary keypad for VT series, 264
　DCS EM220, 160
　editing keypad for VT series, 264
　numeric keypad on VT100/LK201
　　(Table B-1), 220
　PC compared to VT terminal, 159
　Powerstation (KEA Systems), 159
　redefining keys for MAIL
　　(Table B-2), 221
　templates, 159
　VT series audible indicators, 266
　VT series control commands, 267
　VT series function keys, 265
　VT series visual indicators, 266
　VT terminal compared to PC, 159
　VT-Series (Fig. D-4), 263
　VT-Series terminals, 261, 262

Keyboard:, *continued*
  WPS-Plus, 160
KFPQ, 47
Kinetics, 47

LAN, 8
  components, 33
  interface cards, 28
  NetWare/VMS (Fig. 3-6), 48
  network hardware, 33
  network software, 34
  Novell, 166
  PC Network to VAX, 79
  peer-to-peer, 29
  peer-to-peer(Fig. 3-1), 30
  server, 30
  server-based PC LAN (Fig. 3-2), 31
  star configuration, 13
  wiring, 13
LAST, in VMS MAIL, 235
LAT—Local area transport, 48, 185, 187
Line drivers, 300
Local area network, 8
LOGOUT, 136
Long VMS MAIL messages, 224
LPT1-3, 120
LRC—Longitudinal redundancy
    checking, 178

MAIL, reading, 147
Mailbus, 25
Marc Software, 78
Microchannel architecture, 84
  PS/2 models, 83
Microcom, 175, 179
Microsoft, Inc., 116, 174
MicroVAX 3300/3400 family, 105
  DECstation 3100 (Fig. 7-5), 106
  MicroVAX 2000 (Fig. 7-3), 103, 104
  MicroVAX 3000, 104
  MicroVAX 3300 (Fig. 7-7), 108
  MicroVAX 3500 and 3600
      (Fig 7-6), 107
  MicroVAX II (Fig. 7-4), 104, 105

performance, 156
product line (Fig. 7-1), 97
VAXstation 2000, 103
VAXstation 3100, 102
MicroVAX II
  MIPS, 87
  speed, 87
MIPS, 32
  MicroVAX II, 87
  PC MIPS ratings, 83
MIS, needs for communication, 19
MNP, 179
Modem
  212A standard, 283
  acoustically coupled, 293
  alternatives, 299
  amplitude modulation, 61
  AT commands, 297
  bandwidth, 63
  baud rate, 63
  Bell 202 standard, 283
  buying, 289
  callback modem, 133
  direct-connect, 292
  Everex, 163
  frequency modulation, 61
  Hayes, 180
  Hayes modem registers, 298
  Hayes indicator lights, 296
  Hayes standard, 295
  Hayes-compatible, 70
  intelligent, 294
  links, 74
  null, 299
  operation, 61
  phase angle modulation, 61
  short haul, 301
  short haul, 66, 293
  Smartmodem, 296
  specifications, 290
  speed, 291
  standards, 283
  telecommunications expenses
      (Table F-2), 302
  transmission speeds, 62

Modem:, *continued*
  types, 292
  V-series, 180
Modular patch panel (Fig. 2-5), 16
Motherboard, 84, 85, 87
Motorola 68000, 88
Moving VMS MAIL messages, 213
MS-DOS, 4, 87, 88, 182
  batch programming facility, 122
  commands, 117
  command structure, 118
  compared to VMS, 116
  country file, 122
  devices, 119, 120
  directories, 120
  drive letters, 122
  EDLIN, 122
  file extensions, 119
  file names, 119
  files, 118
  modes, 117
  typical directory structure (Fig. 8-1), 121
Multiplexers, 301
Multiprocessor, 32
Multiuser computing, response times, 28

NAK, 178
NCL, 44
NetWare, 47
NetWare/286, 47
NetWare/VMS, 48, 190
  product positioning, 191
  system requirements, 191
Network
  backbone, 12
  bridge, 26
  buffered repeater, 26
  distance limits, 25
  gateway, 26
  interface, 33
  network to host, 80
  PCs in VAX environment, 27
  repeater, 26

  server links, 75
Network cabling
  bus topology, 33
  ring, 33
Network hardware, LAN, 33
Network layer, 23
Network management
  efficiency, 43
  functions, 41
  session control (Fig. 3-5), 42
Network schemes
  peer-to-peer, 29
  server, 29
Network server links, software components, 75
Network software
  LAN, 34
  node software functions, 34
  server software, 34
NEXT, in VMS MAIL, 235
Novell, 47, 166
  interface card (Fig. 5-4), 73
  NetWare, 190
  NetWare Network (Fig. 5-5), 79
NUL, 120

Open system interconnection, *see* OSI. 20
Operating Systems, 115
  MS-DOS, 87, 101
  ULTRIX, 98
  VAX, 97
  VMS, 87, 98, 101
OS/2
  applications, 126
  communications manager, 124
  compatibility with MS-DOS, 124
  database manager, 125
  features, 123
  market penetration, 88
  market position, 125, 126
  presentation manager, 125
OSI, 7
  application layer, 24, 37

## INDEX □ 345

OSI:, *continued*
    data link layer, 22
    DECnet, 37
    DECnet vs. OSI layers (Fig. 3-3), 38
    DECnet/OSI phase V, 40
    Digital and OSI, 20
    link layer, 37
    management layer, 37
    model (Fig. 3-4), 39
    network layer, 23
    physical layer, 22
    presentation layer, 23
    protocols, 21
    semantics, 21
    session layer, 23
    seven-layer model, 21
    syntax, 21
    timing, 21
    transport layer, 23

P-VAX, 102
Packet-switched data networks, 25
PAD — Packet assembler and disassembler, 175
Parity checking, 176
Passwords
    set password, 134
    VMS, 133
PC, 1, 4
    "baby" AT, 86
    clones, 85
    Digital MS-DOS personal computers (Fig. 7-2), 100
    Digital's products, 99, 101
    enhanced PC keyboard (Fig. 10-3), 158
    Ethernet adapters, 72
    Ethernet software, 73
    IBM PC AT, 29, 91
    IBM PS/2, 92
    IBM-PC class motherboard (Fig. 6-1), 85
    keyboard, 158
    MIPS rating, 83
    motherboard, 84

    operating systems, 115
    original IBM, 90
    PC AT class machine (Fig. 10-2), 154
    PC XT, 90
    PC/AT class computer (Fig. 6-3), 87
    PC/AT class motherboard (Fig. 6-2), 86
    perspective, 95
    rebooting, 70
    with VAX host, 76
    VAX-compatible software, 77
    VT family keyboard (Fig. 10-4), 159
    VT terminal keyboard, 159
    in the workplace, 27
PC LAN, advantages, 79
PC network
    advantages, 29
    departmental distributed processing, 28
    distributed processing, 31
    interface cards, 28
PC serial connectors, 69
PC XT, 29
PC-DOS, 4
PC-VAX Communications, 182
    benefits to MIS, 19
    benefits to users, 18
    direct serial link, 9
    MIS needs for communication, 19
    MIS perspective, 19
    technology, 9
    user perspective, 17
    user's need to communicate, 17
PDP, 96
Persoft, 193
Personal computer, 1, 83
    operating systems, 115
PHONE, 149
    answering messages, 149
    in VMS, 245
Physical layer, 22
Polygon, 193
Ports
    asynchronous, 55
    serial, 55
PostScript, 76

Presentation layer, 23
PRINT
  in DCL, 203
  in VMS MAIL, 230
Printing, on VAX, 76
Professional 380, 102
Protocol
  CRC—cyclical redundancy
    checking, 178
  Kermit, 179
  LAP-B, 180
  LRC—longitudinal redundancy
    checking, 178
  MNP, 179
  VRC—vertical redundancy
    checking, 178
  Xmodem, 178
Protocols
  Access (Microsoft), 174
  asynchronous, 169
  bisynchronous, 169, 170
  CSMA/CD, 23
  data compression, 175
  error checking, 175
  handshaking, 172
  MNP (Microcom), 175
  in OSI data-link layer, 22
  PAD—packet assembler and
    disassembler, 175
  Parity checking, 176
  SNA/SDLC (IBM), 175
  Synchronous, 169, 170
  Tymnet network, 174
  X.25, 174
  X.PC, 174
  XMODEM, 23
PS/2, 83
PSDN, 25
Punch down block (Fig. 2-4), 15
PURGE
  in DCL, 203
  in VMS MAIL, 230

QUIT, in VMS MAIL, 231

RAF
  LAT—local area transport, 185
  performance, 186
RAF—Remote Accesss Facility, 184
  Datability Software Systems, Inc., 184
Rainbow, 101
  DECmate III, 102
  Professional 380, 102
READ, in VMS MAIL, 231
Reading MAIL, 210
REJECT, in VMS PHONE, 252
Remote boot, 184
Remote logins, 132
RENAME, 137
  in DCL, 205
Repeater, 26
REPLY, in VMS MAIL, 233
Response times, multiuser
  computing, 28
RJ-11, 292
RS-232C, 278
  cable diagram, 281
  pin assignments (Table E-1), 279
  signal standards (Table E-2), 285
RS-422, 282
RS-423, 282
RTS—Request to send, 173

S-Net, 47
SEARCH, in VMS MAIL, 233
SELECT, in VMS MAIL, 233
Semantics, 21
SEND, extending VMS MAIL
  command, 219
Sending a file
  in VMS PHONE, 250
  in VMS Mail, 216
Sending a VMS MAIL letter, 215
Sending electronic chain letter by
  VMS MAIL, 217
Serial communications
  CCITT, 283
  Centronics connector (Fig. E-1), 286
  Centronics standard, 285

Serial communications:, *continued*
   Centronics standard pin assignments
      (Table E-3), 287
   current loop, 281
   described, 275
   RS-232C, 278
   RS-232C cable diagram, 281
   RS-232C pin assignments
      (Table E-1), 279
   RS-232C signal standards
      (Table E-2), 285
   RS-422, 282
   RS-423, 282
   standards, 275
Serial connector
   DB-9 Connector (Fig. 5-3), 71
   DB-25 (Fig. 5-2), 68
   DB-25 D-shell, 67
   DB-25P, 67
   DB-25S, 67
Serial link, 65
   Serial attachment (Fig. 5-1), 67
Serial port
   finding connectors, 69
   hardware, 66
   software, 71
Session control, network
      management, 42
Session layer, 23
SET and SHOW, in VMS MAIL, 239
Sholkin, Howard, 189
SNA, 20
Software
   low-cost, 82
   PC applications, 82
   protocols, 167
   serial port, 71
   spreadsheets, 78
   terminal emulation, 72, 160, 192
   VAX-compatible, 77
   word processing, 78
Software protocols, 167
   asynchronous, 169
   bisynchronous, 169, 170
   synchronous, 169, 170

Solidus
   in MS-DOS, 128
   in Xenix, 128
SPAWN and ATTACH, in VMS MAIL, 236
Standards
   FTAM, 25
   IEEE 802.4, 25
   IEEE 802.5, 24
   ISO 8802.5, 24
   VTP, 25
   x.25, 25
   X.400, 25
Star configuration, 13
Syntax, 21
System commands in VMS MAIL, 236
System network architecture, 20

TCP/IP, 23, 45
Technology Concepts, Inc., 47
Telecommuications, expenses
      (Table F-2), 302
Telecommunications
   asynchronous, 55
   dedicated/leased line, 74
   hardware, 52
   serial, 55
   theory, 51
   voice frequency, 58
Telephone
   leased lines, 59
   modular patch panel (Fig. 2-5), 16
   PBX, 60
   punch down block (Fig. 2-4), 15
   wall connector (Fig. 2-2), 12
Telephone network, 55
   telephone link, 56
Terminal
   defined, 152
   Digital's VT-300 (Fig. 10-1), 152
Terminal emulation, 151
   advantages, 164
   BitCom, 163
   DataMedia Corporation, 166
   EM220 (Diversified Computer
      Systems), 192

Terminal emulation:, *continued*
  hardware, 165
  Kermit, 165
  modem, 163
  Novell, Inc., 166
  PC-Talk III, 161
  PolyStar/240 (Polygon), 193
  Powerstation 240 (KEA Systems), 192
  Procomm (Datastorm Technologies, Inc.), 162
  Qmodem, 163
  Reflection 4 Plus (Walker, Richer, & Quinn), 194
  set-up screen from Procomm (Fig. 10-5), 162
  SmarTerm 240 (Persoft), 193
  Software, 72, 160, 192
  Tektronix 4208 terminal, 166
  Telix, 163
  Xmodem, 165
Terminal server, 131
Terminals
  in the Digital environment, 111
  VT-series, 255
Terms
  AFP (AppleTalk filing protocol), 46
  ARPAnet, 45
  basic input/output system, 83
  CMIP, 44
  conditioned line, 59
  crossover cable, 299
  DCL—Digital command language, 134
  DECnet, 36
  DSSI—Digital storage systems interconnect, 105
  Freeware, 161
  leased line, 59
  mark, 53
  modem, 60
  modem eliminator, 299
  MS-DOS, 4
  NCL, 44
  PC, 4
  PC-DOS, 4
  space, 53

TCP/IP, 45
UART, 55
  workstation, 4
The Headlands Press, PC-Talk III, 161
ThinWire, 72
Third-party agreements
  Apple, 8
  Compaq, 8
Timing, 21
Transmission control protocol, 23
Transport layer, 23
TSSnet, 47
Twisted pair, 10, 72
Tymnet, 174
TYPE, in DCL, 205

UART—Universal asynchronous reciever/transmitter, 55
Ungermann-Bass (Personal-NIU), 189
Unipress, 78
Unshielded twisted pair, 12
  wiring diagram (Fig. 2-3), 14
User's need to communicate, 17

VAX
  6300 Family (Fig. 7-8), 109
  6300 series, 107
  8650, 111
  8900, 110
  clustered 8900-series (Fig. 7-11), 112
  midrange models, described, 107
  older VAXs, 110
  operating systems, 97
  overview, 96
  as a peer, 78
  as a peripheral, 76
  VAX 11/750, 111
  VAX 11/780, 111
  VAX 11/785, 111
  VAX 6200 family, 18, 107
  VAX 8250, described, 108
  VAX 8350, described, 108
  VAX 8500 series, described, 108
  VAX 8600, 111

VAX:, *continued*
  VAX 8840 (Fig. 7-10), 111
  VAX high-end systems,
    described, 109
  VAX/VMS Services for MS-DOS, 182
  VAXcluster, 110
  virtual addressing, 96
  VMS, 98
VAX/VMS Services for MS-DOS, 182
VAXcluster, 110
VAXmate, LK250 keyboard, 100
VAXstation 2000, 103
VAXstation 3100, 102
Virtual addressing, 96
Virtual terminal protocol, 25
Viruses, 163
VMS
  command structure, 135
  compared to MS-DOS, 116
  DCL operations, 144
  device name, 140
  directories and subdirectories, 206
  file default specifications, 142
  file manipulation, 145
  file names, 141
  file specification, 140
  file type, 141
  files and directories, 139
  global characters, 142
  logging in, 130
  logging on, 130
  node name, 140
  passwords, 133
  security, 131
  signing in, 130
  utilities, 146
  version number, 141
VMS commands
  answering phone messages, 149
  DIR, 136
  HELP, 137
  help word list, 138
  LOGOUT, 136
  MAIL, 147
  PHONE, 148
  RENAME, 137
  set password, 134
  wildcards, 143
VMS MAIL, 209
  ATTACH, 238
  BACK, 234
  COMPRESS, 238
  COPY, 225
  copying a file, 214
  CURRENT, 226
  DELETE, 226
  directory, 210
  EDIT, 227
  ERASE, 228
  EXIT, 228
  extending SEND powers, 219
  EXTRACT, 228
  FILE and MOVE, 229
  FIRST, 235
  FORWARD, 229
  HELP, 242
  key redefinition for MAIL
    (Table B-2), 221
  LAST, 235
  long mail messages, 224
  moving messages, 213
  navigational commands, 234
  NEXT, 235
  PRINT, 230
  PURGE, 230
  QUIT, 231
  READ, 231
  reading mail, 210
  redefining keys, 221
  REPLY, 233
  SEARCH, 233
  SELECT, 233
  sending a file, 216
  sending a letter, 215
  sending electronic chain letter, 217
  SET and SHOW, 239
  SPAWN and ATTACH, 236
  system commands, 236
  using folders, 212
VMS operating system, 129

VMS PHONE, 245
  answering the phone, 249
  commands, 246
  conference calls, 248
  DIAL, 246
  dialing a call, 247
  directory assistance, 248
  hanging up, 249
  HELP, 250
  placing call on hold, 251
  rejecting calls, 252
  sending a file, 250
VRC—vertical redundancy checking, 178
VT terminal, 130
VT-220, described, 256
VT-240, described, 256
VT-241, described, 257
VT-320, described, 257
VT-330, described, 257
VT-340, described, 258
VT-family terminals
  VT100, 112
  VT200, 112
  VT300, 112
VT-series keyboard
  audible indicators, 266
  auxiliary keypad, 264
  control commands, 267
  editing keypad, 264
  function keys, 265
  visual indicators, 266
VT-series terminal, control codes, 131
VT-series terminals, 255
  compatability chart (Table D-1), 259
  composing characters, 270
  keyboard (Fig. D-4), 263
  main keyboard, 262
  multinational characters
    (Table D-2), 272
  operating modes, 261
  standard keyboards, 261
  type ahead buffer, 271
  VT terminals (Fig. D-2), 258
  VT terminals (Fig. D-3), 259
  VT-220, 256

VT-240, 256
VT-241, 257
VT-320, 257
VT-330, 257
VT-340, 258
VT100/LK201, numeric keypad
  (Table B-1), 220
VTP, 25

Walker, Richer & Quinn, 194
Wecker, Stuart, 189
Wildcard commands, 143
Wiring, LAN, 13
WordPerfect, 78
Workstation, 4, 155
  configuring, 157
  defined, 153
  terminal emulating, 157
  terminal to host
    communications, 153

X.25, 25
X.400, 25
XENIX, 116
  commands, 127
  described, 126
  visual editor, 127
Xmodem, 165
  ACK—acknowledge, 178
  EOT—end of transmission, 179
  NAK—negative acknowledge, 178
XON/OFF, 172